Evolving Iran

Evolving Iran

*An Introduction to Politics
and Problems in the Islamic Republic*

Barbara Ann Rieffer-Flanagan

Georgetown University Press
Washington, DC

Library of Congress Cataloging-in-Publication Data

Rieffer-Flanagan, Barbara Ann J.
  Evolving Iran : an introduction to politics and problems in the Islamic republic / Barbara Ann Rieffer-Flanagan.
       pages cm
  Includes bibliographical references and index.
  ISBN 978-1-58901-978-2 (pbk. : alk. paper)
  1. Iran—Politics and government—1979–1997. 2. Iran—Politics and government—1997– 3. Iran—Economic policy—1979- 4. Human rights—Iran—History. I. Title.
  DS318.8.R54 2013
  955.05'4—dc23   2012037548

∞ This book is printed on acid-free paper meeting the requirements of the American National Standard for Permanence in Paper for Printed Library Materials.

15 14 13   9 8 7 6 5 4 3 2 First printing

For James Flanagan for many years of love and support

CONTENTS

PREFACE

This book brings together scholarship from various highly focused academic works and seeks to distill a general and systematic overview of Iran's political and economic system since the 1979 Islamic Revolution. The opening chapters provide the foundation and history to help the reader understand those events that provided the motivation for the Revolution. Next I cover a broad array of subjects, including foreign policy, human rights, women's struggle for equality, the development and evolution of elections and the institutions of the political system, and the economy. My emphasis in this book is to show how and why political decisions are made in the Islamic Republic of Iran.

I have spent a decade studying the Islamic Republic of Iran and grappling with its politics. A number of individuals helped me as I embarked on the long process that led to this book. This book was supported by a grant from the Office of the Dean of the College of the Sciences at Central Washington University. Beyond providing funding for this research project, Kirk Johnson has been a very supportive dean. I will always appreciate his willingness to give his time and advice to a young faculty member. Jean Cahan, Dave Forsythe, Pam McMullin-Messier, and Mahmood Monshipouri were kind enough to read and comment on the earlier materials that went into the creation of this book. I am especially grateful to Dave Forsythe for his encouragement throughout graduate school and beyond. Although his research never focused on the Islamic Republic of Iran, this did not prevent him from reading and offering his advice on numerous drafts on the Revolution, Iranian foreign policy, and human rights. I am grateful that Dave has been a tough but supportive mentor to me over the years. Don Jacobs was an understanding and helpful editor at Georgetown University Press. Finally, I thank my family for putting up with my never-ending comments about Iran. I am sure that they grew tired of hearing me talk about Iran's theocracy and the political leaders that make Iran such an interesting country to study. I will always be grateful for their understanding.

GLOSSARY

Ashura. Shia religious holiday honoring the day of Imam Hosain's martyrdom.

ayatollah. Typically refers to a well-respected and high-ranking religious leader in the Shia tradition. It literally means "sign of God."

basij. Mobilization, a volunteer paramilitary force.

bazaar. A marketplace or area of town where goods are sold.

bonyads. Charitable foundations.

brain drain. The loss of educated people due to emigration.

burka. A loose-fitting garment that covers a woman's body from head to toe, including her face.

chador. A loose-fitting garment that covers a woman's body from head to toe.

exegesis. A critical interpretation of a religious text.

faqih. Jurist or religious scholar.

fatwa. Religious decree; pronouncement.

GDP. Gross domestic product—the production of goods and services within a country.

gharb zadegi. Sometimes translated as "Westoxification," it typically refers to a desire for Western culture and ideas. It is used as a criticism of the loss of Persian culture.

hadith. Stories attributed to the Prophet Muhammad.

haqq. Rights.

hijab. A piece of clothing, typically a veil or scarf, that covers the head and neck.

iefan. Islamic mysticism

ijtihad. The interpretation of religious texts through independent reasoning.

imam. Religious leader.

komitehs. Neighborhood committees.

Majles. Assembly, parliament.

mostaz'afin. The deprived, downtrodden, or the disinherited.

mujtahids. Religious leaders.

Qajar Dynasty. The ruling family in Iran (Persia) from 1794 to 1925.

Qur'an. Holy book for Muslims.

SAVAK. Sazman-i Ittili'at va Amniyat-I Kishvar, the National Intelligence and Security Organization; this security service was created in 1957 and was used to crush any political opposition to the monarchy.

sayyid. Someone who claims descent from the Prophet Muhammad.

shah. A word for king.

shahid. Martyr.

Shari'a. Islamic law; the rules and regulations that guide the life of a Muslim.

taghut. Idolatry, false gold.

talebehs. Religious students.

theocracy. A political system that is governed according to religious principles.

ulema. Religious scholars.

vaqf. Religious endowment.

velayat-e faqih. Guardianship of the jurist.

CHAPTER 1

Introduction

The Incomplete Revolution

The June 2009 presidential elections were a significant event in Iranian politics. These elections offered Iran's political system the opportunity to take another step along a democratic path. The presidential election pitted President Mahmoud Ahmadinejad against a rather uncharismatic former prime minister, Mir-Hossein Mousavi. However, instead of democratic images of people voting, Iranians and observers around the world were left with the image of a young woman in blue jeans.

On June 20, 2009, Neda Agha Soltan walked to a demonstration in Tehran. Many protesters, frustrated with the election results and their lack of political influence, took to the streets after Ahmadinejad was declared the winner. As Neda walked along Kargar Avenue, she was shot by Abbas Kargar Javid, a man associated with the Basijis—a progovernment militia.[1] The video footage captured international attention for the graphic depiction of her death—blood streamed from her nose and chest as she lay dying on an ordinary street in Tehran. The image also captured the brutality of the regime and the numerous human rights violations that the theocratic regime has committed.

This horrific event, captured for all the world to see, offered a number of lessons for all those who were watching. First, it reminded us of the way the regime deals with perceived threats. Neda's senseless death was one of many as the regime crushed a potential political threat in the Green Movement. When the theocratic regime feels threatened, it has often responded in a ruthless manner. Second, demonstrators such as Neda face an uphill battle in their ongoing struggle for democracy. The riots, clashes, and show trials that unfolded in the subsequent months demonstrated the regime's willingness to give up any pretense at being a democracy.[2] Third, and last, it is worth noting that the regime did not justify its use of force with religious references or Islamic tenets.

Themes of This Book

Iran's political system is complex and multifaceted. This book offers an overview of political issues and problems in the Islamic Republic of Iran. It begins with the basic question: How are policy decisions made? To understand the economic situation in Iran, or the human rights violations that exist, one must understand what values guide policymaking and how these decisions affect the policies pursued in Iran.

In Iran one sees that religion is important to politics and is nominally the foundation of the political system. This poses challenges for many in the West who seek to understand how the Iranian political system functions with direct religious influence. When does Shia Islam most strongly influence politics? When do religious tenets take a backseat to the self-interest of political elites? This book is intended to help readers understand how specific religious ideas and themes influence this polity and when they have taken a backseat to other concerns.

Despite the fact that the Islamic Revolution of 1979 ushered in a theocracy, Shia theology did not guide many policies. One goal of this work is to demonstrate a tendency toward pragmatic decision making over religious or ideological beliefs based on a radical form of Islam. A strongly conservative interpretation of Islam has not determined many of the policies in Iran. Since the Revolution, there have been many instances when self-interest and pragmatism have taken precedence over theology and religious values. Thus the reader will see how the regime in Tehran has evolved during the last few decades, and how it has at times evolved in a more pragmatic direction.

A second focus of this book is threats. The evolution of Iran's political and social landscape may be slow, but during the last few decades we have seen significant change. This theocracy continues to reinvent itself as it faces internal and international threats. Iran's political system can be best described as clerical authoritarianism with weak democratic elements. One argument put forward in this book is that various threats to religious leaders and other political elites have affected the domestic and foreign policies adopted by the Islamic Republic of Iran. Thus one needs to understand the evolution of the Iranian political system and its policies in the framework of both real and perceived threats.

In addition, this book considers the democratization process in Iran. Since the early years of the twentieth century, Iranians have attempted to make their political system more democratic. Yet various attempts to move the society in a more democratic and accountable direction have failed to produce a consolidated democratic political system where citizens have a meaningful voice in political decisions. This book argues that greater democratization is unlikely to occur in the short term, especially in light of increased threats from the international community.

An Introduction to the History of Iran

Chapter 2 examines important political events that preceded the Islamic Republic of Iran—the Constitutional Revolution and the reign of the Pahlavis. In the Constitutional Revolution one can see a failed attempt to promote a more democratic polity. The monarchy enacted numerous policies to prevent a genuine democracy from taking hold. This chapter primarily focuses on the major factors that led to the crumbling of the Pahlavi reign. The shah's coziness with the West, his disrespect for Islam, the human rights violations committed by his regime, his unwillingness to share power and engage in meaningful democratic reforms, and the economic problems plaguing the country all led to his removal from the Peacock Throne. The failures of the shah, all criticized sharply by Ayatollah Ruhollah Khomeini, contributed to the Islamic Revolution of 1979.

This chapter also examines the role of Ayatollah Khomeini before the Revolution; his influence during the late 1970s, despite his exile in Turkey, Iraq, and later France; and how his views affected the theocracy that was created. Although the Western media often portrayed Khomeini as a rigid leader and absolute ruler of Iran, that image is misleading. And though Khomeini was highly influential throughout the 1970s and until his death in 1989, he was not in complete control of the creation of this new political system. This work suggests a more nuanced understanding of the role that Khomeini played. Although he was an important figure in the Revolution, he was not the grand puppeteer pulling the strings every step of the way. Other individuals, some of whom were his more radical followers, pushed him into policies that he did not initiate. Furthermore, the image of an inflexible Ayatollah who never compromised misses the mark. Though it may have been a delayed response, accepting the cease-fire (drinking from a poisoned chalice) to end the war in Iraq in the 1980s shows his eventual pragmatism and realism. There are other instances where Khomeini's pragmatism comes through (e.g., evolution on women's voting rights and participation in the political system, and dealings with the so-called Great Satan, America, in the Iran-Contra affair). In this book I use Khomeini's writings to demonstrate not just his profound influence on the Iranian political landscape but also the evolution of his thoughts from a young cleric in Qom to the leader of a unique political system in the 1980s.

The Revolution and the Role of Religion

Chapter 3 explores the role of religion in Iranian politics. Religion, specifically Shia Islam, is a powerful belief system and source of identity in Iran today. And religion's influence on Iranian politics is nothing new. Dating back to the sixth century BCE, Zoroastrianism was an influential religion in Persia, and Zoroastrians believed that religion had political as well as spiritual concerns.[3] Shia Islam supplanted Zoroastrianism to become the dominant religion in the country in the sixteenth century.

In the last century, religion for some became a consuming worldview that provided choices and answers, and that gave meaning to individuals' lives. Although some Enlightenment and contemporary thinkers have argued for the separation of religion and politics, religion continues to be a potent force in politics. Despite the predictions of many that religion will wither away, religion is still an important element in the construction of group identity, and it is a key force in Iran.[4]

For Ayatollah Khomeini, the founding father of the Islamic Revolution of 1979, Islamic law, or shari'a, offered a just political system. That the Pahlavi regime had deviated significantly from the basis of Islamic law demonstrated to Khomeini that the regime was unjust. The grievances of many Iranians against their monarch led to a revolution that was unique in the twentieth century. Many of the revolutions that occurred in the twentieth century were Marxist in orientation. Given that Marx believed that religion was the opiate of the masses, religion was banished by many Marxist revolutionaries. Iranians, conversely, embraced a version of Islam and harnessed its power in their Revolution. Given that more than 90 percent of Iranians follow the Shia faith, it is not surprising that religion provided a frame of reference for many who opposed the shah's rule and demanded political change.

Moreover, by the late 1970s many secular ideologies had failed to bring about social and economic change in the Middle East. Ideas such as communism and modernization did little to improve the lives of many in the region. Aside from the failure of these Western ideas to galvanize or rally many Iranians, there also remained a general resistance to foreign ideologies that were a reminder of Western domination and imperialism. Islam, conversely, was indigenous to the region and familiar to the people. Thus it is not surprising that political Islam would have a following and would be the vehicle for a revolution in Iran.[5]

Given its unique nature and its lasting impact on Iran, the Revolution of 1979 is analyzed in great detail in chapter 3. Specifically, I focus on how— through the ideas, practices, and symbols of Shia Islam, and a grassroots network based on Shia Islam—the revolutionaries were able to overthrow an established monarchy. I also examine how Ayatollah Khomeini came to lead and personify the Revolution in Iran. He also initiated far-reaching political changes upon his return to his homeland in February 1979. Some of the men and women in the streets openly sobbed as he was driven past.[6] He received a hero's welcome from millions of Iranians upon arriving in his native land in February 1979.

The grassroots network and religious ideas based on Shia Islam not only shaped and drove the Revolution of 1979; they also colored the political system that was subsequently created. Understanding the Revolution sets the stage for the theocracy that was established in its aftermath.

Iran has a unique political system in the twenty-first century. As a theocracy, Iran's political system is supposed to be based on and consistent with Islam. In addition, this political system is dominated by religious elites. This is most clearly demonstrated in the office of the supreme leader. Iran created one of the few theocratic political systems in global politics. This demonstrates the importance of religion while also presenting some difficulties for understanding this polity.

Some scholars have described Iran's system as "one of the most complex Byzantine, fragmented, and opaque on Earth."[7] Elements of the political system, such as the Guardian Council and the Assembly of Experts, are unknown or generally misunderstood. Chapter 3 sheds light on the political institutions that were established at the birth of this new regime.

Since 1979, many prominent individuals—Khomeini, Rafsanjani, and the like—have struggled to control the levers of power in Iran. Various domestic factions have vied for power, including neoconservatives and hard-line conservatives who believe in Khomeini's efforts to spread the Revolution and his anti-Western approach. There have also been reformers and pragmatic conservatives who are willing to cooperate with the West and moderate some of the harsher aspects of the theocracy in domestic affairs. The results of these power struggles and the religious ideas that justify various policies have contributed to the country's unique political system. In addressing these different institutions within Iran, chapter 3 explains the factionalism at work and the different centers of power.

Elections in Iran

Despite the criticisms that have been raised regarding Iran's theocracy, Iranians voted to change their political system from a monarchy to an Islamic republic. One very curious element of the foundation of Iran's political system rests on the fact that in 1979, Iranians were consulted and allowed to voice their political preferences in a largely democratic process. One may wonder why the revolutionary leaders decided to *allow* the Iranian public to have a political voice at all. Why did Khomeini and his cadre turn to a referendum to alter the political system? Shia Islam does not emphasize the notion of consultation in the manner that Sunni Islam does. One possible answer was that they were confident of the outcome. People in Iran were so frustrated with the shah, his government, and his policies that the revolutionary leaders were assured of a victory. That the referendum consisted of one narrowly tailored question lends support to this explanation. It simply asked if the people wanted to replace the monarchy and establish an Islamic republic.

Some revolutionary leaders also saw the benefits of a participatory process. Political leaders have often boasted of the fact that more than 90 percent of the eligible public took part in the creation of the Islamic Republic.[8] Elections and referenda, especially when free from manipulation, can confer legitimacy on a political system. Although the system that was created is not a liberal democracy, Iranians participated in a democratic campaign, and there are democratic elements in this resulting political system. Furthermore, no elected official has ever refused to give up office at the end of his term. Thus the peaceful handover of power is a norm of Iran's political system.

Chapter 4 analyzes the presidential and parliamentary elections in Iran since 1980. Some readers may be surprised to learn that since the Islamic Revolution in 1979, Iran has experienced multiple elections for president and for the legislature. This chapter examines why the Islamic Republic continues to stress and hold elections, and it analyzes the role that elections have played in Iran. Chapter 4 also discusses some instances of electoral manipulation.

Human Rights in Iran

Despite the fact that millions of Iranians welcomed Khomeini and voted for the political changes he endorsed, many observers outside Iran have expressed their concerns about the political system that was created after the Iranian Revolution. There are a number of reasons why human rights activists, governmental officials, and scholars share this common concern. Some have complained that the Revolution ushered in discrimination and oppression. Although Iran was not a blossoming liberal democracy under the shah, the monarchy had better relations with many other countries and offered some of its members (women in particular) more freedom than the political system that followed.[9]

This book addresses the importance of human rights in Iran and the global and domestic forces that influence this topic. Since the Islamic Republic transformed Iran's political system, there have been significant violations of human rights, including the right to life, the right to be free from torture, and other basic civil and political liberties. Nongovernmental organizations have consistently criticized Iran's policies over the years, including during the reformist Khatami presidency. Two reasons help explain the Islamic Republic's poor record on human rights: a specific and narrow interpretation of Islam, and perceived domestic and international threats to the regime.

Many of the human rights violations committed by the government during the last thirty years stem from perceived threats. Limitations on political rights occur to limit political opposition to the regime and thus protect the dominant power of hard-line conservatives in the regime. Khatami spoke of encouraging and protecting human rights, including freedom of speech and the press. However, many of the reformists' efforts were blocked by the conservatives on the Guardian Council. Despite human rights violations that occur in the name of Islam—for example, punishing an individual accused of adultery by stoning—Islam may also offer hope for future progress. Because *ijtihad* (i.e., the interpretation of religious texts through independent reasoning) allows for the reexamination of some Islamic doctrines and ideas, this provides an avenue for improving the human rights record in Iran. In sum, this chapter examines the ebb and flow of human rights in Iran since the Revolution, and it concludes with a recounting of the progress that has occurred during the last thirty years.

Religion and Realpolitik in Iranian Foreign Policy

Iran "has long been a scene and a source of instability and tension. Recently, the problem of this area has critically tested the new international order and sharply challenged American statesmanship. In spite of official and unofficial interchanges among the four governments involved—Tehran, Moscow, London, and Washington—and, in spite of discussions in the Security Council of

the United Nations, the problem has not yet been solved."[10] These words written in the 1940s are strikingly reminiscent of the problems facing the United
States and the international community concerning Iran today.

Iran is not the powerful hegemon—the Persian Empire—that once controlled vast territory from the borders of modern Iran to Greece. Although
Khomeini may have talked about spreading the Revolution, no current leader
envisions enlarging Iranian territory as Cyrus the Great did or as Darius and
Xerxes tried to do.[11] Yet that fifth-century empire has not faded from the
minds of contemporary Iranians. The Persian Empire could boast of a fierce
army and vast wealth. It was one of the most impressive civilizations the world
has known. Iranians seek not to reconstitute the empire but rather to gain
respect and influence in the region. Iran's fervent anti-Western stance has contributed to some of its regional stature. Iran is one of the few countries in the
region that is not diplomatically, militarily, or financially dependent on the
West, and especially the United States.

Iran sits on the Persian Gulf in a volatile region. In addition, the strategi-
cally important Strait of Hormuz just off the southern coast of Iran is a narrow channel that connects the Persian Gulf to the Gulf of Oman. Most of the
Middle East's oil must pass through the Strait of Hormuz on supertankers.
The US Energy Information Agency suggested that "15.5 to 17 million barrels
a day have flowed through the Strait to world markets in recent years. This has
been 33 percent to 40 percent of all seaborne traded oil, and some 17 percent
of all oil traded worldwide."[12]

In addition, Iran also exerts or tries to exert its influence over other countries in the Middle East such as Syria, with its support of President Bashir al-
Assad. Furthermore, Tehran has given support to terrorist organizations in the
Middle East such as Hezbollah and Hamas.[13] Finally, Iran is suspected of developing a nuclear weapons program and of continuing to enrich uranium—
one of the ingredients needed to build a nuclear weapon.[14] Many Arab leaders,
including the Saudi and Jordanian kings, have also voiced concerns about the
growing Iranian threat.

Iran has offered rhetorical and financial support to the Palestinians in their
struggle to secure a homeland in the West Bank and the Gaza Strip. Iran's continuing hostility to the state of Israel predates statements by Ahmadinejad that
Israel should be wiped off the map. Ayatollah Khomeini was very explicit in
his anti-Israel remarks. And even more troubling than these remarks is the fact
that Iran has ballistic missiles with the capability and range to reach Israel's
territory, including Tel Aviv and Jerusalem. Given the fact that the Middle

East has experienced much instability in the last five decades—with wars (the Six-Day War, Iraq-Iran War, Iraq War in 2003, Lebanon in 2007, and Gaza in 2008), uprisings (the Intifada in 2000), assassinations (Sadat in 1981, Rabin in 1995, and Hareri in 2005), and the Arab Awakening—Iran's role in the Middle East has the potential to be quite significant. One question this book addresses is whether Iran's future influence will lead to greater regional stability and more cooperation or to more instability and bloodshed.

Assessing Iranian foreign policy in the last thirty years since the Revolution takes us through a number of major wars and conflicts in the region, to Iran's development as a growing regional power. Chapter 6 examines the role that threats have played in the push and pull of Iranian foreign policy. Although religious rhetoric has often billowed from Friday sermons and speeches, pragmatic policies driven by a basic understanding of realism have generally determined Iran's actual foreign policy. Although Islamic language would be employed to defend this policy, as the regime moved further away from the Revolution in 1979, the policies were more often driven by realism than by Islam. Alternatively, one might say that Iran's foreign policy was driven by Islamic realpolitik with more emphasis on power politics than on religious piety. Thus, in dealing with Iran, the proper approach for the United States and other countries is to understand Iran's national interests and to find some common interests upon which to cooperate and reduce tensions.

Economics in the Islamic Republic of Iran

Natural resources offer Tehran another means to influence global politics beyond the Middle East. The Middle East holds vast oil reserves—close to "⅔ of the world's proven oil reserves."[15] Currently, when numerous countries around the world are looking for stable sources of energy, Iran proves to be a curse and a blessing. Iran's resources are a blessing to many energy-dependent countries around the world because Iran has significant deposits of oil and natural gas. Iran supplies roughly 5 percent of the world's oil to global markets and produces more than 2 million barrels of oil per day. In addition, it has largely untapped natural gas resources.

However, Iran's natural resources are also a curse both for Iran and for the world. They have proven to be a curse for foreign diplomats who cannot use economic leverage or economic carrots to induce a change in Iran's behavior. But oil wealth has also proven to be a curse for Iran itself. The oil curse tends to result in the neglect of economic development and investment in other areas of the state's economy. Because oil revenues provide Iran with much income, there have been smaller incentives to develop other industries. Some have also suggested that reliance on oil production tends to inhibit the development of democracy, given that most of the major oil-producing states (Saudi Arabia, Kuwait, Iran, etc.) are far from democratic.[16] States that rely on natural resources to fund the government do not have to ask their citizens for revenue. In states devoid of natural resources, direct taxation of citizens provides the government with revenues to carry out basic functions. Citizens that are taxed will often make demands on the government for greater access or influence. Thus the demand for accountability (sometimes discussed in terms of the unjust nature of "taxation without representation") can influence states that depend on their population's productivity and taxes to function. States that rely on the wealth produced from natural resources are not accountable to their citizens because they do not have to rely on their citizens for wealth creation and taxes. Despite the Iranian government's reliance on oil revenues, Iran has various economic problems that prohibit the government from buying off the population indefinitely.

Chapter 7 considers the economic problems that plague Iran, including sanctions, inflation, and inequality. By looking at a range of economic issues, one can see that some of these economic problems are a long-term threat to the stability of the regime. Iran is far from a free market, capitalist system. The inability of the Iranian government to develop long-term economic plans that produce growth and provide for the basic needs of the people has been a consistent problem during the theocratic regime's last few decades. To explain these issues, chapter 7 looks at the interplay between Islamic tenets and factional infighting. In addition, this chapter analyzes the role of economic threats to the regime in the form of international sanctions. Tehran has adopted a pragmatic policy to deal with international sanctions. Finally, I examine some improvements in basic needs that are not threatening to the regime and are consistent with Khomeini's message of social justice. These problems must be confronted by the regime to create economic growth and prevent an economically frustrated population from expressing its anger at the government. Failure to combat these economic problems will contribute to the regime's lack of legitimacy.

Iran's Future
Will Iran move toward a more democratic political system where human rights are protected, or will Iran increasingly become a religious dictatorship where rights and democratic choice are only a facade? Chapter 8, the conclusion,

suggests that Iran's political system can develop into a society that is more respectful of human rights under certain conditions. Tehran could act in a more cooperative manner with other countries, and it could decrease its support for violent groups in the context of a less threatening environment.

Various threats—real and imagined—to the Iranian regime can explain specific policies. One should not be astonished at the role that threats to the Islamic regime play in Iran. Given Iran's long history of foreign interference, the political sensitivity to threats is unsurprising. In the twentieth century alone, the British Empire and Russian Empire repeatedly meddled in Iranian politics. Whether it was the British concessions on tobacco or the Anglo-Persian Oil Company's domination of the country's oil, the British did not respect Iranian sovereignty. Furthermore, during World War II Iran was occupied by the British in the southern part of the country, and by the Russians in the northern part of the country. When coupled with the American-led coup of Mossadeq in 1953, political leaders in Iran have ample reasons to be concerned about threats to their power and independence. With no long-term, dependable allies, with the possible exception of Syria, the regime is keenly aware of foreign threats. However, Iranian leaders are not only concerned about foreign threats.

Internal threats are also a concern to the regime and help explain policy decisions. As Graeme A. M. Davies notes:

> The social and economic malaise within Iran manifested itself in 1992, 1994, and 1995 as declining living standards resulted in workers rioting in several Iranian cities. Similarly, there were mass student protests in June 1999 which were ruthlessly repressed. While all these riots were overwhelmed by the internal security forces, instability in Iran still provides domestic political incentives for the Iranian regime to manufacture crises with the US and hopefully divert attention from domestic political problems, of which there are many in Iran. The regime in Tehran is very aware of the problems that it is facing as shown by a leaked Interior Ministry document in 2003 that suggested around 90 percent of the population were dissatisfied with the government.[17]

Understanding these threats and how the Iranian regime deals with perceived threats can help to explain its current and future policies.

This book seeks to explain the creation and development of the theocracy in Iran. It explores the influence of religion on the political system and the policies produced in Iran. This project incorporates the role of threats in the development of public policy. In addition, the book examines the pragmatic policies adopted by the government of Iran. Finally, this work addresses those factors that are necessary for Iran to become a more open, democratic, and accountable political regime. Ultimately, more cooperation and fewer threats are more likely to produce moderate responses from Tehran than coercion and threats of military action.

Conclusion

The Islamic Revolution successfully ousted a monarch and developed a new political system, but it did not usher in a democratic political system. Demonstrations in the aftermath of the election in 2009 show Iranians' continuing efforts to have a more accountable government.

In addition to Shia Islam, the real and perceived threats to the Islamic political system are key to understanding Iran's future. Will Iran move toward a more democratic political system where human rights are protected, or will it increasingly become a religious dictatorship where rights and democratic choice are just a facade? This book argues that an increase in threat perceptions will result in further entrenchment of illiberal and confrontational policies.

Notes

1. Martin Fletcher, "The Face of Abbas Kargar Javid: Man Accused of Killing Neda Soltan," *The Times*, August 20, 2009. The Basij are a volunteer paramilitary force under the direction of the Islamic Revolutionary Guards. "Basij" comes from the Farsi word for mobilization. Ali Reza Nader, David E. Thaler, and S. R. Bohandy, *The Next Supreme Leader: Succession in the Islamic Republic of Iran* (Santa Monica, CA: RAND Corporation, 2011), 33.

2. Iranian journalist Masih Alinejad wrote a letter to Ahmed Shaheed, the United Nations' special rapporteur on human rights in Iran. It discusses the human rights violations in the aftermath of the 2009 election. It can be found at www.insideofiran.org/en/human-rights/2215-to-the-un-special-rapporteur-number-of-iranians-killed-is-a-tragedy-not-a-mere-statistic.html. The International Campaign for Human Rights in Iran stated that more than 400 prisoners of conscience have been jailed since the 2009 elections. International Campaign for Human Rights, "UN Resolution Ramps Up Cross-Regional International Pressure on Iran's Human Rights Crisis," November 21, 2010.

3. Sandra Mackey, *The Iranians: Persia, Islam and the Soul of a Nation* (New York: Plume, 1998), 17.

4. Mary Ann Tetreault, "God, the State, and Mammon: Religious Revivalism and the Modern World," paper prepared for the International Studies Association meeting, New Orleans, March 25, 2002, 3.

5. Some have even suggested that political Islam gained strength in regions such as the Middle East because it challenged the hegemonic ideology of the West and the United States. Mohammed Ayoob, "Challenging Hegemony: Political Islam and the North-South Divide," *International Studies Review* 9 (2007): 629–43, at 631; Ray Takeyh, *The Guardians of the Revolution* (Oxford: Oxford University Press, 2009), 21.

6. The description of Khomeini's return to Iran in 1979 is derived from Robin Wright's account. Robin Wright, *In the Name of God* (New York: Simon & Schuster, 1989), 35–37.

7. Kenneth Pollack, Daniel Byman, Martin Indyk, Suzanne Maloney, Michael O'Hanlon, and Bruce Riedel, *Which Path to Persia? Options for a New American Strategy towards Iran* (Washington, DC: Brookings Institution Press, 2009), 17.

8. Nikki Keddie, *Modern Iran: Roots and Results of Revolution* (New Haven, CT: Yale University Press, 2003), 247.

9. United Nations, "Report of UN Secretary General on the Situation of Human Rights in Iran at the Human Rights Council in Geneva," March 28, 2011, A/HRC/16/75; Mahmood Monshipouri, *Islamism, Secularism, and Human Rights in the Middle East* (Boulder, CO: Lynne Rienner, 1998), chap. 6.

10. Harold Moulton, "Foreword" to Arthur C. Millspaugh, *Americans in Persia* (Washington, DC: Brookings Institution Press, 1946), iii.

11. Herodotus, *The Histories*, details the expansion of the Persian Empire and Darius's attempt and failure to conquer the Greek city-states in 490 BCE and Xerxes' attempt and failure in 480–479 BCE. The last three books of *The Histories* are devoted to Xerxes' attempt to conquer Athens and the other Greek city-states. Herodotus, *The Histories*, translated by Aubrey de Selincourt (New York: Penguin Books, 2003). See also J. M. Cook, *The Persian Empire* (New York: Schocken Books, 1983).

12. Alexander Wilner and Anthony Cordesman, "US and Iranian Strategic Competition: The Gulf Military Balance," Center for Strategic and International Studies, November 2, 2011, 129.

13. Jeffrey Feltman, "Acting Assistant Secretary, Bureau of Near Eastern Affairs, Testimony before the Subcommittee on Near Eastern and South Central Asian Affairs of the Senate Committee on Foreign Relations," Washington, DC, June 8, 2010; Thanassis Cambanis, *A Privilege to Die* (New York: Free Press, 2010), 221.

14. The International Atomic Energy Agency (IAEA) noted its concerns about Iranian nuclear programs in its November 15, 2004 report, "Implementation of the NPT Safeguards Agreement in the Islamic Republic of Iran," www.iaea.org/Publications/Documents/Board/2004/gov2004-83_derestrict.pdf. An IAEA report in November 2007 also complained that "the Agency's knowledge about Iran's current nuclear programme is diminishing" due to the lack of complete cooperation on the part of Tehran. IAEA, "Implementation of the NPT Safeguards Agreement and relevant provisions of Security Council Resolutions 1737 (2006) and 1747 (2007) in the Islamic Republic of Iran." November 15, 2007. See also Joseph Cirincione and Elice Connor, "How Iran Can Build a Bomb," *Foreign Policy*, July 1, 2010.

15. Ayoob, "Challenging Hegemony," 631.

16. See, e.g., Michael Ross, "Blood Barrels," *Foreign Affairs* 87 (May–June 2008): 2–8.

17. Graeme A. M. Davies, "Inside Out or Outside In: Domestic and International Factors Affecting Iranian Foreign Policy towards the United States 1990–2004," *Foreign Policy Analysis* 4 (2008): 209–25, at 214.

PART I

The Past

CHAPTER 2

Pahlavi Power and the Alienation of the Masses

Iranian history is filled with foreign interventions, political infighting, coups, and political upheavals—none more earthshaking than the Islamic Revolution of 1979. To understand the Revolution, which was orchestrated by Ayatollah Khomeini and his supporters, it is necessary to explain a number of important events that occurred earlier in the twentieth century. These seminal events will help the reader comprehend why millions of Iranians flocked into the streets to welcome Khomeini home in February 1979, and why they endorsed the theocratic changes he advocated.

On a number of occasions during the last 125 years, Iranians have gone into the streets to demonstrate for political change and a more accountable government. In 1905, 1953, and 1979, and again in 2009, many Iranians voiced their political frustration with the authoritarian leaders running the country. The year 2009 was just the latest phase in Iran's incomplete Revolution. Since the early years of the twentieth century, Iranians have articulated a desire for a democratic political system. Unfortunately, these desires remain largely unfulfilled.

The Constitutional Revolution

At the beginning of the twentieth century Iranians first attempted to fundamentally alter their political system and move toward a more liberal, accountable regime in the Constitutional Revolution (1905–11). This political activity was reminiscent of the political agitation in 1890 over a tobacco concession. The Qajar monarchy had inflamed many segments of the population by granting a tobacco concession to a British company. The Qajar monarch offered a monopoly on buying and selling tobacco to a British company in return for money, which the Qajars perpetually needed.

Members of the bazaar (i.e., *bazaaris*) and other segments of society rejected this proposal emphatically. Not only were their economic interests at stake, but they also rejected further foreign interference in the country. The *bazaaris* successfully mobilized various aspects of society, including segments of the clergy:

> The *bazaaris* also solicited the backing of the clergy by arguing that the concessions violated the Islamic principles of free trade and were an affront to the independence of the nation and Muslim community. While many clergy remained indifferent or sided with the government, a number of clerics encouraged the protests out of political conviction or economic calculation (tobacco was an important cash crop grown on land held as private property by many clerics or as trusts bequeathed as support for religious institutions). Finally, a number of clerics, including one of the leading Ayatollahs, issued religious decrees forbidding the consumption of tobacco. The tobacco trade in the bazaars ceased and its consumption in the coffee houses and homes came to a halt; the Shah was forced to rescind the concessions.[1]

This political activism at the end of the nineteenth century enabled the mobilization of much of the population in the Constitutional Revolution that followed a decade later. The unification of clerics, *bazaaris*, and intellectuals (many who had studied in the West) centered on their criticism of Western interference in Iran and the authoritarian nature of the Qajar regime. Western-educated intellectuals promoted ideas about accountability and political freedom that found receptive ears in Iran. The political protests at the heart of the Constitutional Revolution emphasized Iran's sovereignty and democracy.[2] These demands for a political system that was responsive to the people made some limited progress when the king agreed to the creation of a Parliament and sowed the seeds for future change: "The intellectual critique of absolute monarchy came from Western-educated and inspired thinkers and segments of the Shiite clergy who were sympathetic to tenets of consultation and the rule of law. Together they introduced the urban population to the principles of accountability, representative government, and political participation. Along with pressure from the urban population this coalition was able to formally end the arbitrary role of the Qajar monarchy by establishing an elected parliament and drafting a constitution."[3]

However, this coalition proved unable to prevent the rise of the Pahlavi monarchy, which came to power and quashed the desire for a vibrant, accountable democratic political system for many decades. Yet one can see in the tobacco revolt, and in the Constitutional Revolution, the seeds of the Islamic Revolution of 1979.

The Pahlavi Regime

Political power in Iran was rarely transferred democratically in the twentieth century. Mohammad Reza Pahlavi became the ruler of Iran on August 25, 1941, after the Soviet Union and the United Kingdom invaded the country and orchestrated his father's (Reza Shah) abdication. Likewise, his father did not rise to power on the basis of the ballot box. Reza Shah (1925–41) had come to power through his position as a military leader. On February 21, 1921, he took over Tehran with his Cossack Division and began to dominate politics.[4] His influence over Iranian politics gradually increased as he accumulated political offices. First, he became army commander, then minister of war, then prime minister, and eventually this culminated in his becoming the king of Iran.[5] Reza Shah was an elusive political figure who initially appealed to many in Iran: "Many nationalists, socialists, and clerics backed the new monarch. Nationalists admired him for unifying the nation. Clerics hoped he would stop Mustafa Kemal Ataturk's secularizing reforms from spreading to Iran. Leftists hoped he would dismantle the archaic agrarian relations and usher in a new era of capitalist development that would eventually lead to socialism. But the Shah disappointed and surprised both his admirers and his critics."[6]

The Islamic Consultative Assembly (Majles-e Shorâ-ye Eslami, or simply Majles) ended the Qajar Dynasty in 1925, and in 1926 Reza Khan was officially crowned king.[7] This process, as described by the prominent scholar Ervand Abrahamian, echoed many of the power grabs by strong men in the past: "He did not openly venture on to the central stage until 1925–26 when he convened a Constituent Assembly, deposed Ahmad Shah, accepted the crown, named his son heir apparent, and crowned himself monarch—much in the fashion of his heroes, Napoleon and Nader Shah."[8]

Reza Shah's coup fundamentally set back the progress of the Constitutional Revolution of 1905, which had sought a more accountable and representative government. While allowing elections for the Majles, he also manipulated these parliamentary elections from 1925 to 1940 in order to ensure that he had malleable lawmakers with whom to work.[9]

Despite his centralization of power at home, aspects of his foreign policy would contribute to his political downfall. Before World War II he appeared too friendly with Hitler's Germany for the Allies' liking. Trade demonstrated the growing ties between the two countries. By the end of the 1930s almost one-third of Iran's trade was with Germany.[10] The Allies feared losing Iran's natural resources—especially its oil—and its strategic location to the Nazis. So as part of the war effort in 1941, they sent Reza Shah into exile, where he died in 1944, and replaced him with his son—Mohammad Reza Pahlavi.

The removal of Reza Shah in favor of his inexperienced son demonstrates not only the realism of the great powers to do as they wished with a weak state but also the limited support Iranians had for their king. Ansari notes this in *Modern Iran since 1921:* "It was an exercise in realpolitik in which Reza Shah Pahlavi became expendable in the interests of the wider international imperatives. The fact that it happened so easily, with so little domestic opposition, is a testament to the hollowness of the regime that had been constructed: solid in appearance but devoid of the moral fiber or nationalist fervor necessary for its sustenance."[11]

The young king who inherited the throne pursued many policies that alienated his people and contributed to his demise. During the almost four decades of Mohammad Reza Pahlavi's rule (1941–79), a number of factors contributed to events that led to the Islamic Revolution of 1979, and the loss of the shah's throne (all further references to the shah refer to Mohammad Reza Pahlavi). The first of these problems concerns the relationship between the shah and the West. He was too friendly with the West and Western leaders. The perception of many Iranians was that the shah was reluctant to defend the rights of Iranians if it meant that he would alienate his supporters in the West. The second issue concerned the economy. The shah seemed either indifferent to the economic and social woes of the majority of Iranians, or impotent to improve the economic situation of the people of his country. The failure of the White Revolution to significantly improve health care, expand education, and create jobs was symptomatic of the shah's ineffective economic and social policies.

The shah was also criticized for the cultural and religious policies that he pursued on the throne. For many conservative Iranians the prohibition of the veil for women and the use of civil courts instead of Islamic courts were attacks on Islam and Iranian identity. Finally, the shah faced repeated condemnation for the human rights violations that occurred at the hands of the National Intelligence and Security Organization (Sazman-i Ittili'at va Amniyat-I Kishvar), better known as SAVAK. All these criticisms were justifications for the Revolution that ultimately replaced him and changed the political system from a monarchy to a theocracy. This chapter chronicles the shah's evolution from a weak monarch to an authoritarian leader who refused to engage in democratic reforms and share power with his political opponents, and to the beginnings of the Revolution that would result in his exile. The chapter also focuses on the two key actors in this prerevolutionary drama: the shah and Ayatollah Khomeini. In addition, it examines the domestic factors—economic stagnation and human rights violations—that caused millions of Iranians to gravitate toward Khomeini and his religious-political views.

Attacking Islam

Many Iranians, and especially clerics such as Khomeini, viewed the policies of the Pahlavis as an attack on Islam. Mohammad Reza Pahlavi, like his father before him, embarked on a program to remake Iran along Western lines. The West, for Reza Shah, was the height of progress and innovation, and he wanted to lead his people down this path. Thus he tried to mold Iran into a more modern and powerful state. These efforts would push Iran toward the image of the West, and this inevitably meant pushing Iran in a more secular direction. Although Reza Shah would engage in a frontal assault on Islam's influence in Iran, his initial steps on becoming king were far more respectful than what would follow. In April 1924 he offered a rather gracious speech on the importance of Islam: "My special attention has been and will continue to be given to the preservation of the principles of religion and the strengthening of its foundation because I considered the complete reinforcing of religion one of the most effective means of achieving national unity and strengthening of the spirit of the Iranian society."[12]

Despite these initial courteous efforts, during the 1930s Reza Shah started to emasculate the clergy in Iran. In this he was similar to Ataturk's approach to Turkey decades before.[13] Even the name "Pahlavi" had a pre-Islamic origin.

To achieve a modern, secular society Reza Shah gradually replaced the authority of Islamic courts with secular courts. He wanted to greatly reduce the influence of the clergy in Iran. To do so, he attempted to diminish their legal status in society. The judicial transformation and its consequences were profound. Under the Civil and Penal Codes of 1939 and 1940, the secular authorities took over the responsibilities of the religious courts.[14] He also established a national bank modeled on European banks. Furthermore, he tried to fundamentally change education in Iran by establishing a public education system that would compete with religious schools.[15] He created an Education Ministry that required religious schools throughout Iran to conform to a standardized curriculum. This curriculum was developed in Tehran in an attempt not only to control what children learned but also to create a new generation of modern Iranians. These policies were alienating for a population more comfortable with Islam and the local mosque than a Western-based system.

Finally, Reza Shah was also viewed by many in Iran in a negative light because he attacked Islamic practices. He prohibited the teaching of the Qur'an in schools. In 1929 he limited the practice of self-flagellation associated with the reenactment of Hussein's death during Ashura.[16] Ashura is one of the most sacred holidays in Shia Islam because it honors Hussein—the son of Ali, who was martyred at Karbala. Ali was the cousin and son-in-law of the Prophet Muhammad. In this the king was deliberately limiting Shia religious practices. Islam had been part of the foundations of Iranian society for centuries; however, Reza Shah wanted to see his country become more Western in orientation.

In the West women did not wear veils or other conspicuous religious symbols, and Reza Shah wanted his society to replicate the West. So women were told to take off their veils or chadors. The veil has been a controversial topic over the years. For some in the West it is a mark of oppression, whereas for others it has empowered women to receive an education and a professional occupation. States such as France and Turkey have required women to take off the veil in some public settings. Other countries, such as Saudi Arabia, require women to be covered in public. At the start of the twentieth century, the veil said more about one's economic and social standing in Iran than it did about religion. During Reza Shah's regime the state sought to control women's attire.[17] In 1935 Reza Shah mandated, by a government decree, that women in Iran remove their veils.[18] In March 1935 the police were ordered to forcibly remove a woman's veil if she appeared in public wearing one. Women could not enter many public places—including stores, theaters, and bus stations—if they were wearing a veil.[19] Forcibly removing the Islamic symbol was a direct attack on Islam and on Shia clerical authority in Iran.[20] These policies were enacted because the Pahlavis—both father and son—"perceived Shiism as a stumbling block to their modernizing agenda."[21]

After Mohammad Reza Pahlavi accepted the throne, he also demonstrated his dislike of the clergy. His first moves as a hand-picked monarch without any base of support was to show deference to Islam and its followers. He allowed women to wear the chador in public. He reversed his father's policy and allowed the passion play associated with Ashura to resume.[22] As his confidence in his throne grew, especially after 1953, he took a more confrontational approach to the clergy and various aspects of Islam. And he further antagonized the clergy by directing the Awqaf organization—a body that controlled religious endowments. In doing so, he limited the financial means of the clergy.[23] He also limited the religious literature that was published by closing publishing houses. Beyond this, the monarchy also detained, tortured, jailed, and executed hundreds of clerics in the 1960s and 1970s. In one incident in March 1963, soldiers killed two students at a theological school in Qom.[24] Rafsanjani and Khameini, two clerics who would occupy prominent positions of power after the Revolution, were imprisoned during the shah's time on the throne.[25]

Khomeini's Critique

These various actions by father and son were seen by many in Iran, including Khomeini, as an attack on the indigenous religious beliefs of the people. Ruhollah Khomeini was the epitome of a pious Iranian. Born in 1902 to a religious family (both his father and grandfather were religious scholars), he studied at Arak and Qom. He served as a popular teacher of ethics in Qom before gaining national recognition for his criticisms of the shah. Khomeini's defense of Islam arose from its endangered status in Iranian society. As the prominent scholar Arjomand notes, "He [Khomeini] was moved first to protest in the early 1960s and then to revolutionary action in the 1970s to preserve the Shi'ite tradition, which had nourished him and which he now saw as threatened with extinction. What Khomeini was taking on was thus no less than the whole twentieth-century idea of modernization that had become entrenched in the political culture of Iran since the Constitutional Revolution (1906–1911)."[26]

To address this assault on Islam, Khomeini repeatedly criticized the anti-Islamic stance of the Pahlavi monarchy. On June 3, 1963, he stated: "We come to the conclusion that this regime also has a more basic aim: They are fundamentally opposed to Islam itself and the existence of the religious class. They do not wish this institution to exist; they do not wish any of us to exist, the great and the small alike."[27]

Khomeini also wrote numerous letters and articles criticizing the king: "The ruling circles have violated the sacred rules of Islam and are heading for trampling underfoot the very tenets of the Holy Qur'an. . . . They considered Islam and the *ulema* hostile to their plans and interests. . . . In order to warn the Muslim *ummah* of the imminent dangers facing the Qur'an and this country of the Qur'an, I declare the New Year to be a period not of festivities but of mourning."[28]

For his constant verbal and written assault on the monarchy, Khomeini was arrested in June 1963 and sent into exile. Yet despite the monarchy's efforts to rid Iran of Khomeini and limit the influence of religion, the Pahlavi regime failed to fundamentally crush Shia Islam within society. These incomplete and ineffective efforts led to the Revolution of 1979, and are discussed further in chapter 3.

The Influence of the West

Foreign interference in Iran's domestic affairs has a long history. Whether in the form of capitulations or concessions, Iranians resented the privileged treatment accorded to, or in some cases demanded by, foreign actors. The legal arrangements called capitulations were particularly troubling because they exempted foreign nationals from local laws. Capitulations, which existed throughout the Middle East, were often articulated in treaties and prevented local courts from trying foreigners in the indigenous legal system.[29] Additional anger was directed at the economic concessions given to foreign businesses. These concessions provided the Qajar monarchy with a much-needed source of revenue. In the nineteenth century a number of concessions were given to British and Russian companies for the development of Iran's infrastructure. For example, a concession went to the British to establish the Imperial Bank of Persia in 1889. This was only twenty years after another British company received a telegraph concession.[30] A tobacco concession to a British company in 1890 led to protests, and then to a fatwa forbidding the consumption of tobacco. Ultimately, this pressure forced the monarch to withdraw the concession.[31] Thus Western influence in Iran in the twentieth century drew on a long narrative.

Many Iranians felt alienated from their monarch. This stemmed, in part, from his relationship with the West. Mohammad Reza Pahlavi was increasingly viewed as beholden to the West. This was especially true after the United States restored him to the throne in 1953 in the coup of Mordad 28, 1332.

Prime Minister Mohammad Mossadeq—elected to the Majles in 1941—was selected to be premier in 1951 after Prime Minister Razmara was assassinated. Mossadeq resigned in 1952, but protests in Tehran led the shah to recall him as prime minister.[32] He battled with the shah over various policies including foreign involvement in the oil industry. Since the early years of the twentieth century, Mossadeq had consistently argued that Iran should end the misguided policy of giving in to the great powers.[33] Iranian oil was dominated by the Anglo-Iranian Oil Company (AIOC), which was later renamed British Petroleum and is now known simply as BP. This was a result of an oil concession dating back to 1901.[34] This British company treated Iranian workers poorly and took the bulk of the oil revenues back to London. Ansari notes the extent of British audacity: "Many professional Iranians considered the AIOC to be an affront to national dignity because of the colonial manner in which it operated in Abadan—including the importation of Indian labor—and because of its increasingly blatant exploitation of Iranian resources. It was widely known, for example, that AIOC paid more in taxes to the British exchequer than it did in royalties to the Iranian government. . . . The sense of grievance ran deep."[35]

In 1949 Iran sought to renegotiate the profit-sharing agreement with AIOC but was rebuffed. The British viewed the oil to be a result of British ingenuity, and hence it was more British than Iranian in their eyes. Donald Ferguson, permanent undersecretary at the Ministry of Fuel and Power, captures this sentiment: "It was British enterprise, skill and effort which discovered oil under the soil of Persia, which has got the oil out, which has built the refinery, which has developed markets for Persian oil in 30 or 40 countries, with wharves, storage tanks and pumps, road and rail tanks and other distribution facilities, and also an immense fleet of tankers. . . . None of these things would or could have been done by the Persian government or the Persian people."[36]

By the middle of the twentieth century AIOC's revenues from Iranian oil came to £200 million. Iran, however, received less than £20 million.[37] Mossadeq resented Western interference in Iran and the unwillingness of AIOC to compromise. His response, in 1951, was to nationalize the oil industry through the Iranian Oil Nationalization Act. This did not sit well with Washington or London. They feared that Mossadeq would adopt more friendly policies with the Soviet Union. Policymakers in the United States were also concerned with the possibility of a communist takeover of the Iranian government due to the instability in the country. In a statement by the US National Security Council in November 1952, one sees this concern articulated: "It is of critical importance to the United States that Iran remain an independent and sovereign nation, not dominated by the USSR. Because of its key strategic position, its petroleum resources, its vulnerability to intervention or armed attack by the USSR, and its vulnerability to political subversion, Iran must be regarded as a continuing objective of Soviet expansion."[38]

In the midst of the Cold War, the United States was not about to lose Iran to the communists as it had lost China a few years earlier. In reality the Tudeh Party (i.e., the Iranian Communist Party) was not on the verge of taking over power in Iran. It was far weaker due to internal disagreements than the United States imagined.[39]

The shah tried to replace Mossadeq with Qavan (a previous prime minister) because of the nationalization policy. Mossadeq and the nationalization act were popular with Iranians, including many *bazaaris* who offered financial support, and they took to the streets to support him.[40] The shah, due to a lack of domestic support, took refuge in Rome for a short period but was returned to power after a United States–orchestrated coup d'état in August 1953. The US Central Intelligence Agency (CIA), with British assistance, ousted the prime minister and restored Mohammad Reza Pahlavi to his throne in Operation Ajax. The goals of Operation Ajax (also referred to as TPAJAX) were outlined by Donald Wilber in the CIA Clandestine Service History "Overthrow of Premier Mossadeq of Iran, November 1952–August 1953." In Wilber's summary, he states:

> By the end of 1952, it had become clear that the Mossadeq government in Iran was incapable of reaching an oil settlement with interested Western countries; was reaching a dangerous and advanced state of illegal, deficit financing; was disregarding the Iranian constitution in prolonging Premier Mohammed Mossadeq's tenure of office; was motivated mainly by Mossadeq's desire for personal power; was governed by irresponsible policies based on emotion; had weakened the Shah and the Iranian Army to a dangerous degree; and had cooperated closely with the Tudeh (Communist) Party of Iran. In view of these factors, it was estimated that Iran was in real danger of falling behind the Iron Curtain; if that happened it would mean a victory for the Soviets in the Cold War and a major setback for the West in the Middle East. No remedial action other than the covert action plan set forth below could be found to improve the existing state of affairs. It was the aim of the TPAJAX project to cause the fall of the Mossadeq government; to reestablish the prestige and power

of the Shah; and to replace the Mossadeq government with one which would govern Iran according to constructive policies. Specifically, the aim was to bring to power a government which would reach an equitable oil settlement, enabling Iran to become economically sound and financially solvent, and which would vigorously prosecute the dangerously strong Communist Party.[41]

As one of the CIA agents involved, Kermit Roosevelt (the grandson of President Teddy Roosevelt) bragged that with a few thousand dollars they had managed to bring about the coup. The United States (with the help of the British, who were still furious with Mossadeq over the nationalization program) funded newspapers to criticize the prime minister on a daily basis. They also reached out to General Zahedi to encourage a military coup.[42] The United States also had domestic actors (the Rashidian family) organize demonstrators on the streets of Tehran to denounce Mossadeq.[43] Thus the United States received assistance from domestic sources as well. After clashes in Tehran between pro-Mossadeq and pro-shah forces, the prime minister was arrested, which allowed the shah to return to Iran and to his throne. He thanked Roosevelt, saying, "I owe my throne to God, my people, my army—and to you!"[44] Mossadeq was placed under house arrest following a trial.

Removing a popular prime minister who had the support of the bazaar and the middle class (teachers, civil servants, and lawyers), and restoring an unpopular monarch did not enamor many Iranians with the United States.[45] It reminded Iranians of Russian and British interference in the nineteenth century. The coup halted any further progress on the road to democracy. This act set the stage for the Revolution that took place twenty-five years later and for general Iranian hostility toward Washington.[46] Furthermore, the legitimacy of the shah was undermined by this act.

In the aftermath of the coup in 1953, the shah increasingly grew more confident. He received financial and military support from the United States. He aggressively promoted his modernization programs as a way to keep up with the West.[47] Aside from his restoration to the throne, the presence of Americans working in Iran also reminded the Iranian people of America's influence. Iranians would not have to look far to see an influx of foreign workers in various professions in Iran.[48] One observer estimates that there were 50,000 Americans in Iran in the mid-1970s.[49] That the shah in 1964 also pushed a revision to a bill—the American-Iranian Status of Forces Agreement—through Parliament that expanded the number of American personnel immune from prosecution made him look like a lackey of the United States.[50] The fact that the bill appeared to be linked to a $200 million loan from Washington only furthered the image of the Iranian leader doing Washington's bidding.[51]

The cozy relationship between the shah and the West was also evident from frequent visits by American presidents. Both presidents Nixon and Carter visited Tehran during the shah's reign. President Carter noted, somewhat ironically in retrospect, that the shah had created "an island of stability in a turbulent corner of the world. This is a great tribute to you, Your Majesty, and to your leadership and to the respect, admiration and love which your people give to you."[52] These visits and international meetings, all hyped in the state-run media, did not help the shah's image with average Iranians. That Iran, under the shah, was an ally of Israel contributed to Iranians' disdain for their ruler. This resentment was further fueled by Ayatollah Khomeini.

Khomeini's Critique

Khomeini repeatedly criticized the shah's pro-Western policies, including his support for Israel and the United States. For example, he was critical of the Status of Forces Agreement: "The government has sold our independence, reduced us to the level of a colony, and made the Muslim nation of Iran appear more backward than savages in the eyes of the world!"[53] Khomeini also criticized the foreign influence in the country and its colonial status. He "denounced the shah for supporting Israel against the Muslim world; allying with the West in the Cold War; undermining Islam by blindly imitating all things foreign and thereby spreading *gharb zadegi* [plague from the West]."[54]

What also disturbed the clergy, including Khomeini, was Western cultural influence in the form of books, movies, and music. This encouraged a relaxation of proper social norms—a form of moral corruption. He criticized the shah for allowing the cultural pollution of Iran with Western thoughts, books, and movies. Not only did Iranians need to protect themselves against the imperialism of Western foreign policy, but they also needed to guard against accepting alien concepts and desires in their lives.[55]

Other writers and intellectuals, such as Ali Shariati, also criticized the Westernization of Iran. Jalal al-e Ahmad and Ali Shariati developed the concept *gharb zadegi*—Westitis or Westoxification. "Westoxification" referred to "an excessive dependence on the West that threatened to strip Iranians of their independence and cultural identity."[56] In *Gharbzadegi* (Plagued by the West), Ahmad explains: "Today we stand under that [Western] banner, a people alienated from themselves; in our clothing, shelter, food, literature, and press.

And more dangerous than all, in our culture. We educate pseudo-Westerners and we try to find solutions to every problem like pseudo-Westerners."[57]

His concern with the Westoxification of Iran, as explained by Soroush, "was the coming of Western customs, manners, and technology, causing our eviction from our native home, the sacrifice of our noble and gracious traditions at the feet of the Western practices and industry. It meant the nauseating limitation of everything Western even at the expense of immolating the most eminent cultural assets and legacies of our own."[58] Thus for Khomeini, and many others in Iran, the fear of Western domination also included the degradation of Iranian culture through Western ideas and practices.

Economic Problems

Iran faced numerous economic problems despite a decade of sustained economic growth.[59] Many Iranians were unable to find a job and affordable housing. Furthermore, their basic needs (including access to health care) were not being met, and inflation was often a problem. There was a growing gap between the rich and the poor.[60] One study concluded that expenditures in the wealthiest households grew, while declining in the bottom 40 percent of the population: "On the basis of household expenditure surveys carried out by the Statistical Center of Iran in urban and rural areas, it is easily seen that while the expenditure share of the top 20 percent of households in urban and rural areas rose from 50 percent in 1969 to 54 percent in 1973, the expenditure share of the bottom 40 percent of households declined from 17 percent to 13 percent over the same period."[61] Another study suggested that the top 20 percent of the population had more than 60 percent of the country's income in 1975 compared with the lowest 40 percent, which had 11 percent.[62] Additionally, corruption was an endemic problem in Iran. One scholar estimates between $13 and $15 billion was lost in waste and corruption in the years 1977–78 alone.[63]

The Iranian people resented their king because the economic policies that were enacted failed to deliver economic benefits to the people. Although the shah wanted to move Iran from an agricultural society to a modern industrial power, his efforts were ineffective.[64] Ultimately, the Shah and his advisers fundamentally mismanaged the economy and were incapable of using the country's oil wealth to improve the long-term prospects of Iran's economy.

One of the initial economic problems that Iranians faced was the lack of jobs. The economy was driven by the oil sector, which did not produce many jobs. In the 1970s some 40,000 people were employed in the oil industry. This was less than 1 percent of the population.[65] Those Iranians fortunate enough to have a job often did not receive a sustainable living wage. Protests to demand better wages occurred throughout the shah's reign. One example was in May 1961, when more than 50,000 teachers in Tehran demanded better pay.[66]

In many small towns and villages throughout Iran, the people lacked access to electricity, sanitation, and health care.[67] In addition, in the early 1970s more than 40 percent of Iranians were undernourished by the World Health Organization's standard.[68] The shah's agricultural policies unintentionally enhanced Khomeini's grassroots network. When the agricultural reforms failed to provide farmers with an adequate standard of living, many moved to the cities to search for work. Some 2 million Iranians moved to urban centers between 1966 and 1978.[69] This created additional problems.

In the cities many Iranians also found it difficult to secure affordable housing. Between 1967 and 1976 close to 40 percent of Iranian families lived in a one-room apartment; and in Tehran, Iranians spent 50 percent of their income on housing.[70] Because demand for housing exceeded supply in Iran's major cities, housing was unaffordable for many Iranians. Many scholars have noted that rents in the major cities rose at least 100 percent annually.[71]

In addition to having trouble finding affordable housing, these peasants struggled to satisfy their basic needs, especially food and medical services. Having left their rural communities, many felt isolated and disoriented in the cities. And because they had left their families, these individuals could no longer rely on communal ties to help in desperate times. Therefore, when rural Iranians who had migrated to cities such as Tehran experienced economic hardships, it was religious institutions that provided social services to help the newcomers get by. And given that the government had failed to develop policies to help these vulnerable individuals, they often turned to their local mosque for food subsidies or medical assistance.[72] The mosques were a community and a familiar institution where new arrivals to the city could feel comfortable and receive much-needed assistance.

Inflation was also a problem throughout the last two decades of the shah's reign. By 1962 the government admitted that inflation was more than 10 percent, although some believed that it was much higher.[73] The Iranian government claimed that inflation was 14.2 percent in 1974 and more than 27 percent in 1977. However, the International Monetary Fund estimated that the actual numbers were much higher. To give one example, food prices increased about 30 percent per year in the mid-1970s.[74] Inflation in Iran was largely the result of easy access to credit, few productive investments, and the purchase of nonessential imports.[75] The middle and lower classes often bore the brunt of the inflationary problems in Iran.

Government Policies

One of the basic problems with Iran's economy was the lack of development and growth in the private sector. In 1963 the shah created the Ministry of the Economy, which was headed by Alinaqi Alikhani. Alikhani attempted to foster economic growth and industrialization, but he ultimately failed due to political interference. He gradually lost the political support of the shah for his developmental policies. The increase in oil revenues in the 1970s contributed to the demise of Alikhani and his ministry.[76] As Nasr notes, increased oil wealth led the shah to the conclusion that he could guide economic policy:

> After 1966–67, when the growth of the preceding four years had relieved economic pressures on the state, and after 1971, when the price of oil would begin to enrich the state, the Shah's attitude toward economic growth and its institutional foundations changed drastically. He began to view growth as self-sustaining and confused oil wealth with development (especially in the heady years of the 1970s). He then concluded that growth, as well as revenue and employment generation, did not need a private sector—which is why Alikhani's attempts to protect it were deemed overzealous. In the 1970s, these conclusions would lead the Shah to question the wisdom of his economic planners. He came to believe that he knew more about industrialization than did the economists, and he began to credit himself with having resolved problems of growth.[77]

Iran in the 1950s and 1960s benefited from its natural resources, especially oil, which brought the government its main source of revenue. Oil revenues rose from $90 million in 1955 to more than $485 million a decade later.[78] By 1970 Iran was making close to $800 million from its oil resources. In the last year of the monarchy Iran made more than $20 billion from oil exports.[79]

The shah used much of this oil revenue to build up Iran's military. Between 1953 and 1963 spending on the military increased more than $100 million (from $80 million to $183 million).[80] During the Kennedy administration a quarter of the national budget was going toward military spending.[81] And the shah also added 80,000 men to the armed forces.[82] He bought the newest military technologies from the West, and especially the United States. Between 1970 and 1976 American arms sales to Iran were more than $12 billion.[83]

This military equipment was purchased to deal with the perceived threat from the USSR and communism.[84] The United States, especially during the Nixon administration, sought to use Iran (and Saudi Arabia) to secure stability in the Middle East. This was known as the two-pillar policy. Although the Shah embraced this role, Iranians felt alienated by it. Although the shah may have welcomed the enhanced role offered to him to increase his regional power, many Iranians simply viewed this as further evidence of Iran's subservience to the United States.[85] The Nixon administration—unlike the Eisenhower, Kennedy, and Johnson administrations—allowed the shah to purchase whatever nonnuclear weapons and military equipment he wanted.[86]

The shah wanted and purchased the latest in military technology, including 7 airborne warning and control system aircraft ($1.23 billion) and 160 F-16 fighter-bomber aircraft ($1.8 billion). The shah in 1978 alone ordered naval destroyers, nuclear submarines, and F-16s totaling $12 billion worth of arms.[87] This money could have been spent on improving the lives of Iranian citizens, who had numerous basic needs. Money was needed to improve the country's infrastructure and educational system and to create jobs. When combined with Iranians' perception that there was no immediate military threat to the country's borders, these expensive military purchases were incomprehensible.

The White Revolution

In the 1960s the shah embarked on an ambitious series of programs to reform Iranian society in a more progressive direction.[88] He appeared to be motivated in part by the desire to create a more just and equal society. Discussing the White Revolution, Mohammad Reza said, "As long as wealth is not justly distributed among the people, its abundance is meaningless."[89] One reason why Mohammad Reza Pahlavi waited two decades to develop these economic and social policies was his initial powerlessness. He needed to consolidate his power after his father abdicated and Mossadeq's power grab in the 1950s.[90] Some of the impetus for these programs also stemmed from pressure from the Kennedy administration.[91] The fear in Washington, which was in the midst of the Cold War with Moscow, was the potential spread of communism among the Iranian masses. To deal with this potential threat the Kennedy administration encouraged the monarch to undertake some reform efforts, specifically land reform.

Land reform became one of the centerpieces of the White Revolution, and its intent was to redistribute land held by large landowners to help peasants in rural areas. From an economic point of view, reallocating land to the poor would improve their economic well-being. Politically, this also offered the shah an opportunity to weaken wealthy landowning opponents of the regime, including the members of the *ulema* (religious scholars), who were also landowners. Not only would the redistribution of land weaken political opponents; it also had the potential to create a group of people who would be loyal to the king.

Additional aspects of the White Revolution included the nationalization of forests, profit sharing for workers, and the creation of a Literacy Corps to help develop reading and writing in the countryside. This Army of Knowledge, as it was known, sent more than 70,000 people into rural villages to encourage a literate population.[92] By sending college graduates into the rural areas, the monarchy would not only improve literacy but also reach into the countryside and demonstrate the concern for people outside the cities. A Health Corps similar to the Literacy Corps was also established to extend health care services to those in rural areas.

Political reforms were also an aspect of the White Revolution, especially as they pertained to women's rights. In 1963 women were given the right to vote, albeit in a political system that was something less than a full-fledged democracy. Women were also offered the right to hold political and legal offices, such as judges. Furthermore, women were offered more rights in the area of family law. With the passage of the 1967 Family Protection Law women began to enjoy more custody rights and the ability of men to get a divorce was limited.[93]

The White Revolution never lived up to expectations and hence did not produce the large-scale improvements throughout society that Iranians were hoping for and desperately needed. Although the Literacy Corps did contribute to a more literate population, the results were limited. In 1966 approximately 30 percent of the population was literate. A decade later 60 percent of the population was still illiterate.[94] Land reform, the centerpiece of the White Revolution, failed miserably. The land reform efforts were unable to distribute enough land to peasants to improve their lives. Thus the small plot of land that they were given was unable to provide a living for a family. Furthermore, only half the people living in rural areas received land under this program.[95] Last, some large landholders were exempted from the land distribution whereas others sold off their worst lands. Thus the land reforms had less of an impact than initially hoped for. The result was an influx of peasants migrating to cities to improve their economic conditions.[96] When placed in the context of a country that enjoyed enormous oil wealth, this only exacerbated the failure of the government to live up to expectations. The oil wealth did not appear to be trickling down to the people. The shah's lavish spending on a variety of things, including the 2,500th anniversary of the Iranian monarchy, only fueled the belief that the shah did not care about the material well-being of his people. This led to more disillusionment with the shah.

Ultimately, the shah's efforts at economic reform and modernization failed to bring much needed relief to his people. There were many reasons for this failure, including the fact that the shah ignored the bazaar. His expressed his disdain for the *bazaaris* when he referred to them as "a fistful of bearded bazaar idiots." He believed that his modernization policies would lead to the withering away of the bazaar. These policies did not allow this prominent element of Iranian society to take part in the country's much-needed economic improvement.[97] Ignoring the bazaar would have additional consequences for the shah, as we will see in the next chapter. Many members of the bazaar helped to fund the Revolution that would overthrow the Pahlavi regime.

Khomeini's Critique

Khomeini was also very critical of the monarchy's economic policies because they failed to address the needs of the poor. In *Islamic Government* he raised this issue: "Do you imagine all that bombastic propaganda being broadcast on the radio is true? Go see for yourself at first hand what state our people are living in. Not even one out of every two hundred villages has a clinic. No one is concerned about the poor and the hungry, and they do not allow the measures Islam has devised for the sake of the poor to be implemented. . . . Islam is aware that first, the conditions of the poor must be remedied. But they (the Shah's government) do not allow the plans of Islam to be implemented."[98]

The shah, in Khomeini's view, failed to bring basic services to people. Most problematic was the lack of schools, health clinics, and clean water for villages across Iran.[99] Khomeini's theocracy would over time improve Iranians' access to basic needs.[100]

Furthermore, the clergy, and especially Khomeini, criticized the White Revolution as an attack on Islam. Khomeini criticized the White Revolution as "the revolution intended to spread the colonial culture to the remotest town and villages and pollute the youth of the country."[101] Various aspects of the White Revolution were troubling to conservative religious leaders including giving women greater political rights. Furthermore, the land reform efforts would have reduced the financial standing of various religious leaders who received money from the landlords. This also affected the clergy who owned land.[102] Thus these attempts at reform "limited the property, revenue and power of the *ulema*."[103] In response to Khomeini's forceful verbal attacks on the shah, he was arrested in June 1963 and spent ten months in jail. He was then sent into exile on November 4, 1964, in Turkey. He was later allowed to resettle in Iraq. This made a martyr out of Khomeini and enhanced his status.

Human Rights Violations

An additional problem with the shah's leadership concerned the various human rights violations that occurred during his rule. Iran under Mohammad Reza was a police state.[104] Although some groups were better off under the shah than in the years that followed the Revolution—women in particular—we should not forget the illiberal nature of the monarchy. As Esposito and Voll note: "The shah's government had been denounced by its critics for repression and massive violation of human rights: censorship; the banning of political parties; the arrest, imprisonment, torture, execution and assassination of opposition members; and the creation of a society in which the fate of individuals personally and professionally was dependent on royal favor."[105]

The shah tolerated no real meaningful political opposition and did not want to share power. The US Embassy in Tehran recognized this in the late 1950s. A report from the embassy in Tehran in 1957 notes: "Upon the Shah's return to Tehran, he has apparently strengthened his determination to rule as well as reign and to reduce the Prime Minister to political impotence. This decision has grave connotations for the future political stability in Iran."[106]

Although individuals had the right to vote—including women—voting in an illiberal polity where the king refuses to relinquish power means little. As Pollack notes, the parties "contesting" elections were often referred to as the "yes and yes sir" parties because the shah had created both of them (the National Party and the People's Party) to suit his interests.[107] However, Iranians were not fooled by these blatant antidemocratic efforts on the part of the shah and resented him all the more for it.

Furthermore, the shah had various elections rigged. In 1954, on the heels of his return to power, he set out to prevent another "Mossadeq" from challenging him. To assure his dominance of the political system, Mohammad Reza Pahlavi rigged the Majles elections in 1954. In 1960, despite the shah's pledge of free elections, his people doubted that there would be a meaningful voting process. Many Iranians simply did not bother voting in what they considered to be a rigged process.[108] Elections for the Majles in 1963 were also rigged to ensure a complacent political body. Thus the shah refused to allow an independent parliament to develop that would help in governing the country.

Various human rights violations were also committed by the National Intelligence and Security Organization, better known as SAVAK, which was created in 1957. The shah did not tolerate dissent from any quarter. His regime stifled efforts to develop a free press. SAVAK was employed to limit political opposition to the regime, and it suppressed the creation of a vibrant civil society (labor unions, civic associations, etc.).[109] It did this through the use of informants, intimidation, and fear. For example, Ali Shariati, an Islamic philosopher and an influential leftist intellectual, was jailed by SAVAK for his subversive activities.[110] Thousands were jailed and tortured.[111] Many political prisoners were tortured with electric shocks and beatings and even the use of drills. Among those jailed and tortured included the future president and later Supreme Leader Ali Khamenei. Expressions of political dissent were often dealt with brutally. For example, in June 1963 antigovernment demonstrations occurred in Tehran. Some 3,000 protesters lost their lives, and SAVAK proceeded with a harsh crackdown in the aftermath of the marches.[112]

Although the shah eased some of the worst violations due to the incoming US presidency of Jimmy Carter, these reforms hardly turned Iran into a liberal democracy. For example, he invited prominent human rights and humanitarian nongovernmental organizations, including the International Committee of the Red Cross and Amnesty International, to visit Iran to survey the political landscape.[113] The International Committee of the Red Cross opened an office in Tehran in 1977, and it issued a number of reports suggesting the regime had made substantial changes to its prisons and improvements had occurred.[114] In August 1978 the shah decided to allow independent opposition parties to develop and participate in elections.[115] Reforms concerning due process of law and greater press freedoms were undertaken in the late 1970s; however, they were too little too late as far as the Iranian people were concerned.

By 1978 the shah's attempts at political reform and improving human rights were halted, and on September 7, in response to protests, he declared martial law. On September 8, a protest in Tehran in Jaleh Square was met with bullets from troops sent to deal with the demonstrators. There were many casualties, and the event became known as Black Friday.[116]

Khomeini's Critique

In addition to the criticisms of the reforms of the White Revolution, Khomeini also criticized the various human rights violations in the country. He denounced the shah for allowing SAVAK to trample on his people. As mentioned above, Khomeini, like many other Iranians, was tortured by SAVAK.[117] The fact that SAVAK was trained by and cooperated with Israel's Mossad was another mark against this security force. This again demonstrated the harmful Western influences in Iran.

Conclusion

Throughout his reign, Mohammad Reza Pahlavi planted the seeds that would lead to his destruction. His weakness and indecisiveness as a leader only worsened the policies that were enacted. The shah would vacillate between frustration and paralysis. Over the course of his time on the throne, many makers of foreign policy would criticize the king for his personal weakness. One American ambassador to Iran, Loy Henderson, commented: "I am becoming more and more convinced that he [the shah] is lacking in courage and resolution; that he is conscious of his weaknesses and that he is inclined to endeavor to conceal his true character by finding excuses for inaction and even by laying blame for past mistakes on those around him."[118] The shah reportedly wept after the killings on Black Friday. The influence of the West, including his friendly relations with Israel and the United States, offered an image to some Iranians of a king more foreign than Iranian. The inability of the king and his ministers to substantially improve the lives of the poor, coupled with the lavish lifestyles of the rich, including the royal family, suggested a monarch who was out of touch with his people.

Many Iranians frustrated with the lack of jobs and housing and with the endemic corruption also had to deal with the inability to influence the political system. The shah offered no meaningful political participation, and efforts to engage in freedom of speech or freedom of expression were often dealt with harshly by SAVAK.

All these depravations might have been tolerated if the Pahlavi regime (both father and son) had not challenged the role of Islam in society. Efforts to modernize and invariably Westernize society were an affront to the Iranian people. The frontal assaults on the Shia hierarchy, including the detention and torture of religious leaders, were too much to ask a pious population to bear. The decision to send Ayatollah Khomeini into exile only contributed to the view that the shah was disrespectful of Islam. The perception that Mohammad Reza Pahlavi, like his father before him, was not a just and pious ruler contributed to the Revolution that would force him to relinquish the Peacock Throne.

Notes

1. Arang Keshavarzian, *Bazaar and State in Iran* (Cambridge: Cambridge University Press, 2007), 235.

2. Janet Afary, *Sexual Politics in Modern Iran* (Cambridge: Cambridge University Press, 2009), 125.

3. Keshavarzian, *Bazaar and State*, 235.

4. Ervand Abrahamian, *A History of Modern Iran* (Cambridge: Cambridge University Press, 2008), 65. See also Said Amir Arjomand, *The Turban for the Crown: The Islamic Revolution in Iran* (New York: Oxford University Press, 1988), 68.

5. Ali Ansari, *Modern Iran since 1921: The Pahlavis and After* (London: Pearson Education, 2003), 20.

6. Afary, *Sexual Politics*, 143.

7. Ali Ansari, *Confronting Iran* (New York: Basic Books, 2006), 22; Michael Axworthy, *A History of Iran: Empire of the Mind* (New York: Basic Books, 2008), 219.

8. Abrahamian, *History of Modern Iran*, 65.

9. Ibid., 73. Keddie describes the Majles as a "rubber stamp." Nikki Keddie, *Modern Iran: Roots and Results of Revolution* (New Haven, CT: Yale University Press, 2003), 88.

10. Vanessa Martin, *Creating an Islamic State: Khomeini and the Making of a New Iran* (New York: I. B. Tauris, 2000), 16. Keddie suggests that Germany controlled almost 50 percent of Iran's foreign trade between 1939 and 1941. Keddie, *Modern Iran*, 101.

11. Ansari, *Confronting Iran*, 72.

12. Prime Minister's Proclamation from Sitareh Iran, April 1, 1924. Quoted by Arjomand, *Turban for the Crown*, 81. See also Ansari, *Modern Iran since 1921*, 38.

13. Martin, *Creating an Islamic State*, 9.

14. Arjomand, *Turban for the Crown*, 66; Sandra Mackey, *The Iranians: Persia, Islam, and the Soul of a Nation* (New York: Plume, 1998), 179.

15. Kenneth Pollack, *The Persian Puzzle: The Conflict between Iran and America* (New York: Random House, 2004), 36.

16. Mackey, *Iranians*, 180. See also Arjomand, *Turban for the Crown*, 82.

17. Afary, *Sexual Politics*, 13. After the Revolution Khomeini and other religious leaders would also control women's attire via state policies.

18. Azar Nafisi, *Reading Lolita in Tehran* (New York: Random House, 2003), 112. See also Arjomand, *Turban for the Crown*, 68; and Mackey, *Iranians*, 181. This decree would be rescinded due to its unpopularity.

19. Afary, *Sexual Politics*, 156.

20. Arjomand, *Turban for the Crown*, 82.

21. Vali Nasr, *The Shia Revival* (New York: W. W. Norton, 2006), 123.

22. Mackey, *Iranians*, 189.

23. Ibid., 267; Pollack, *Persian Puzzle*, 118.

24. Mackey, *Iranians*, 225.

25. Pollack, *Persian Puzzle*, 119.

26. Said Amir Arjomand, *After Khomeini: Iran under His Successors* (Oxford: Oxford University Press, 2009), 17.

27. Khomeini, *Islam and Revolution: Writings and Declarations of Iman Khomeini*, translated and annotated by Hamid Algar (Berkeley, CA: Mizan Press, 1981), 177.

28. Amir Taheri, *The Spirit of Allah: Khomeini and the Islamic Revolution* (Bethesda, MD: Adler & Adler, 1985), 127.

29. Arthur C. Millspaugh, *Americans in Persia* (Washington, D.C.: Brookings Institution Press, 1946), 13.

30. Ibid.

31. Keshavarzian, *Bazaar and State*, 234–35; Karl E. Meyer and Shareen Blair Brysac, *Kingmakers: The Invention of the Modern Middle East* (New York: W. W. Norton, 2009), 299; Keddie, *Modern Iran*, 61.

32. Pollack, *Persian Puzzle*, 56, 62.

33. Abrahamian, *History of Modern Iran*, 114.

34. Meyer and Blair Brysac, *Kingmakers*, 305.

35. Ansari, *Confronting Iran*, 26. See also Ansari, *Modern Iran since 1921*, 107–8; and Keddie, *Modern Iran*, 123.

36. Quoted in Meyer and Blair Brysac, *Kingmakers*, 328.

37. Ray Takeyh, *Hidden Iran* (New York: Times Books, 2006), 86.

38. Statement of Policy proposed by the National Security Council on *The Present Situation in Iran*, NSC 136/1.

39. Maziar Behrooz clearly demonstrates the fears of the Tudeh Party were overblown. "The 1953 Coup in Iran and the Legacy of the Tudeh," in *Mohammad Mossadeq and the 1953 Coup in Iran*, edited by Mark J. Gasiorowski and Malcolm Byrne (Syracuse, NY: Syracuse University Press, 2004), 102–25.

40. It is worth noting that Mossadeq was no great democrat. He engaged in electoral manipulations in 1952 to ensure that he would not lose power.

41. See "Summary," www.gwu.edu/~nsarchiv/NSAEBB/NSAEBB28/summary.pdf.

42. Abrahamian, *History of Modern Iran*, 121; Pollack, *Persian Puzzle*, 63; Ansari, *Confronting Iran*, chap. 2.

43. Mark J. Gasiorowski, "The Coup d'État against Mossadeq," in *Mohammad*, ed. Gasiorowski and Byrne, 227–60, at 237.

44. Meyer and Blair Brysac, *Kingmakers*, 338.

45. Arjomand, *Turban for the Crown*, 72. However, it is also true that there were many Iranians, including the Rashidian brothers, who were also actively involved in the coup against Mossadeq. For a further discussion of the domestic opposition see Fakhreddin Azimi, "Unseating Mossadeq: The Configuration and Role of Domestic Forces," in *Mohammad* ed. Gasiorowski and Byrne, 27–101.

46. In March 2000, almost fifty years after the fact, Secretary of State Madeleine Albright acknowledged the United States' role in the coup and its assistance to the shah's regime. In an effort to improve US–Iranian relations and in an act of political contrition she said: "In 1953, the United States played a significant role in orchestrating the overthrow of Iran's popular prime minister, Mohammad Mossadeq. The Eisenhower administration believed its actions were justified for strategic reasons; but the coup was clearly a setback for Iran's political development. And it is easy to see now why many Iranians continue

to resent this intervention by America in their internal affairs. Moreover, during the next quarter century, the United States and the West gave sustained backing to the Shah's regime. Although it did much to develop the country economically, the Shah's government also brutally repressed political dissent. As President Clinton has said, the United States must bear its fair share of responsibility for the problems that have arisen in US–Iranian relations" (Pollack, *Persian Puzzle*, xxv). The speech had little effect on US–Iranian relations. Supreme Leader Ayatollah Khamenei rejected it as meaningless. Ironically, many clergy were opposed to Mossadeq or largely indifferent in the early 1950s. Takeyh, *Hidden Iran*, 91; Arjomand, *Turban for the Crown,* 81.

47. Robin Wright, *In the Name of God* (New York: Simon & Schuster, 1989), 49.

48. Arjomand, *Turban for the Crown*, 105.

49. Mackey, *Iranians*, 251.

50. John Limbert, *Negotiating with the Islamic Republic of Iran*, Special Report 199 (Washington, DC: US Institute of Peace, 2008), 10.

51. Khomeini, *Islam and Revolution*, 182. See also Wright, *In the Name of God*, 52; Martin, *Creating an Islamic State*, 64; and Keddie, *Modern Iran*, 148.

52. *New York Times*, January 2, 1978; Pollack, *Persian Puzzle*, 124.

53. Khomeini criticized this agreement in a speech on October 27, 1963. Khomeini, *Islam and Revolution*, 182.

54. Abrahamian, *History of Modern Iran*, 147.

55. Fred Halliday, *Nation and Religion in the Middle East* (Boulder, CO: Lynne Rienner, 2000), 137.

56. Mahmood Monshipouri, *Muslims in Global Politics: Identities, Interests, and Human Rights* (Philadelphia: University of Pennsylvania Press, 2009), 167; Keddie, *Modern Iran*, 189.

57. Jalal Al-e Ahmad, *Plagued by the West*, translated by Paul Sprachman (New York: Caravan Books, 1982), 33.

58. Abdolkarim Soroush, "The Three Cultures," in *Reason, Freedom, and Democracy in Islam: Essential Writings of Abdolkarim Soroush*, edited by Mahmoud Sadri and Ahmad Sadri (New York: Oxford University Press, 2000), 156–70, at 160.

59. M. H. Pesaran discusses fifteen years of economic growth, from 1963–64 to 1977–78. Pesaran cites the growth in GDP at 9 percent a year and the rise in per capita income from $176 to $2,160. M. H. Pesaran, "The System of Dependent Capitalism in Pre- and Post-Revolutionary Iran," *International Journal of Middle East Studies* 14, no. 4 (November 1982): 501–22.

60. Fred Halliday, "Iran: The Economic Contradiction," *MERIP Reports*, no. 69 (July–August 1978), 9–18; Keddie, *Modern Iran*, 158–62.

61. Pesaran, "System of Dependent Capitalism," 507.

62. Barry Rubin, *Paved with Good Intentions* (New York: Penguin Books, 1981), 268.

63. Patrick Clawson, "Iran's Economy: Between Crisis and Collapse," *MERIP Reports*, no. 98 (July–August 1981): 11–15. For a discussion of the widespread corruption in Iran, see also Keddie, *Modern Iran*, 160.

64. Keshavarzian, *Bazaar and State*, 4.

65. Halliday, "Iran," 11.

66. Pollack, *Persian Puzzle*, 82; Keddie, *Modern Iran*, 142.

67. Mackey, *Iranians*, 220.

68. Pollack, *Persian Puzzle*, 113.

69. Afary, *Sexual Politics*, 204.

70. Pollack, *Persian Puzzle*, 110–12.

71. Arjomand, *Turban for the Crown*, 111; Halliday, "Iran," 16. Some put the number even higher. Pollack suggests that rents rose nearly 300 percent in the 1970s.

72. Afary, *Sexual Politics*, 201.

73. Ansari, *Modern Iran since 1921*, 151–52; Pollack, *Persian Puzzle*, 83.

74. Halliday, "Iran," 16; Pollack, *Persian Puzzle*, 111.

75. Keddie, *Modern Iran*, 141.

76. Vali Nasr, "Politics within the Late-Pahlavi State: The Ministry of Economy and Industrial Policy, 1963–1969," *International Journal of Middle East Studies* 32 (2000): 97–122.

77. Ibid., 112.

78. Rubin, *Paved*, 130; Pollack, *Persian Puzzle*, 75.

79. Clawson, "Iran's Economy," 11–15.

80. Martin, *Creating an Islamic State*, 20. The United States also gave the shah "approximately $500 million in military assistance" from 1953 to 1961. Pollack, *Persian Puzzle*, 77.

81. Rubin, *Paved*, 112.

82. Pollack, *Persian Puzzle*, 77.

83. Rubin, *Paved*, 128.

84. Pollack, *Persian Puzzle*, 76. The shah stressed how important Iran was to limiting Soviet expansion in the region. In truth, this desire for the latest weapons had more to do with the shah's desire to be a great leader than an actual threat from the Soviets.

85. "The Shah dreamed of making Iran one of the five conventional military powers of the world, and Washington fueled his ambitions to some extent by anointing his regime the policeman of the Persian Gulf. Many Iranians saw this surrogacy of the shah's regime as a sign of Iran's complete subservience to the United States and its loss of independence. This popular perception developed into a profound source of alienation." Ramazani quoted by John Esposito and John Voll, *Islam and Democracy* (Oxford: Oxford University Press, 1996), 60.

86. Pollack, *Persian Puzzle*, 104; Gary Sick, *All Fall Down* (New York: Penguin Books, 1986), 17.

87. Abrahamian, *History of Modern Iran*, 125.

88. Arjomand, *Turban for the Crown*, 72–73.

89. Mohammad Reza Pahlavi, *The White Revolution* (Tehran: Kayhan Press, 1967), quoted by Ferydoon Firoozi, "Income Distribution and Taxation Laws of Iran," *International Journal of Middle East Studies* 9, no. 1 (January 1978): 73–87.

90. Rouhollah Ramazani, "Iran's White Revolution: A Study in Political Development," *International Journal of Middle Eastern Studies* 5 (1974): 124–39.

91. Keddie, *Modern Iran*, 144.

92. Ramazani, "Iran's White Revolution," 132.

93. Abrahamian, *History of Modern Iran*, 134; Keddie, *Modern Iran*, 167.

94. Halliday, "Iran," 16.

95. Ibid., 10.

96. Arjomand, *Turban for the Crown*, 73.

97. Keshavarzian, *Bazaar and State*, 20, 133.

98. Quoted by Algar, in *Islam and Revolution*, by Khomeini, 120.

99. Abrahamian, *History of Modern Iran*, 147.

100. This is discussed in greater detail in chapter 7.

101. Quoted by Arjomand, *Turban for the Crown*, 99.

102. Pollack, *Persian Puzzle*, 88.

103. Esposito and Voll, *Islam and Democracy* (Oxford: Oxford University Press, 1996), 55.

104. Rubin, *Paved*, 177.

105. Esposito and Voll, *Islam and Democracy*, 69.

106. Philip Clock, "First Secretary of Embassy, Report from American Embassy in Tehran," July 20, 1957, RG 469 Records of the US Foreign Assistance Agencies 1948–61, Office of Near East and South Asia Operations, box 20, ARC 4240159.

107. Pollack, *Persian Puzzle*, 78; Keddie, *Modern Iran*, 140.

108. Ansari, *Modern Iran since 1921*, 145; Mackey, *Iranians*, 219.

109. Mahmood Monshipouri, *Islamism, Secularism, and Human Rights in the Middle East* (Boulder, CO: Lynne Rienner, 1998), 173.

110. Kasra Naji, *Ahmadinejad: The Secret History of Iran's Radical Leader* (Berkeley: University of California Press, 2008), 11.

111. Pollack, *Persian Puzzle*, 139; Rubin, *Paved*, chap. 6; Sick, *All Fall Down*, 26; Keddie, *Modern Iran*, 134.

112. Rubin, *Paved*, 109.

113. Pollack, *Persian Puzzle*, 121.

114. Manoucher Ganji, *Defying the Iranian Revolution* (Westport, CT: Praeger, 2002), 2–3. Ganji worked for the shah. Keddie, *Modern Iran*, 217.

115. Arjomand, *Turban for the Crown*, 109.

116. Ibid., 114. Pollack puts the number of killed at more than two hundred. See Pollack, *Persian Puzzle*, 130.

117. Karim Sadjadpour, "The Supreme Leader," in *The Iranian Primer: Power, Politics and US Policy*, edited by Robin Wright (Washington, D.C.: US Institute of Peace, 2010), 11.

118. Quoted by Fakhreddin Amizi, "Unseating Mossaddeq: The Configuration and Role of Domestic Forces," in *Mohammad*, ed. Gasiorowski and Byrne, 54.

CHAPTER 3

The Islamic Revolution and the Birth of a New Political System

The Pahlavi Dynasty had crumbled before an "Islamic Revolution" that promised greater political participation, the preservation of national identity and independence, and a more socially just society.
—John Esposito and John Voll, *Islam and Democracy*

I ask the government that, fearing neither East nor West and cultivating an independent outlook and will, it purge all remnants of the tyrannical regime, which left deep traces upon all the affairs of our country. It should transform our educational and judicial systems, as well as all the ministries and government offices that are now run on Western lines or in slavish imitation of Western models, and make them compatible to Islam, thus demonstrating to the world true social justice and true cultural, economic, and political independence.
—Ayatollah Khomeini, "Declaration on April 1, 1979"

Throughout history, religion has inspired its followers to great accomplishments. Religion has also been the motivation for wars, peace movements, and, in Iran's case, a revolution. In a religious political movement or revolution, religious ideas and symbols, practices and beliefs, leaders and institutions are essential for the development and success of the political project. Religion is so important for the revolution that religious language and modes of religious communication are adopted. Furthermore, a religious identity, a religious community, and religious language all become the basic elements of the political cause.[1]

Religion is a useful tool for achieving political goals because many religious traditions have a well-established grassroots network that can be unleashed in the political realm. Religious leaders already have institutional resources such as meeting places, fund-raising techniques, and a network of followers with a shared identity. For any revolution to be successful, it must have a popular base of support. Revolutions without regiments of revolutionaries have an inherent weakness and are more likely to fail. In Iran, these elements proved to be essential for the Islamic Revolution in 1979, which had developed over the course of two decades.

This chapter examines the Islamic Revolution that overthrew the shah and the political system that followed. Numerous revolutions have been attempted without success. Especially important for the success of this revolution was the religious leadership, which mobilized demonstrations that ended the monarchy. Beyond individual religious leaders, this chapter also examines domestic factors—including the role of religious ideas, such as good and evil, and martyrdom—in Shia Islam. These ideas unified the Iranian population and can help explain the success of the Islamic Revolution.

The second half of this chapter examines the dysfunctional political system that was created in the aftermath of the Revolution. The theocracy that was created in 1979 evolved in conjunction with domestic factors. Domestic threats in the form of institutional stagnation and impasse, along with political opponents who undermine the foundations of the regime, have led to political and institutional changes. This evolution has not been an entirely stable, gradual progression. In addition to examining the contradictions inherent in the Constitution, the chapter also looks at the creation and powers of the major political institutions in Iran. Finally, the chapter considers the current political polarization in Iran and how the clerical regime has tried to neutralize perceived domestic threats.

Creating the Islamic Movement

Revolutions do not arise naturally; they require nurturing and development. The Islamic Revolution of 1979 took decades to develop. It was effective in ousting a monarch from his throne because of the religious actors, beliefs, and movement that had developed, along with resentment of the king's policies.

Anger at the Shah

The religiously inspired movement that took to the streets of Iran at the end of the 1970s was motivated by a number of different factors. Many Iranians felt alienated from their monarch. The shah's Westernization programs, which aimed to redesign Iranian society in the image of the West, were not well received by the vast majority of Iranians.[2] The restructuring of the curriculum of religious schools and the replacing of traditional Islamic courts with civil courts were not welcome developments for many Iranians.[3] Mohammad Reza Shah Pahlavi's restoration to the throne by the United States also proved difficult to accept.[4] Instead of the Western style of the shah, the people turned to what they knew, to that with which they were most comfortable: Shia Islam and its religious leaders.

Religious Leaders: The Influence of Khomeini

In many societies, religious leaders are often the most respected members of the community. This was also true in Iran because many placed their trust in Shia clerics. The most important figure in the Islamic movement in Iran was Ayatollah Khomeini. His significance stemmed from his charismatic leadership and his austere lifestyle, as well as his decades-long opposition to the shah and the Westernization of the country. Khomeini was viewed as a spiritual leader who led a simple life and defended the oppressed and the poor. This helped to cultivate the image of him as an imam—a religious leader and guide for the community. This was an image and a religious vocabulary that ordinary Iranians could relate to and support.[5]

Khomeini influenced the Revolution not only as a charismatic leader but also with the ideas and an ideology that would transform Iran from a monarchy to a theocracy. His beliefs formed the backbone of the Revolution and of the political system that followed. Some of his views, as explained in *Secrets Revealed* in the early 1940s, would change by the time of the Revolution (e.g., concerning an elected assembly), whereas others concerning adherence to Islamic laws remained consistent throughout his life.

Despite Khomeini's criticism of the Western influence in Iran, he himself was influenced by Western political thought. He believed that society needed a strong and virtuous leader, which he found in Plato's philosopher-king. In the *Republic*, Plato argued that a just society would only be possible if a philosopher with decades of training in mathematics, ethics, and governance were to rule the society.[6] Unless philosophers controlled the polity, Plato believed that justice was unobtainable: "Until philosophers rule as kings in their cities, or those who are nowadays called kings and leading men become genuine and adequate philosophers so that political power and philosophy become thoroughly blended together, while the numerous natures that now pursue either one exclusively are forcibly prevented from doing so, cities will have no rest from evils, . . . nor, I think will the human race."[7]

The idea of a supreme leader developed by Khomeini was influenced by the Platonic notion of the philosopher-king who ensures justice within the Republic.[8] For Khomeini, a virtuous individual could lead the community if he had the proper knowledge of religious truth and justice. His adaptation was to require the person holding this position to have the highest Islamic credentials and an understanding of Islamic law to guide the community. His *velayat-e faqih* (i.e., guardianship of the jurist) added a religious element to Plato's philosopher-king.

Khomeini stressed a set of specific values, which included justice, independence, self-sufficiency, and Islamic piety.[9] He rejected the influence of Western culture and the secularization programs of the twentieth century. He portrayed himself as the conscience of a nation that was being led by the shah down the path of the devil. Khomeini sought to change the regime in order to save the people. Thus he wrote: "Wherever you go and whomever you encounter from the street sweeper to the highest official, you will see nothing but disordered thought, confused ideas, contradictory opinions, self-interest, lechery, immodesty, criminality, treachery, and thousands of associated vices. . . . Given such circumstances, it should not be expected that the government would be regarded as just and legitimate in religious circles."[10]

For his criticism of the White Revolution, of the monarchy, and of the Western influence taking hold of the country, Khomeini was exiled from Iran for more than fourteen years. Yet despite his exile, he was still enormously influential in Iran. He lectured Iranians on the importance of religious identity and social justice and on the need for political participation to address the corruption and oppression in Iran through the medium of audiotapes that were smuggled into Iran. By integrating religious, social, and economic themes, he developed a large following.

In developing these economic themes and themes of social justice, one can also see the influence of Marxist ideas. Marxist thought had infiltrated Iran through the Soviet Union's meddling and through the Tudeh Party. Other intellectuals and thinkers, such as Ali Shariati, would also talk about exploita-tion. Khomeini, who had the political acumen to see the appeal of these ideas, would incorporate the notion of *mostaz'afin* into the political discourse.[11]

Khomeini the Maverick

Although Khomeini's religious ideas were the foundation of the Revolution, he did not always promote traditional Shia theology. He was considered some-thing of a maverick in theological circles in Iran.[12] The framework he devel-oped produced a very innovative religious-political system. He developed a theory of clerical rule in his treatise *Islamic Government* (*Hukoumat-e Islami*). In this book he explained the need for rule by the *ulema* (i.e., religious schol-ars). Nasr summarized the basic argument as follows: "God has sent Islam for it to be implemented. No one knew religion better than the *ulema*, who were trained in its intricacies and who carried the Twelfth Imam's mandate to safeguard its interests. God had commanded an Islamic government, and the *ulema* had to rule if that command was to be executed. Shia *ulema* had always been the guardians; Khomeini argued that that function could now be properly performed only if they ruled. With this theory of 'guardianship of the jurist' (*velayat-e faqih*), Shiism would look to its *ulema* as a class—and among them the most respected cleric—rather than its shahs to rule and protect its interests and identity."[13]

The essence of Khomeini's thought rejected the separation of religion and politics. Instead, religious leaders would interpret and implement Islamic law in the absence of the twelfth imam. This was the only way to promote a just social order. Further, he added that members of the Shia hierarchy had a duty to follow the *velayat-e faqih*.

For Khomeini a just society required that the clergy play a significant political role. However, the notion of an Islamic cleric at the center of po-litical power in a capacity to oversee the political system was not embraced by all Shia clerics. Some viewed the *velayat-e faqih* as a departure from tradi-tional Shia doctrine.[14] Ayatollah Golpaygani believed Khomeini's views veered on sacrilege.[15] Grand Ayatollah Abol-Qasem al-Khoi criticized the *velayat-e faqih* "as an innovation with no support in Shia theology or law," and Grand Ayatollah Mohammad Kazem Shariatmadari was ultimately defrocked for his opposition to *velayat-e faqih*.[16]

Many Shiite clerics adhere to the quietist school. The concept of quietism within Shia Islam is based on the belief that clerics should not take an active role in politics. Because the only definitive authority is Allah, all man-made attempts to govern would be imperfect. In the absence of the divine, clerics should focus on religious matters and avoid assuming positions of political authority. Given the fact that power has the ability to corrupt political leaders, religious leaders should avoid political positions to maintain their spiritual commitments. The corruption inherent in Iran's political system would give justification for many Shia religious leaders' opposition to the Iranian theocratic system. Khomeini's Supreme Leader was not only involved in politics but was also at the center of political power. Khomeini rejected the quietest approach, and his regime would harass and imprison many, including those clerics who criticized his political creation.

Religious Ideas

The religious movement that Khomeini inspired stressed the importance of a number of ideas central to Shia Islam. Given its historical roots, Islam is an easy way to integrate the religious and the political. Although Christians have sought to separate the religious and the political and have cited biblical references—such as Jesus' injunction, "Give unto Caesar what is Caesar's, Give unto God what is God's"—Islam has a different tradition. Muhammad was not only a prophet; he was also a soldier and the political leader of his community of believers.[17] Muhammad and the religious tenets derived from his message addressed spiritual as well as political and economic matters.

Khomeini offered a simple religious message concerning good and evil to which Iranians could easily relate. The "dualistic idea of a cosmic clash of good versus evil, light and darkness, order and chaos, truth and falsehood" has been prevalent in Iranian society for centuries.[18] This Manichean worldview can motivate individuals. If Muhammad's fight was for God and goodness then by implication the enemy was aligned with the forces of evil.

By employing the imagery of light versus darkness and good versus evil, this message offers a religious leader the ability to develop a group of loyal followers. It was easy for Iranians to understand one of Khomeini's central themes: the implicit call to fight against evil. The shah was referred to as *taghut* (false god)—a title reserved for Satan in the Qur'an.[19] Furthermore, because the shah was depicted as evil, then naturally Khomeini was Allah's representative in the fight for justice. Khomeini argued: "It is the duty of all of us to overthrow the *taghut;* i.e., the illegitimate political powers that now rule the entire Islamic world. The government apparatus of tyrannical and antipopular regimes must be replaced by institutions serving the public good and administered according to Islamic law."[20]

By depicting the shah and his regime as evil and un-Islamic, Khomeini put forth a discourse that prevented any possibility of compromise. Although some individuals, such as Karim Sanjabi (a member of the National Front) and Mehdi Bazaragan (of the Liberation Movement of Iran), might have allowed the shah to remain on the throne and reign instead of ruling, Khomeini was adamant that the king must go. Not only should the monarchy be abolished, but Mohammad Reza Pahlavi should be punished.[21] Social justice was a significant element of Khomeini's arsenal of criticism against the monarchy.

The Importance of Shiism

Although Islamic thought was important to this movement, Shia tenets were especially crucial to Khomeini's Revolution.[22] Shiism was declared the state religion in the sixteenth century and has been influential ever since.[23] The division within Islam between Sunnis and Shiites, which arose over a dispute regarding the rightful successor to lead the Muslim community after the death of the Prophet Muhammad, laid the foundations for social protest within the Shia community. Though the Shiites argued that a member of Muhammad's family—Ali, his cousin and son-in-law—should lead the Islamic community, Sunni Muslims selected the Umayyad family to succeed Muhammad through a council of religious scholars.[24]

When Hosain, the grandson of Muhammad, challenged the rule of the Umayyads as the rightful Muslim rulers, he and his followers were massacred at Karbala in 680.[25] This religious holiday for Shiites is called Ashura. This event laid the foundation for the role of martyrdom within the Shia faith. An individual's sacrifice for the faith is not only a noble gesture but also a duty to God.

Shia Islamic themes and ideas were repeatedly invoked throughout the last years of the 1970s. Khomeini reminded his followers of the unjust nature of the regime, which he tied to the martyrdom of Hosain.[26] Traditional and familiar notions of sacrifice and injustice, illegitimate rulers and oppression were referenced to mobilize the Iranian public. Khomeini told his followers, "You should pray to Allah to grant you the honor of becoming a martyr."[27] By giving up one's life for this cause, Khomeini argued, one was living an honorable life.[28] This message found a receptive audience. Mossoumeh Ebtekar, one of the students involved in holding Americans hostage at the US Embassy in Tehran, explains: "For everyone here in Iran, the analogy with Imam Hossein was clear to see . . . the people's uprising was like that of Imam Hossein and his companions. They were fighting for justice, democracy, for their rights and dignity, for their independence. Against them was a dictator who had all the power, and the support of a foreign superpower, the United States. The analogy was perfectly clear then: It was necessary to sacrifice our lives, to accept martyrdom."[29]

This emphasis on martyrdom is especially true when fighting an unjust system.[30] Khomeini continuously criticized the shah's regime as an unjust political system. In addition, some in the Shia tradition argued that the "active opposition to corrupt sovereign powers" was a way to quicken the return of the twelfth imam.[31]

Ayatollah Khomeini also referred to the twelfth imam as a reason for clerical rule. For Shiites the correct succession of Muslim rulers begins with Ali and Hosain and continues through the twelfth imam, Mohammad al-Mahdi, who in 939 CE was withdrawn into a state of occultation.[32] The twelfth imam will return on Judgment Day; however, in his absence, *mujtahids* (religious leaders) should lead the faithful. Shia Islam more than Sunni Islam has a more active role for the *ulema* in leading the faithful.[33] Khomeini used this religious tenet to justify his leadership as a representative of the twelfth imam: "When a Mujtahid who is just and learned stands up for the establishment and organization of the government, he will enjoy all the rights in the affairs of society that were enjoyed by the Prophet, and it will be the duty of the people to listen and obey and this *faqih-and-mujtahid* ruler will hold the supreme power in the government and the management and control of social and political affairs of the people in the same way as the Prophet and Hazrat Ali (used to do)."[34]

The Grassroots Network

In the 1960s Khomeini was deliberately trying to create a grassroots movement to develop an Islamic government. A decade before the Revolution, he understood the power of Islam in Iran:

> You must teach the people matters relating to worship, of course, but more important are the political, economic, and legal aspects of Islam. These are, or should be, the focus of our concern. It is our duty to begin exerting ourselves now in order to establish a truly Islamic government. We must propagate our cause to the people, instruct them in it, and convince them of its validity. We must generate a wave of intellectual awakening, to emerge as a current throughout society, and gradually, to take shape as an organized Islamic movement made up

of the awakened, committed and religious masses who will rise up and establish an Islamic government.[35]

This goal was accomplished by regular religious services: "We must take advantage of these assemblies (congregational prayer) to propagate and teach religion and to develop the ideological and political movement of Islam."[36] Thus prayer and political mobilization went hand in hand.

Khomeini's students were the foundation of the grassroots base that was essential to his success in 1979. In the twentieth century the monarchy limited the role of religion in society. However, it failed to eradicate religion from the population. More than 90 percent of Iranians are Shia Muslims.[37] These believers continued to embrace their faith. As Ahmad noted, for some Iranians it was all they had: "The lives of 90 percent of the population of this country are still guided by religious values and standards. By 90 percent I mean all of the villagers, combined with the urban mercantile classes, servants, and the aggregate of people who make up the lower strata of the country. These classes of people because of their poverty, have nothing to rely on for survival but their religious beliefs. They are compelled to find today's unattainable happiness in heaven, religion, and the hereafter."[38]

Shia clerics connected to the faithful in the thousands of mosques that dotted the Iranian landscape and in religious schools. The mosques of Iran were largely free of SAVAK interference, and thus they were one of the few places people could speak freely about politics.[39]

This proved to be an advantage that Khomeini had over other elements of the opposition in Iran. Although communists and liberal groups also opposed the shah, they did not have the ability, as the clerics had, to mobilize the public. Khomeini drew on a preestablished base—a grassroots network—in overthrowing the shah. The shah's policies also helped to consolidate the Revolution's religious orientation and its ties throughout the population:

> After the Shah's government banned all independent political parties and trade unions in 1953, seminaries, mosques, and religious institutions with relative financial independence from the state gradually became centers of political dissent. . . . After 1965, modern *hussiniyeh*, or centers for the commemoration of Imam Hussein, mushroomed in urban centers. The benefactors of these centers, often bazaar merchants, also provided the poor and the needy with a variety of financial and health services, sometimes including a state-of-the-art hospital,

which treated the poor without charge. The regime exiled dissident religious figures to small provincial towns, but this policy only helped spread the Islamist message more widely.[40]

Political repression in secular areas helped the Islamic movement spread and gain loyal followers.

Furthermore, Khomeini's grassroots network drew upon preestablished religious ceremonies and holidays to mobilize the people to protest. This movement profited from the religious gatherings that occur during the holiday season and during mourning rituals. The mourning process in the Shiite tradition incorporates not only the rituals that occur immediately after a person's death but also additional ceremonies and gatherings forty days later. This assisted the Islamic Revolution by providing individuals with a religious obligation to gather and to continue their protests. After a large group attended these religious events, its members would march through the streets vetting their anger and frustration at their government.[41] For example, when Mustafa Khomeini, the ayatollah's son, died in October 1977, the mourning rituals continued forty days after his death. This proved to be a defining moment, for it was after Mustafa's death that Khomeini became the focal point of the Revolution.[42]

These gatherings presented additional problems for the government. The mourning rituals were often met with violence from the security forces. This led to more deaths and more mourning rituals and hence more protests.[43] In a four-month time span, the Iranian authorities confronted a series of protests. In February 1978, the regime had to deal with demonstrations in a number of cities including Tabriz. In January 1978, a group of *talebehs* in Tabriz demonstrated against the depiction of Khomeini in the newspaper *Ettelaat*. More than a dozen protesters were killed by the police.[44] The violence encountered at these demonstrations led to more protests in March and again in May. Some have estimated that this series of clashes left more than two hundred people dead.[45] It was a seemingly endless cycle of mourning and protest. To further complicate matters for the government, many *bazaaris* aligned with the demonstrators. Toward the end of 1978 the *bazaaris* engaged in a series of strikes, which resulted in economic paralysis. These strikes—such as the one on October 16, 1978, in response to Black Friday—demonstrated the crippling effect that the bazaar could have on the economy.[46]

The grassroots network encouraged people to become more politically active and to oppose the regime at sermons during Friday prayers. Individuals who attend religious services once a week are a captive audience. This opportunity mobilized people to their political cause. During the Revolution more than 2,000 demonstrations were organized by clerics or *bazaaris*.[47] That Khomeini's students would use the Qur'an and the traditions of the Prophet Muhammad and the martyrdom of Hosain to demonstrate the injustices of the Pahlavi regime gave the movement legitimacy.

The Success of the Revolution:
The Shah Is Gone—Now What?

This remarkable protest movement ushered the shah from the height of political power to exile abroad. It also ended the two-thousand-year history of the monarchy in Iran. In 1978 Iranians took to the streets to protest their nation's flawed political leadership. They demanded change. And they were ultimately successful when the Pahlavi Dynasty, which had ruled Iran for more than five decades, crumbled. Khomeini and his religious followers, as well as liberal intellectuals and communists, pushed the monarch from his throne despite the fact that the shah commanded the sixth-largest military in the world in 1978. The Iranian military held one of the most extensive arsenals in the Middle East, one largely purchased from the United States.[48]

Once the shah left the country on January 17, 1979, the process began to create a new political system. Most Iranians were clear in their rejection of the Pahlavi monarchy, but what they wanted to replace the monarchy with was not clear. There were many divergent views as to what should come next: "The revolutionary forces—nationalist, leftist, religious—that combined to overthrow the Pahlavis were multiple and varied, but united in their main aim: to reject the autocratic, unjust and unaccountable Pahlavi monarchy, the inequalities in society, and the overwhelming influence of the United States. But the alternatives they sought were as varied (and often-contradictory) as they were themselves: a popular democracy; a classless society; a socialist state; national autonomy; an Islamic government, with rulers guided by the *ulema* and the *sharia*."[49]

The Islamic Revolution of 1979 was not unique in this respect. The French Revolution and the Russian Revolution were far clearer about what form of rule they did *not* want than what form of political system should replace the ancien régime. The disparate groups opposing the monarchy (nationalists, leftists, religious) were clear that they wanted to influence their political system through meaningful political participation. The form that this participation should take was indeterminate at the time of the Revolution. Khomeini spoke of a more Islamic system, but the process of institutionalizing his ideas was not automatic. To create a new political system, his ideas had to be translated into a functioning political system.

This lack of clarity about what government structure would follow the overthrow of the shah was the result of vague statements by Khomeini, and of the conflicting desires of the monarchy's opponents. Although the dominant motif of the Revolution was based on Islamic, and specifically Shia, characteristics, it was not entirely clear how this would translate into the political framework of the postrevolutionary system. Many Iranians were unaware of the specifics of Khomeini's theology. They had some vague idea that Khomeini supported an Islamic government. But the details of what that would unfold were not well known in the years 1978–79. This ignorance had many consequences, as demonstrated by the political turmoil of the theocracy's early years.

Furthermore, despite all the religious influence during the Revolution, Ayatollah Khomeini and followers tried to reassure the public that the clerics would not dominate politics. As Abol Hassan Bani-Sadr, Iran's first elected president after the Revolution, stated: "For several months Khomeini met with reporters from all over the world. To allay fears, he insisted that the mullahs would not interfere in government affairs."[50] In an interview with *Le Monde* while Khomeini was in exile, he said, "Our intention is not that religious leaders should themselves administer the state."[51] In Paris he expressed his intention to return to his theological work. Given his age (he was close to eighty years old at the time of the Revolution), many Iranians could have been forgiven if they had believed that he would retire to a quiet life. The desire for a more democratic and participatory political system was reinforced by a declaration issued from Neauphle–Le Chateau (where Khomeini was residing in exile in France) that spelled out support for elected political institutions. The new government would be entrusted with the following tasks:

1. The formation of a Constituent Assembly composed of the elected representatives of the people in order to discuss for approval the new Constitution of the Islamic Republic.
2. The implementation of elections based on the principles approved by the Constituent Assembly and the new Constitution.
3. The transfer of power to the representatives chosen in those elections.[52]

These statements gave those interested in democracy the hope that a democratic political system would be created in the aftermath of the Revolution. Elements of democracy, including popularly elected branches of government (president/parliament), would be incorporated into the new political system.

Adding further difficulties to this process were the initial actions of Khomeini. Khomeini, upon his return from Paris, did not immediately spell out all the political changes he wanted to see. In fact, the opposite was true. His initial statements, made in Paris before his return to Iran, suggested a more passive role, not only for himself but also for clerics more generally. The role that Khomeini would play in this new political system was not established at the time of the Revolution. After the Revolution he returned to the holy city of Qom. This suggests that he did not initially seek to play an active role in the government. In the aftermath of the Revolution nonclerics such as Bazargan and Bani-Sadr led the government in various political positions.[53] Khomeini specifically rejected the notion that a cleric should be president, and he also rejected Ayatollah Beheshti's candidacy for president.[54]

While in Qom he had various visitors come to him when disputes in Tehran could not be solved. Thus, numerous politicians had to travel to Qom to persuade Khomeini to intervene politically. Although cumbersome, Khomeini remained in Qom until health problems required a visit to a hospital in Tehran.[55] This provides some evidence to suggest that Khomeini's original goals and actions demonstrated a desire for a supervisory role for clerics as opposed to running the daily operations of government. However, some of his more devoted followers wanted Khomeini and his ideas to play a major role in Iran's new political system.

The New and Unique Creation: The Islamic Republic

The political system that developed in the aftermath of the Revolution was unique in that it combined elements of Shia Islam with a Western-style democracy. This theocracy that allowed for political participation would blend ideas from both East and West and would be forced to deal with the resulting contradictions.

The Political System

The political system created in 1979 was heavily influenced by Khomeini's writings, especially *Islamic Government*. It was also the result of a democratic process. A referendum was held a short time after Khomeini returned from exile. In March 1979, Iranians were presented with a political choice: Should Iran's political system remain a monarchy, or should it be changed to an Islamic Republic? Of the 20 million Iranian citizens who voted in the referendum, more than 98 percent endorsed the idea of an Islamic Republic.[56] Iranians voted to create an Islamic Republic through a somewhat limited democratic process. In truth, most Iranians did not fully understand what an "Islamic Republic" meant. Khomeini admitted as much in an interview on December 29, 1978: "Everywhere the goal is the same: an Islamic government. It is possible, of course, that some people understand and accept the principle of an Islamic government without knowing the details of its functioning, but what is certain is that the whole of Iran—including townspeople, peasants, tribesmen, and mountaineers—is unanimously proclaiming its demand for an Islamic government."[57] Although anyone familiar with Khomeini's writings or speeches would have known that he believed that a legitimate government must govern according to shari'a, the details of his political system were not widely known throughout the population.[58]

The Constitution

Once the Iranian people decided that they wanted an Islamic Republic, the basic elements of this political system had to be defined and established. To accomplish this task a new Constitution was drafted in the aftermath of the referendum. The Constitution created in 1979 has been in effect since December 1979, although it was modified in the late 1980s. The first draft of the Constitution was in many respects more moderate than the later version that became law. The first version included some basic rights and freedoms, and provided for a supervisory role for religious leaders. Although Islamic law was not explicitly established in the document, a Guardian Council of clerics was created to assure that the laws of Iran would not violate shari'a.[59] Though Khomeini supported the first version of the Constitution, many other leaders had reservations. Some of the nonclerical leaders, including Bazargan and Bani-Sadr, rejected the proposed draft.

However, these nonclerical leaders were not the only ones who were unhappy with the original document. Some of Khomeini's more radical followers felt that the draft did not go far enough in creating an Islamic state. An Assembly of Experts was elected in August 1979 for the purpose of drafting a new Constitution for the Islamic Republic. The Assembly of Experts was dominated by clerics (fifty-five of seventy-three seats were won by clerics), many of whom supported Khomeini's idea of *velayat-e faqih*.[60] The chairman of the assembly was Ayatollah Montazeri. The result was a Constitution that placed more power in the hands of clerics and especially Khomeini. A supreme leader would wield far-ranging powers dealing with foreign policy and national security and would oversee the political system to ensure that it was consistent with Islamic law. In many respects the revised Constitution was closer to Khomeini's political vision as laid out in *Islamic Government.*

Remarkably, though Khomeini steered the Revolution and the ousting of the shah, he did not dominate the drafting of the Constitution. He was willing to accept a political document (the first draft of the Constitution) that did not faithfully stick to his own political writings. The first draft of the Constitution did not include Khomeini's theological principle of *velayat-e faqih.* He was shown a draft of the Constitution and did not object to the omission of *velayat-e faqih.*[61] His pragmatism shows in his decision to accept an Islamic-lite political creation rather than demand the more radical political system that ultimately developed in the second document. It also demonstrates that he was not always directing the political system but was also, at times, being pushed and pulled by various elements among his supporters.

Many influential individuals who supported the Revolution did not support the idea of a government run and dominated by clerics. Besides secular figures such as Bani-Sadr and Bazargan, ayatollahs including Shariatmadari and Taleqani also rejected clerical rule and believed "that *ulema* involvement in government should be restricted to an advisory committee on the legislation and its compatibility with Islam."[62] This was similar to ideas previously established in the 1905–6 Constitution. Although some members of the Assembly of Experts wanted a secular government and rejected the role of a supreme leader, the more radical and religious clerics in the assembly won the day and ultimately had a strong influence on the final draft of the Constitution.

This Constitution was then put for approval before the Iranian people, who ratified it in another referendum. More than 16 million Iranians voted in favor of the document.[63] It is worth noting that this was a fairly inclusive political process. Many women endorsed and supported these political changes. It was only after the Family Protection Law of 1967 was repealed that some Iranian women began to criticize the political direction in which Iran was heading. Minority religious groups were represented and allowed to voice their concerns and objections while the Constitution was being drafted.

The Constitution articulates a hybrid system that includes both democratic and nondemocratic elements. The democratic elements allow Iranians to influence the government. Specifically, Article 6 states "in the Islamic

Republic of Iran, the affairs of the country must be administered on the basis of public opinion expressed by the means of elections, including the election of the President, the representatives of the Islamic Consultative Assembly."[64] The Iranian political system also included, in Principle 3, the importance of political self-determination. This principle states that Iranians have the right to determine their political, economic, and social destiny.

The democratic offices that are a part of Iran's political system include the presidency and the Parliament. These popularly elected bodies allow for the *potential* of checks and balances within the political system. Although Iran's president may resemble an institution in many Western political systems, in Iran's political system the unique office of the supreme leader retains most of the powers traditionally reserved for a head of state. The Guardian Council, a body constituted by senior clerics, is also not directly elected by the citizens of Iran. Ultimately, the traditional republican institutions, such as the president and Parliament, have had to share power, if not cede power, to a series of unelected supervisory bodies such as the Guardian Council. The theocratic and nondemocratic aspects tend to overpower the democratic ones.

The Constitution has many elements of Western constitutions and borrowed from the French and Belgian models. This is ironic given Khomeini's criticism of the Western influence in Iran during the Pahlavi regime. There are, however, a few articles and clauses that would be very unfamiliar to Western readers.

The language of Iran's Constitution of 1979 sets out the importance of Islam in the Iranian nation:

> Article 1: The form of government of Iran is that of an Islamic Republic, endorsed by the people of Iran on the basis of their longstanding belief in the sovereignty of truth and Qur'anic justice.

> Article 4: All civil, penal, financial, economic, administrative, cultural, military, political, and other laws and regulations must be based on Islamic criteria. This principle applies absolutely and generally to all articles of the Constitution as well as to all other laws and regulations.[65]

In addition, the Constitution sets out the basic rights and liberties of Iranian citizens. These rights include the right to freedom of belief and assembly. Iranians also have the right to an education. Furthermore, procedural rights to due process before the law are also articulated. For example, Article 32 explains that individuals are considered equal before the law and "no one may be arrested except by the order and in accordance with the procedure laid down by the law." Although these rights are enumerated in this founding document, they are limited by the phrase "in accordance with Islamic principles." Thus they have proven to be more far-reaching on paper than in practice.

The foundation of Iran's political system is Islam. Unlike in many Western democratic systems, sovereignty does not lie with the people. Although Iranians have some influence on their government, sovereignty in Iran rests with Allah and is protected and executed by clerics. More accurately, the foundation is the religious elite's interpretation of Islam, which at times has appeared less driven by Islamic tenets and more driven by a desire to retain power. Although influential political leaders have often ignored aspects of the Constitution, or have reinterpreted it to suit their political aims, this does not render the document meaningless. The Constitution spells out the basis for a participatory political system with basic rights and freedoms. These articles can be used as the basis to reform the system in a more democratic direction.

Although Islam was established as the foundation of Iran's political system in 1979, even the role of shari'a has changed. In January 1988 Khomeini issued a fatwa elevating the state and especially the supreme leader over religion and religious law. In his declaration, *velayat-e faqih* had absolute authority and, as noted by Martin, "in effect amounted to altering the Shari'a as a result of political exigency."[66] His statement was remarkable in its demotion of Islam: "Our government . . . has priority over all other Islamic tenets, even over prayer, fasting and the pilgrimage to Mecca."[67] Khomeini elevated government decisions and policies over the five pillars of the Islamic faith. In this statement we can see the Supreme Leader promoting the survival of the government over policies consistent with and required under Islam. Thus upholding Islamic tenets was less pressing than the survival of his political project. This also demonstrates just how far Khomeini's views on politics had evolved. In his early work *Secrets Revealed*, Khomeini argued that "any sovereignty except the sovereignty of God is against the well-being of the people and is tyranny, and except for the laws of God, all laws are void and useless."[68] Khomeini had come a long way from the early 1940s.

Branches of the Government

The political system established by Khomeini and his followers includes a democratically elected parliament and president, as well as some unelected political bodies including the supreme leader and judiciary. Understanding how these political bodies interact with one another and compete for power is essential to comprehending this unique political system. We begin with the most powerful political actor in Iran: the supreme leader.

The Supreme Leader

The unique position of the supreme leader seeks to create a religious authority to guide Iran by "determining the general policies of the system of the Islamic Republic."[69] As the religious guide of the country, this cleric has the ability to determine a broad range of policies based on his understanding of the religious requirements of Shia Islam. The role of the *velayat-e faqih* is to ensure that all government institutions are operating in a manner that is consistent with Islamic principles. Khomeini argued that Shia Islam requires that an Islamic jurist or group of jurists be guardian or custodians over those in society who need it (figure 3.1).[70]

Figure 3.1. Iran's Unelected and Elected Political Institutions

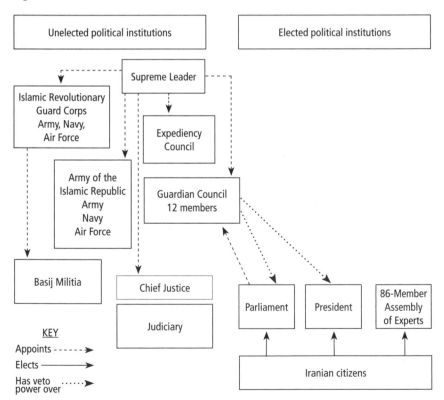

The supreme leader has various constitutional powers that make this office the most powerful in the Iranian political system. The vast powers of the supreme leader are established in Article 110 of the Constitution: "the power to determine the general policies of the system of the Islamic Republic of Iran; supervise the good performance of the regime's general policies; hold the supreme command of the Armed Forces; declare war and peace."[71] The supreme leader controls the armed forces, national security, and foreign policy. His ability to name individuals to serve as national security advisers and military commanders, including the head of the Islamic Revolutionary Guard Corps (IRGC), not only gives him a large degree of control over Iran's hard power but also ensures that the military and security forces will be loyal to him.

The supreme leader has the power to appoint individuals to various positions of power in the political system, including the Guardian Council, Expediency Council, and the Judiciary. Although the president has the power to appoint cabinet ministers, historically supreme leader Khamenei has influenced the selection of the most important cabinet ministers, including the defense and interior minister and the intelligence and foreign affairs ministers. He can also remove a sitting president if he finds just cause. Thus, despite some effort to develop checks and balances with the political system, the supreme leader has tentacles in most branches of the government. The supreme leader also appoints the head of radio and television broadcasting, Islamic Republic of Iran Broadcasting, which can influence what information is available to Iranians.[72] He also has control over charitable foundations that have considerable assets to distribute. There are almost no checks on the power of the supreme leader. The supreme leader typically serves for life.

Ayatollah Khomeini became the supreme leader after the Revolution and the constitutional changes in 1979. He served until his death in 1989. Khomeini had embodied the Revolution, and he steered domestic and foreign policy for a decade. He was able to balance the different factions from the left and the right in the political arena. Despite the vast concentration of power in the hands of the supreme leader, Khomeini tried to stay above politics by never throwing his support completely behind one faction. His death left a power vacuum in Iran.

Khamenei was selected by the Assembly of Experts to succeed Khomeini. Khamenei's elevation to supreme leader in the wake of Khomeini's death was not a surprising political choice. He had been president from 1981 to 1989, and he had served Khomeini loyally since the Revolution. Khamenei's ascension to the position of supreme leader did not immediately elevate him to

Khomeini's stature. In truth, it would be difficult to fill Khomeini's shoes because Khomeini was an icon of the Revolution, but Khameini lacked the adequate religious credentials for the position. Khamenei was not an ayatollah before Khomeini's death. Furthermore, he had not produced any of the major religious scholarship (books, compilations of religious edicts, etc.) that is typical of the most learned and respected Shia jurists.[73] His quick elevation to ayatollah was based on political necessity rather than religious credentials. This further cast doubt on the political position of the supreme leader in the eyes of other Shia jurists in Iran. Furthermore, he lacked Khomeini's charisma and loyal following. It would take Khamenei a few years to build up his base of support and a network of allies throughout the political system.

This position is not one of the democratic elements of the political system. There have been discussions within Iran as to whether this position with all its unchecked powers should be an elected office. However, the possibility of direct elections for the supreme leader of Iran seems rather unlikely. It is doubtful that Khamenei or the next person to hold this office will voluntarily relinquish power. Having to campaign and compete to assume this office would place some political limitations on the officeholder. Furthermore, the idea behind the supreme leader is a moral authority who should decide issues based on Islam, not public opinion polls.

The President

The president is directly elected by the people of Iran and serves a four-year term. Presidents are limited to serving two consecutive terms. They may run for reelection at a later time, as Rafsanjani did in 2005 (he had been president in the early 1990s). The president selects a cabinet to help him govern the country. He has the legal power to fire cabinet members, although the supreme leader can overrule him. The primary responsibility of the president is to execute the laws of Iran. He is responsible for the budget, which he submits to parliament. He can propose legislation, although any legislation proposed must be consistent with Islamic laws. The president can also play a role in foreign policy by selecting ambassadors and speaking to the rest of the world at international forums such as the United Nations. However, if the president strays too far in foreign policy from the will of the supreme leader, these efforts will be nullified.

The presidency has undergone a significant transformation since the early days of the Revolution, not only in the powers of the office but also in the officeholders. The first president of Iran, Bani-Sadr came to office having

Table 3.1 Presidents of Iran since the 1979 Revolution

President	Years in Office
Bani-Sadr	1980–81
Rajai	August 1981 (assassinated)
Khamenei	1981–89
Rafsanjani	1989–97
Khatami	1997–2005
Ahmadinejad	2005–13

won the January 1980 election with 70 percent of the vote. He had the support of Khomeini, who initially prohibited clerics from running from office. Khomeini supported Bani-Sadr to such an extent that the supreme leader relinquished command of the armed forces to the new president in February 1980.[74] However, some of the more radical clerics feared losing their influence over the political system if Bani-Sadr was fully able to consolidate his powers. By June 1981 Bani-Sadr had fallen from power.[75] He lost favor with Khomeini due to the president's support of secular individuals at the universities. The fall of Bani-Sadr, and Khomeini's change of heart, further demonstrate that Khomeini did not dictate on all political matters to a docile group of supporters. At numerous times the supreme leader altered his political position due to pressure from some of his more radical supporters.

Khamenei served as president for most of the 1980s. During his time in office, he was overshadowed by other political figures, including Khomeini. Rafsanjani's years in office (1989–97) were often marked by pragmatism and an attempt at economic development. Some progress was made to improve relations with other countries and to encourage economic growth after the long war with Iraq. Rafsanjani was succeeded by Mohammad Khatami (1997–2005), whose lofty rhetoric inspired many younger Iranians to believe in his reform platform (table 3.1). Unfortunately, the reform efforts never matched the results, given the opposition from other branches of the Iranian government. Many conservatives in the Guardian Council and judiciary saw the reformists' efforts as a threat to their hold on power.

Parliament: The Islamic Consultative Assembly
The Islamic Consultative Assembly (Majles-e Shorâ-ye Eslami, or simply Majles) resembles many legislatures around the world in that it passes legislation,

approves international treaties, confirms ministers selected by the executive, approves the budget, and can dismiss a cabinet member through a vote of no confidence. The Majles is a directly elected unicameral body led by the speaker. There are 290 members, who serve four-year terms. Specific seats are reserved for members of Iran's minority communities, including Jews, Assyrian Christians, Armenian Christians, and Zoroastrians. The Parliament must approve the president's cabinet. At first glance the Majles appears to be a traditional legislative body. However, its ability to propose and develop legislation is limited in two ways. First, any laws that are drafted must be a reflection of and consistent with shari'a. And second, all legislation is vetted by the Guardian Council, which must approve of any legislative acts.

The Majles is not completely impotent in the Iranian political system. There have been many fierce debates in the legislature concerning the direction of the war with Iraq and the economy. Numerous criticisms have been leveled at ministers whose departments underperform. And this had been true when both conservatives and reformists controlled Parliament. The members of Parliament, under both reformists and conservatives, have let their voices be heard when they have felt dismissed by other branches of government. For example, in March 2012, the Majles summoned President Ahmadinejad to answer questions about his management of the economy and his political appointments. Some legislators criticized his mishandling of the economy and the significant increases in the prices of basic goods. Although Ahmadinejad answered these questions in a dismissive and at times condescending manner, this was an example of Parliament challenging another branch of government.[76]

Parliament can also impeach a cabinet minister. An example of this occurred in November 2008, when Parliament, by an overwhelming majority, dismissed the interior minister, Ali Kordan, who had lied about various university degrees. A total of 188 lawmakers out of the 247 who were present voted to dismiss Kordan.[77] The impeachment proceedings also allowed Majles Speaker Ali Larjani to score a victory against Ahmadinejad.

At the end of 2010 conservative lawmakers criticized Ahmadinejad for ignoring the constitutional limits of the power of the president. A number of representatives from the Majles sent a letter to the Guardian Council complaining of abuse of power, financial irregularities, and failing to implement a variety of laws.[78] This is another example of how Parliament asserts itself. Although some of the Majles' policy efforts have been stymied in the past, this does not mean that Parliament will agree to be a rubber stamp. In fact, Iran has arguably had some of the most robust debates in all the Middle East (with the exception of Turkey and Israel). However, beyond a certain degree of debate, the powers of Parliament can be severely curtailed by the Guardian Council.

The Guardian Council

The Guardian Council is one of the most powerful bodies within the Iranian political system. The idea of a supervisory council of senior clerics to "safeguard the Islamic ordinances and the Constitution" (Article 91) has a long history in Iran. It arose during the Constitutional Revolution of 1905–11. The Constitution that was created at the beginning of the twentieth century provided for a Council of Guardians in Article 2. These religious figures would ensure that all laws passed by the legislature were consistent with Islamic law.[79]

The Guardian Council is composed of twelve senior religious figures who serve six-year terms. Six members of the Guardian Council are selected by the supreme leader. An additional six jurists are chosen by the chief justice and approved by the Majles. This again demonstrates the extended powers of the supreme leader. Their job is to ensure that all legislation is compatible with Islam. The Guardian Council also has veto power over legislation developed in the Majles.[80] The Guardian Council is also responsible for supervising elections according to Article 99 of the Constitution. The Guardian Council has interpreted this clause to mean that it can vet and veto candidates based on their loyalty to the Islamic Republic. Thus no individual can be elected to parliament and no act of parliament can become law without the approval of the Guardian Council, which thereby carefully supervises and can curtail the elected legislative branch.

This unaccountable part of government has vetoed legislation passed by the reformists in parliament concerning women's rights, family law, the prevention of torture, and electoral reform.[81] In response, President Khatami and the reformists in Parliament attempted through legislation to remove the veto power of the Guardian Council. Their efforts in 2002 failed. The Guardian Council recognized this political threat and vetoed the legislation that would have diminished their powers. The Guardian Council has been able to marginalize the Majles and has stalled many legislative initiatives due to the fact that there are few institutional checks on its power.

The Judicial System

Another unelected political body in Iran is the judiciary. It is headed by the chief justice, who is selected by the supreme leader. The chief justice serves a five-year term and is responsible for supervising the court system, including the Supreme Court. Ayatollah Shahroudi, the former chief justice (1999–2009), interpreted the supervisory function to give him the power of judicial review. Thus he claimed to have the authority to review the constitutionality of laws.[82] The Supreme Court is the highest appeals court in Iran. The judiciary is composed of senior clerics who are supposed to have knowledge of Islamic law. They are also typically chosen due to their loyalty to the regime. Article 61 of the Constitution sets out the functions of this body: "The functions of the judiciary are to be performed by courts of justice, which are to be formed in accordance with the criteria of Islam, and are vested with the authority to examine and settle lawsuits, protect the rights of the public, dispense and enact justice, and implement the Divine limits."

The Constitution also sets out the duties of the independent judiciary in Article 156. These duties include "promoting justice and legitimate freedom," "supervising the proper enforcement of laws," "prosecuting, punishing and chastising criminals," and "prevent the occurrence of crime." Many conservatives in the judiciary have used their judicial powers to punish political opponents, especially reformists and those protesting the June 2009 election. The judiciary has also closed newspapers and handed out sentences to publishers and political groups for insulting religious values.[83] Some preemptive actions taken by the judiciary were meant to prevent crime.[84]

The Assembly of Experts

Eighty-six members make up the Assembly of Experts. These individuals, who are elected by the people, serve an eight-year term of office. The individuals who run for the Assembly of Experts are limited to senior clerics and must be vetted by the Guardian Council before being allowed to run. Thus the Assembly of Experts has been controlled by conservative religious leaders.[85] The assembly, in theory, oversees the work of the supreme leader.[86] This body selects the supreme leader and has the power to remove him. The assembly is supposed to select an individual who is a learned Islamic jurist and whose ethics are above reproach. Although the assembly is constitutionally empowered to remove the supreme leader if the leader is unable to uphold all the religious duties contingent on the office, this is unlikely. The Assembly of Experts is also empowered to amend the Constitution. For much of the history of the Islamic Republic, the assembly has not acted as an independent check on the powers of the supreme leader. Rafsanjani led the assembly as chairman from 2007 to 2011. In 2011 an election within the assembly replaced Rafsanjani with Ayatollah Mohammad Reza Mahdari Kani. This was viewed by some in Iran as a sign that Rafsanjani's power and influence was in decline.[87]

The Expediency Council

The Expediency Council was created in 1988 by Khomeini due to the disputes between different political organs in Iran. Article 112 gives the supreme leader the power to appoint members of this body. Policy differences between the Majles and the Guardian Council had developed in the 1980s, and this would be repeated in the 1990s. Without some mechanism to resolve these disputes, politics was in danger of coming to a standstill. The Expediency Council was created to resolve differences and to deal with stalled legislation.[88] When a bill passed by the Majles is rejected by the Guardian Council, the Expediency Council can try to find a solution to deal with the legislative impasse. The Expediency Council is therefore an additional legislative body, although one that is not reviewed by other political institutions. Thus the Expediency Council has the last word and its decisions are binding.

The Military and Paramilitary Forces

Gaining a sense of Iran's military capabilities is important for understanding how Iran's political system functions. It is also important for assessing the potential threat that Iran poses to its neighbors and other countries around the world. Iran is not a regional hegemon, but Tehran can cause problems throughout the region through its actions.[89] Although Iran has more than half a million soldiers and an advantage in manpower, its conventional forces and military equipment are relatively weak compared with some countries in the region such as Turkey and Saudi Arabia, not to mention Israel. And Iran's military capabilities are no match for American forces in the region. Although Tehran is concerned about the threat from the United States, it is also concerned about an internal rebellion, and its military forces have been used to suppress internal unrest.

Iran has conventional forces, including an army, navy, and air force. As explained in Article 143 of the Constitution, the military serves to protect "the independence territorial integrity of the country." There are approximately 400,000 personnel in the army, navy, and air force.[90] These forces have limited combat experience, as Iran's last major military battles were fought in the 1980s against Iraq. An additional weakness of these forces is that much of their military equipment was purchased by the shah and is thus outdated.[91] Given Iran's hostile relations with the West, Iran has not been able to purchase new weapons or military technology from the West. Ultimately, Iran's conventional forces are weak.

Of greater concern to the region is Iran's ballistic missile program. Since the time of the shah, Tehran has been developing short- and medium-range missiles with foreign assistance from countries such as North Korea. These missiles can act as a deterrent and a threat to neighboring countries. The Shahab-1 and Shahab-2 have a range of 185 miles and 310 miles, respectively. Thus they are capable of hitting a number of countries in the Middle East, including Saudi Arabia.[92] The Ghadr-1 missile, a modified version of the Shahab-3, has a range of about 1,000 miles, whereas the Sajjil-2 has a range of 1,375 miles.[93] Thus the more technically proficient Tehran gets at developing missiles such as the Sajjil-2, the more likely it will be that Tehran can hit countries as far away as Israel.

Also of concern to states such as Israel and Saudi Arabia is the IRGC and its influence and extended reach within Iran's political system. The IRGC was created in the aftermath of the Revolution to protect the new political system from a counterrevolution. Khomeini and many other revolutionary figures did not trust the military due to their historic ties to the shah. The shah had cultivated the military with both military purchases and pay. Thus it was not surprising that the new leaders would seek to eliminate this potential threat. Those high-ranking military officials who did not go into exile were treated brutally. The purges that occurred within the army are an example: "By the end of 1979 between 8,000 and 12,000 officers, including all those ranking above brigadier, had been retired or cashiered. Of the 80 or so generals who had formed the top brass of the Shah's army, at least 70 were executed, together with more than 200 other officers and NCOs [noncommissioned officers]."[94] Thus Khomeini created the IRGC because he wanted a force he could trust.

During the last few years, and especially in the aftermath of the 2009 presidential elections, the IRGC has expanded its political and economic influence throughout the country. The 120,000 members of the IRGC were instrumental in cracking down on protesters in the aftermath of the June elections.[95] Beyond their interference in the political sphere, the IRGC has also entered the economic sphere. It has purchased companies, often in no-competition bids. It is involved in infrastructure projects and nuclear developments. Its economic holdings include telecommunication companies and a variety of other enterprises, including a construction firm—Khatam al-Anbia. One study noted how extensive the IRGC's tentacles were in the economic realm: "From laser eye surgery, and construction to automobile manufacturing and real estate, the IRGC has extended its influence into virtually every sector of the Iranian market."[96] One estimate suggested that the IRGC controlled a third of Iran's economy.[97] The more power the IRGC has, the less it needs the clerics.

Today the IRGC is more than simply a paramilitary force to protect the ideological foundations of the political system from internal and external threats. The IRGC acts like an independent multinational corporation that has not only education programs, media resources, economic investments, and business partnerships but also a well-armed militia that is more powerful than the country's conventional forces.

Factional Political Infighting and Perceived Threats to the Regime

At various times during the last thirty years, key political figures in positions of power have encountered a perceived political threat. These threats have taken the form of direct challenges to the foundations of the regime—secularists who disapproved of a theocracy, as well as opposing political factions that want to readjust the power distribution within the system. In both instances the response to the threat was often decisive and potent. Violence or a prison sentence was often a result. In the early 1980s political infighting took place between the religious revolutionaries and the secular leftists. The religious revolutionaries did not want to share power with anyone who was not committed to the theocracy. They tried to silence many secular critics. In response some of the more radical leftists struck back. One prominent example was the attack on the Islamic Republic Party on June 28, 1981, which killed some prominent members of the party.[98]

Factional differences in Iran revolve around ideological and policy differences. There have been three main divisions within Iranian politics of the last few years: reformists, conservatives, and neoconservatives. On the political spectrum neoconservatives, also sometimes referred to as hard-line conservatives or principlists, are on the far right. Reformists, sometimes called the Islamic left, are the furthest away from the neoconservatives, with pragmatic conservatives falling somewhere in between the two.

Neoconservatives, such as Ayatollah Yardi, take a hard line on both domestic and foreign policy. They are the most socially conservative of the three factions and believe in the strict enforcement of social morality, including separation of the sexes and strict veiling. In foreign policy they are often anti-Western and resist compromise with the international community. Neoconservatives are more nationalist and protectionist in their economic orientation. They have placed more emphasis on the Islamic nature of the political system. They resist "reforms" and believe that Iran should return to the foundational principles of the Revolution, including the social justice message of Khomeini, which they have used to justify the redistribution of Iran's oil wealth.[99] Especially in the early years of his presidency, Ahmadinejad was considered a neoconservative.

Pragmatic conservatives are far less confrontational in foreign policy and have argued for economic cooperation with the rest of the world, including the West. They have traditionally had strong ties to the bazaar and have supported a free market economy. Conservatives are also concerned with social norms within society. They place less emphasis on expanding the democratic elements in the political system. They have been more reluctant to demonize opponents. There is also a generational divide between conservatives and neoconservatives. Traditional conservatives tend to be older, and their formative experience was the Revolution. Neoconservatives tend to be younger (forties and fifties), and their formative experience was the Iran-Iraq War.

Reformists, led by Khatami and Mousavi, have argued for a more open, democratic political system. Many of the reformists were part of the Islamic left during the 1980s. They emphasize the republican aspects of the political system more than the Islamic ones. They have supported a more open and transparent system, including greater freedom of the press. They are more interested in better relations with the global community, including the West. They would like to see more power vested in the democratic branches of government. Students and women's groups have given their support to the reform movement. They have tried to encourage the development of a vibrant civil society. Some reformists have even argued for a supreme leader who is more accountable to the people. Ayatollah Montazeri, who was initially selected by Khomeini to succeed him, argued that the supreme leader should be the result of an electoral process and should be accountable to the people.[100] Shahram Chubin offers a summary of these political divisions:

> Ahmadinejad's opponents seek to stabilize the system, in contrast, by redefining and reorienting Iran through evolutionary change focusing on public accountability and a more open, normal interaction with a globalized world. For them, this is the path to renewing the legitimacy

of the Iranian system that has eroded dangerously. The hard-liners in Iran see this approach as doubly dangerous, for ejecting 'revolutionary values' risks losing control and power. Regime survival, equated with their primacy, depends upon embattlement. Legitimacy for them comes not from the citizenry, many of whom advocate accommodation, but from resistance. Advocates of moderation, therefore, threaten the control of the hard-liners and their definitions of regime.[101]

In the wake of President Khatami's surprising victory in presidential elections, hard-line conservatives initiated a crackdown on many reformists and their supporters. The reformists were a political threat because they wanted a more democratic system, which could have limited some of the power of conservatives. Further, they argued for significant social and cultural changes. The reform movement is also known as The Second of Khordad (Dovvom-e Khordad), which refers to the date of his election in 1997. One target was the vibrant free press that had developed in the aftermath of the 1997 elections. The numerous magazine and newspapers that sprung up investigated the irregularities, corruption, and numerous government figures. These embarrassing details and investigations were a threat to the political and economic power of many. Thus hard-line conservatives in the judiciary had to deal with them. The result was that many reformist newspapers were closed and their publishers were punished with jail sentences or fines.

Salam, for example, published stories about the 1998 serial murders and was shut down. The judiciary was not going to tolerate a free press that aired the regime's dirty laundry. To combat this judicial activism, Reformists in parliament tried to pass a revised law on press freedom in 2001. However, the supreme leader intervened. He directed the speaker of Parliament, Mehdi Karroubi, to prevent any further debate on the revised press law.[102] The supreme leader's legislative intervention demonstrated two things. First, ultimate power in the political system does not rest with the elected bodies. And second, Khamenei and other hard-line conservatives would not tolerate any threat to their power.

Additional examples demonstrate just how far members of the regime are willing to go to retain their power. When university students protested the closure of newspapers such as *Salam* in 1999, they were met with a swift and brutal response. Many were beaten in the street or in their dormitory rooms.[103] A few students were killed as a result. Hard-line conservatives recognized the student protests as a threat to their power. Students were an important part of the Revolution that ousted the shah. The hard-line conservatives were not going to risk another major protest.

Additional acts of violence and murder have been carried out to intimidate political opponents. Five political dissidents had their throats cut in 1998, and Said Hajjarian, a prominent political strategist for the reformists, was almost assassinated in Tehran in March 2000. As one observer noted, this was a strategy of violence:

> The attempt on Hajjarian's life was a part of a strategy of violence, clearly designed to suppress any form of opposition to the clerical state. It was not long before people began drawing connections to a series of murders perpetrated a few years earlier with the intent of creating an atmosphere of terror. In November 1998, five dissident intellectuals, members of a tiny political party tolerated by the Islamic regime, were found with their throats cut in their Tehran homes. The discovery of their mutilated bodies touched off shockwaves, not only among political circles but also among the citizenry at large. . . . An investigation commissioned by President Khatami revealed that the murders had been the work of "rogue elements" belonging to the security police.[104]

More recently, during the Ahmadinejad presidency, there have also been more political clashes between conservatives and hard-line conservatives. As the reformists have been marginalized and become less of a threat, the political competition within the conservative camp has intensified. We can see this in the clashes in the spring of 2011 between the supreme leader and the president. Ahmadinejad fired his cabinet minister, Haydar Moslehi. Moslehi, the head of the Intelligence Ministry, was supported by the supreme leader, who intervened on his behalf and essentially ordered Moslehi to stay at the helm of the Intelligence Ministry. President Ahmadinejad responded to this public rebuke by not going to work for eleven days.[105] This was not the first time the supreme leader ordered the president to reinstate an official. In May 2009 Ahmadinejad removed the official who organizes the annual pilgrimage to Mecca and was promptly ordered to reinstate him by Ayatollah Khamenei. This demonstrated a very public disagreement between two conservatives and a very direct challenge to the supreme leader, who acted quickly to put Ahmadinejad back in his place. These actions demonstrate Ahmadinejad's attempt to assert his power at the expense of the supreme leader. It also shows that the supreme leader will not remain quiet while his power is being threatened.

The competition between conservatives associated with the supreme leader and neoconservatives associated with the president was on display again in the March 2012 parliamentary elections. Reformists and those associated with the Green Movement encouraged their supporters to boycott the election.[106] The president and his supporters drew the short end of the stick in this election. Many of his associates were barred from running for office. The results of the elections strengthened the Ayatollah Khamenei as many of his political supporters were elected.

Aside from political figures, some members of the regime were also willing to confront and neutralize clerical figures who dared to criticize the regime. One of the most prominent religious leaders who was neutralized was Ayatollah Hossein Ali Montazeri, who at one point was Khomeini's handpicked successor. However, in the late 1980s Montazeri became more outspoken in his criticism of the regime. Some of his criticisms were aimed at the way the war in Iraq was conducted. He also condemned the assassinations and political violence that occurred under the cover of the wars, specifically the thousands of political prisoners who were killed in 1988.[107] He would also challenge the very heart of the regime and thus argue that the supreme leader should be an elected office accountable to the people. For these heretical statements Montazeri lost Khomeini's support, was rejected as a possible successor, and was placed under house arrest in 1997. Despite spending more than five years under house arrest, he continued to criticize the regime and the leadership of Khamenei. In an interview in 2005, he said that "a government system cannot and must not be concentrated in the hands of one person. . . . We need a collective government in which the people play a dominant role. . . . The clergy's absolute power is bad."[108] His criticism at the lack of democracy is a nuisance; his criticism of the legitimacy of the Islamic nature of the regime is more potent due to the fact that he has the highest religious credentials in Shia Islam and he was one of the key figures of the revolution.

Conclusion

The Revolution of 1979 succeeded because it had a grassroots network and a homogenous base of supporters—the faithful—who were available to mobilize.[109] Furthermore, the Iranian people were led by clerics who had the ability to influence the public in mosques and religious schools. This political movement expressed the people's resentment and frustration.[110] It was also the only aspect of civil society that was left after the monarchy had crushed other associations in society. The Tudeh Party (communist) was weakened significantly after the coup in 1953. Iran did not have any independent political parties. SAVAK spied on the population, and there was no free media. So the only aspect of civil society that remained were the Shia networks.

In addition, Khomeini drew on an established religious discourse to motivate his followers. His claims of social injustice, oppression, sacrifice, martyrdom, and foreign influence were themes to which Iranians could relate.[111] These ideas were framed in terms of a Manichean worldview of good and evil. Fighting against evil was not only easy to relate to, but it was also understood as a basic religious obligation.

Finally, Khomeini's disdain for the West and Western culture helped to guide not only the Revolution but also Iran's foreign policy in the decades to follow. He criticized the shah for allowing the cultural pollution of Iran with Western thoughts and books and movies. Not only did Iranians need to protect themselves against the imperialism of Western foreign policy, but they also needed to guard against accepting alien concepts and desires in their lives.[112] Although the Revolution's Shia foundations, ideas, leadership, and grassroots network were essential to the success of the movement, it was also helped by the weakness of the monarch. The shah often found it difficult to take decisive action. He was battling cancer at the time of the Revolution. Furthermore, unlike some dictators, he was unwilling to unleash the military upon the protesters. He did not want to see bloodshed on the streets of Tehran.

The political system that was created in the aftermath of the Revolution incorporates two competing ideals: democracy and Islam. Democratic elements can be seen in the presidency and the Parliament, which are two of the elected branches of government. The democratic aspects of this political system are limited by Islamic values that are protected by the Guardian Council and the supreme leader. Thus democracy is contained by religious elites.

Notes

1. Barbara Ann J. Rieffer, "Religion and Nationalism: Understanding the Consequences of a Complex Relationship," *Ethnicities* 3, no. 2 (June 2003): 215–42.

2. John Esposito and John Voll, *Islam and Democracy* (Oxford: Oxford University Press, 1996), 58.

3. See Eliz Sanasarian, *Religious Minorities in Iran* (Cambridge: Cambridge University Press, 2000), 15; and Ali Akbar Mahdi, "Iranian Women: Between Islamicization and Globalization," in *Iran Encountering Globalization: Problems and Prospects*, edited by Ali Mohammadi (New York: RoutledgeCurzon, 2003), 50.

4. Kenneth Pollack, *The Persian Puzzle* (New York: Random House, 2004), 65. See also Elton Daniel, *The History of Iran* (Westport, CT: Greenwood Press, 2001).

5. Vanessa Martin, *Creating an Islamic State: Khomeini and the Making of a New Iran* (New York: I. B. Tauris, 2000), 40–41.

6. Plato, *Republic*, translated by C. D. C. Reeve (Indianapolis: Hackett, 2004).

7. Ibid., book 6, 473d, p. 166.

8. Khomeini was also influenced by *irfan*. For a full discussion of the influence of *irfan* on Khomeini, see Martin, *Creating an Islamic State*, chap. 2.

9. Karim Sadjadpour, *Reading Khamenei: The World View of Iran's Most Powerful Leader* (Washington, DC: Carnegie Endowment for International Peace, 2008), 9.

10. Khomeini, in *Islam and Revolution: Writings and Declarations of Iman Khomeini*, translated and annotated by Hamid Algar (Berkeley, CA: Mizan Press, 1981), 171. Robin Wright, *In the Name of God* (New York: Simon & Schuster, 1989), 46.

11. Ray Takeyh, *Guardians of the Revolution* (Oxford: Oxford University Press, 2009), 15.

12. Vali Nasr, *The Shia Revival* (New York: W. W. Norton, 2007), 121; Gary Sick, *All Fall Down* (New York: Penguin Books, 1986), 232.

13. Nasr, *Shia Revival*, 125.

14. Even Rafsanjani noted how radical a theology this was: "The writing of *The Mandate of the Jurist*, itself at that time in Najaf was a great revolution: that he should come from the jurists and write on such a topic!" Quoted by Said Amir Arjomand, *After Khomeini: Iran under His Successors* (Oxford: Oxford University Press, 2009), 22.

15. Nasr, *Shia Revival*, 144.

16. Although Shariatmadari was implicated in an assassination attempt on Khomeini in 1982, his religious demotion was based on his unwillingness to accede to Khomeini's interpretations of Shia theology. Nasr, *Shia Revival*, 126–27; Wright, *In the Name of God*, 106; Ervand Abrahamian, *A History of Modern Iran* (Cambridge: Cambridge University Press, 2008), 181.

17. Khomeini often drew parallels between his life and Muhammad's, because both were exiled and later returned to lead their communities. Bernard Lewis, "The Roots of Muslim Rage," *Atlantic Monthly* 266, no. 3: 47–60.

18. Lewis, "Roots," 53.

19. Amir Taheri, *The Spirit of Allah: Khomeini and the Islamic Revolution* (London: Hutchinson, 1985), 172. See also Nasr, *Shia Revival*, 131. *Taghut* can also be translated as idolatry. Said Amir Arjomand, *The Turban for the Crown: The Islamic Revolution in Iran* (New York: Oxford University Press, 1988), 103.

20. Khomeini, *Islam and Revolution*, 147.

21. Barry Rubin, *Paved with Good Intentions* (New York: Penguin Books, 1981), 221.

22. Mohammad Manzoor Nomani, *Khomeini, Iranian Revolution and the Shi'ite Faith* (London: Furqan, 1988), 13.

23. Esposito and Voll, *Islam and Democracy*, 53.

24. Nasr, *Shia Revival*, 35; Wright, *In the Name of God*, 47.

25. Nasr, *Shia Revival*, 32; Wright, *In the Name of God*, 47.

26. Khomeini stated: "Everyday is Ashura and every place is Karbala." Wright, *In the Name of God*, 48. The relationship between the shah and Khomeini was in fact more complicated than generally acknowledged. In the mid-1940s Khomeini made several visits to Tehran to speak with the shah. On one occasion Khomeini asked for a pardon for Hussein

Emami. This request was granted. On another occasion he was sent by Ayatollah Borujerdi to ask for financial support for the construction of a new mosque in Qom. He again received what he asked for. See also Taheri, *Spirit of Allah*, 108.

27. Taheri, *Spirit of Allah*, 121.

28. Despite Khomeini's calls for martyrdom, Harold Brown, the defense secretary in the Carter administration, noted ironically, "A man with a martyr complex rarely lives to be seventy-nine." Mark Bowden, *Guests of the Ayatollahs* (New York: Grove Press, 2006), 379.

29. Jean-Daniel Lafond and Fred A Reed, *Conversations in Tehran* (Vancouver: Talon Books, 2006), 38.

30. The notion of martyrdom is also evident in Christianity. Shi'ite Muslims celebrate the festival of Ashura by reenacting the martyrdom of Hosain in Karbala in a similar way that Christians remember the crucifixion every Easter. Nasr, *Shia Revival*, 57.

31. Marvin Zonis and David Brumberg, "Shi'ism as Interpreted by Khomeini: An Ideology of Revolutionary Violence," in *Shi'ism, Resistance, and Revolution*, edited by Martin Kramer (Boulder, CO: Westview Press, 1987), 47–67, at 49.

32. Nasr, *Shia Revival*, 67.

33. Ibid., 38–39.

34. Quoted from Khomeini's *Al- Hukumat- ul –Islamia*, by Nomani, *Khomeini*, 20–21.

35. Khomeini, *Islam and Revolution: Writings and Declarations of Iman Khomeini*, translated and annotated by Hamid Algar, 126–27.

36. Ibid., 130.

37. In the 1980s, out of a population of roughly 55 million, 98 percent were Muslims, and 93 percent of these adhered to the Shi'ite faith. Eliz Sanasarian, *Religious Minorities in Iran* (Cambridge: Cambridge University Press, 2000), 9.

38. Jalal Al-e Ahmad, *Plagued by the West*, translated by Paul Sprachman (New York: Caravan Books, 1982), 47.

39. Nasr, *Shia Revival*, 118.

40. Janet Afray, *Sexual Politics in Modern Iran* (Cambridge: Cambridge University Press, 2009), 237.

41. Taheri, *Spirit of Allah*, 218.

42. Sandra Mackey, *The Iranians: Persia, Islam and the Soul of a Nation* (New York: Penguin Books, 1986), 277.

43. Nasr, *Shia Revival*, 129. Rubin, *Paved with Good Intentions*, 205.

44. Mackey, *Iranians*, 278.

45. Abrahamian, *History*, 159.

46. Arang Keshavarzian, *Bazaar and State in Iran* (Cambridge: Cambridge University Press, 2007), 243; Mackey, *Iranians*, 281.

47. Martin, *Creating an Islamic State*, 152.

48. Wright, *In the Name of God*, 37.

49. Ziba Mir Hosseini and Richard Tapper, *Islam and Democracy: Eshkevari and the Quest for Reform* (London: I. B. Tauris, 2006), 15.

50. Abol Hassan Bani-Sadr, *My Turn to Speak: Iran, the Revolution and Secret Deals with the US* (Arlington, VA: Brassey's, 1991), 1.

51. Robin Wright, *The Last Great Revolution: Turmoil and Transformation in Iran* (New York: Alfred A. Knopf, 2000), 14. Khomeini also articulated this point in 1941 in his book *Kashf al-Asrar*, 170: "We do not say that government must be in the hands of the *faqih*; rather we say that government must be run in accordance with God's law, for the welfare of

the country and the people demands this, and it is not feasible except with the supervision of the religious leaders."

52. "Formation of the Council of the Islamic Revolution," by Khomeini, *Islam and Revolution*, 246–47.

53. Esposito and Voll, *Islam and Democracy*, 62.

54. Hosseini and Tapper, *Islam and Democracy*, 112.

55. Ibid.

56. Wright, *In the Name of God*, 65; Nasr, *Shia Revival*, 145, 152; Abrahamian, *History*, 163.

57. Khomeini, *Islam and Revolution*, 325.

58. Some scholars have suggested that Khomeini was being deliberately deceptive in his speeches in 1978, concealing his true aims.

59. Martin, *Creating an Islamic State*, 158.

60. Esposito and Voll, *Islam and Democracy*, 62; Martin, *Creating an Islamic State*, 158; Abrahamian, *History*, 163.

61. Hosseini and Tapper, *Islam and Democracy*, 113; Keddie, 247.

62. Esposito and Voll, *Islam and Democracy*, 63.

63. Ibid., 62.

64. The Iranian Constitution can be found at www.servat.unibe.ch/icl/ir00000_.html.

65. Ibid.

66. Martin, *Creating an Islamic State*, 41.

67. Wright, *In the Name of God*, 173. See also Hosseini and Tapper, *Islam and Democracy*, 22.

68. Quoted by Martin, *Creating an Islamic State*, 106.

69. Article 110, "Functions and Authorities of the Leader: Iranian Constitution—Moslem," 278. Quoted by Mehdi Moslem, *Factional Politics in Post-Khomeini Iran* (Syracuse, NY: Syracuse University Press, 2002), 225.

70. See Dmitri Trenin and Alexey Malashenko, "Iran: A View from Moscow," Carnegie Endowment for International Peace, 2010, 12.

71. See Article 110, 26.

72. Abrahamian, *History*, 164.

73. Lafond and Reed, *Conversations*, 158.

74. Martin, *Creating an Islamic State*, 166.

75. Ibid., 169.

76. Alan Cowell, "Iranian Parliament Questions Ahmadinejad," *New York Times*, March 14, 2012, www.nytimes.com/2012/03/15/world/middleeast/iran-ahmadine. . . .

77. "MPs Showed Their Mettle in Impeachment of Interior Minister: Larijani," *Tehran Times*, November 5, 2008, www.tehrantimes.com/Names/2007.asp?code=181662; Nazila Fathi, "Minister's Dismissal Is Setback for Iran's Leader," *New York Times*, November 5, 2008, www.nytimes.com/2008/11/05/world/middleeast/05iran.html? . . .

78. William Yong, "Iranian Lawmakers Complain about Ahmadinejad," *New York Times*, November 23, 2010, www.nytimes.com/2010/11/24/world/middleeast/24iran.html.

79. Martin, *Creating an Islamic State*, 7.

80. In 1996 the Council of Guardians prohibited more than 5,000 candidates from running in parliamentary elections. Mahmood Monshipouri, *Islamism, Secularism, and Human Rights in the Middle East* (Boulder, CO: Lynne Rienner, 1998), 178, 186.

81. Human Rights Watch, *World Report 2003: Iran* (New York: Human Rights Watch, 2003). This report can be accessed at www.hrw.org; US State Department, "Country Reports on Human Rights Practices: 2003–Iran," www.state.gov/g/drl/rls/lurrpt/2003/27927 .htm.

82. Said Amir Arjomand, "Constitutional Implications of Current Political Debates in Iran," in *Contemporary Iran: Economy, Society, Politics*, edited by Ali Gheissari (Oxford: Oxford University Press, 2009), 247–74, at 255.

83. Bureau of Democracy, Human Rights, and Labor, US Department of State, "International Religious Freedom Report," October 7, 2002.

84. Said Amir Arjomand, "Constitutional Implications of Current Political Debates in Iran," in *Contemporary Iran*, ed. Gheissari, 247–74, at 255.

85. Mir Hosseini and Tapper, *Islam and Democracy*, 18.

86. Lafond and Reed, *Conversations*, 19.

87. "Mahdavi Kani Replaces Rafsanjani as Assembly of Experts Chief," *Tehran Times*, March 9, 2011, www.tehrantimes.com/NCms/2007.asp?code=237109. See also Alan Cowell, "Rafsanjani Loses Key Post in Iranian Religious Assembly," *New York Times*, March 8, 2011, www.nytimes.com/2011/03/09/world/middleeast/09iran.html? . . .

88. Wright, *In the Name of God*, 173.

89. Anthony Cordesman and Martin Kleiber, *Iran's Military Forces and War Fighting Capabilities* (Westport, CT: Praeger Security International, 2007), 26.

90. Anthony H Cordesman, "The Conventional Military," in *Iran Primer*, ed. Robin Wright (Washington, DC: US Institute of Peace Press, 2010), 66.

91. Cordesman and Kleiber, *Iran's Military Forces*, 41.

92. Michael Elleman, "Iran's Ballistic Missile Program," in *Iran Primer*, ed. Wright, 87. See also Cordesman and Kleiber, *Iran's Military Forces*, 136.

93. Elleman, "Iran's Ballistic Missile Program," 87.

94. Taheri, *Spirit of Allah*, 257.

95. Alireza Nader, David E. Thaler, and S. R. Bohandy, "The Next Supreme Leader: Succession in the Islamic Republic of Iran" (Santa Monica, CA: RAND Corporation, 2011), 2. Some have put the number of Guardsmen higher at 150,000. Ali Reza Nader, "The Revolutionary Guards," in *Iran Primer*, ed. Wright, 59.

96. Fredric Wehrey, Jerrold Green, Brian Nichiporuk, Ali Reza Nader, Lydia Hansell, Rosool Nafisi, and S. R. Bohandy, *The Rise of the Pasdaran: Assessing the Domestic Roles of Iran's Islamic Revolutionary Guards Corps* (Santa Monica, CA: RAND Corporation, 2009), xv.

97. Mark Gregory, "Expanding Business Empire of Iran's Revolutionary Guards," BBC, July 26, 2010. www.bbc.co.uk/news/world-middle-east-10743580? . . .

98. Bani-Sadr, *My Turn to Speak*, 45: "The attack on June 28, 1981 that caused the death of Beheshti and numerous officials of the Islamic Republic Party was undoubtedly the result of one group fighting the other."

99. Nader, Thaler, and Bohandy, *Rise of the Pasdaran*, 14.

100. Geneive Abdo, "Re-Thinking the Islamic Republic: A Conversation with Ayatollah Hossein Ali Montazeri," *Middle East Journal* 55, no. 1 (Winter 2001): 9–24.

101. Shahram Chubin, "The Iranian Nuclear Riddle after June 12," *Washington Quarterly* 33, no. 1 (January 2010): 163–72, at 165.

102. Lafond and Reed, *Conversations*, 63.

103. Ibid., 55.

104. Ibid., 54.

105. Neil MacFarquhar, "Power Struggle in Iran Enters the Mosque," *New York Times*, May 6, 2011, www.nytimes.com/2011/05/07/world/middleeast/07iran.html? . . .

106. Robert Worth, "Iran's Government Declares Huge Turnout in First National Vote since '09 Protests," *New York Times,* March 2, 2012, www.nytimes.com/2012/03/03/world/middleeast/iran-elections-pa. . . .

107. Lafond and Reed, *Conversations*, 171–72.

108. Shahrough Akhan, "The Thought and Role of Ayatollah Hossein ali Montazeri in the Politics of Post-1979 Iran," *Iranian Studies* 41, no. 5 (December 2008): 645–66, at 648.

109. Wright, *In the Name of God*, 42.

110. Michael Axworthy, *A History of Iran: Empire of the Mind* (New York: Basic Books, 2008), 261.

111. Ali Akbar Mahdi, "Iranian Women: Between Islamicization and Globalization," in *Iran Encountering Globalization: Problems and Prospects*, edited by Ali Mohammadi (New York: RoutledgeCurzon, 2003), 47.

112. Fred Halliday, *Nation and Religion in the Middle East* (Boulder, CO: Lynne Rienner, 2000), 137.

PART II

The Present Political Regime

CHAPTER 4

Elections in Iran
Predicting Iranian Politics

Many in the West may be surprised to learn that since the Islamic Revolution in 1979, Iran has experienced more than a dozen elections for president and for the legislature. The Iranian Constitution specifically states the importance of elections in Article 6: "In the Islamic Republic of Iran, the affairs of the country must be administered on the basis of public opinion expressed by the means of elections, including the election of the President, the representatives of the Islamic Consultative Assembly, and the members of councils." Elections are open to most of the population. Any Iranian who is eighteen years of age can vote in presidential and parliamentary elections. Men won the right to vote during the Constitutional Revolution (1905–6), and women during the White Revolution in 1963. Many political leaders in Iran have put a lot of emphasis on these controlled elections. For example, in January 2008, Supreme Leader Ayatollah Ali Khamenei addressed a crowd in Yazd Province in central Iran and explained to them that a large turnout in the March parliamentary elections was of vital importance. He went on to stress the value of Iran's religious democracy: "The Iranian nation, inspired by its faith in God, has opted for the dear Islam as a platform of democracy, presenting the world with religious and Islamic democracy."[1] In 2012 Khamenei reiterated the obligation of Iranian citizens to vote in parliamentary elections: "Elections are an important pillar of the system and religious democracy is founded on elections. Therefore, anybody who believes in the Islamic system considers participating in elections as his duty even if he has objections to certain issues."[2]

Why do leaders such as Ayatollah Khamenei stress the importance of elections and participation in elections? Why would Iranian leaders put so much emphasis on elections and encourage turnout? Elections are not an endogenous feature of Shia Islam, so why stress and continually hold elections that are a product of the West?

Elections can offer political leaders legitimacy and given the restraints on who can run for office, it is understandable why elections have been a continual aspect of the theocracy. As one scholar put it, "elections are indispensable to the Islamic Republic" because they provide a source of legitimacy to the political system.[3] Elections can also offer citizens a means to register their political preferences and express their grievances.[4] This chapter examines how elections have evolved since 1979 and the role that elections have played in the Islamic Republic of Iran. Understanding these changes will help us to understand the direction in which Iran is heading. This chapter also explores how religion and political threats have affected elections in Iran. Although some figures have used religious rhetoric for political gain, Islam has had a limited impact on the election process. Further, there has been a decline in the number of clerics elected to political positions. To explain the evolution of elections, the chapter examines various parliamentary and presidential elections and the role of political infighting.[5] The chapter puts more emphasis on recent elections as they indicate the present state of political affairs in Iran. Iranians have seen more competition in recent elections, including more competition between conservative factions. The more competitive the electoral process is in Iran, the more likely that Iran will develop a more open political system in the long run. The more political figures engage in electoral manipulation and fraud, the less likely that Iran will shed its authoritarian nature. This chapter chronicles the power struggle for the political direction of the country.

Elections

A variety of elements are needed for a legitimate, democratic election. Citizens must be allowed to participate. Participation cannot be limited to a small percentage of the population or to a single ethnic or religious group. Encouraging voter participation, as Khamenei has done, is important, but equally important is a fair process. Democracy is not simply about voting; it is also about competition and counting the votes. Meaningful elections require an independent media to help keep citizens informed about their choices. Thus the government should not monopolize the media during an election campaign. The individuals and organizations that make up civil society must have the freedom to assemble and promote their political messages. Thus basic rights such as freedom of speech and assembly must be respected. Furthermore, the rule of law must be upheld so that any attempts at voter fraud or intimidation can be addressed to provide a fair playing field.

Iran has upheld some of these electoral aspects and has failed miserably in others. Although elections are not a rubber stamp in Iran, they are best understood as semicompetitive affairs with significant limitations on participation. The fundamental flaw with elections in Iran is the limitations on which candidates can run for office. Besides filling out the appropriate paperwork, a candidate must go through a number of procedural hurdles before he or she can run for office. The Ministry of the Interior and the Council of Guardians both review candidates before an election to see if the candidates are qualified and loyal to the Islamic Republic. Candidates register to run with the Ministry of the Interior. The ministry then submits the list of candidates to the Guardian Council for approval.

The Constitution gives the Guardian Council a supervisory role over elections in Article 99.[6] The Guardian Council has interpreted this article to allow it to directly assess the qualifications of candidates. However, some have criticized this interpretation as exceeding its constitutional authority. Ayatollah Montazeri, for example, has argued that it is the responsibility of the Interior Ministry to see if candidates are eligible to run for political office. The original intention was an oversight role, not a vetting procedure.[7] Despite the original intention of those who drafted the Constitution, the Guardian Council has asserted its right to disqualify candidates, and it has rejected many. Women have been barred from running for the office of the president, and many reformists have been prevented from running in parliamentary elections. In 2004 approximately 40 percent of the candidates for the Majles were rejected. In 2008, more than 2,000 reformist candidates were prevented from competing in parliamentary elections including Ali Eshraghi, the grandson of Ayatollah Khomeini.[8] Preventing some candidates from competing in the electoral process will obviously limit the democratic quality of the regime.

The History of Elections in Iran

Elections have been held throughout the twentieth century, and most have been tainted with corruption and fraud. At times free and fair elections were held in Iran; however, many elections (1954, 1963, 1971) were rigged and were far from a legitimate process. For example, in the legislative elections in 1952, Prime Minister Mohammad Mossadeq manipulated the voting process to ensure that his supporters would fill the seats of Parliament. He had voting stopped before rural areas could turn in their ballots, which thereby assured that opposition figures who were strongest in rural areas would not be elected.[9] Some political leaders in Iran viewed elections with much skepticism. The shah sought to control the outcome of elections to prevent another Mossadeq-like figure from challenging him. He rigged parliamentary elections in 1960.[10] American diplomats noted that parliamentary elections in 1967 were controlled affairs that Iranians would not view as legitimate. In a memorandum an American diplomat recalled a conversation with Abdolrese Ansari, the interior minister: "We started out by discussing what people expect, and whether those expectations are important, and quickly agreed that there is a tremendous difference if people have the impression that they are given a genuine choice or if they feel that the results of the elections are precooked. Ansari said it is his understanding that HM [His Majesty] wishes the candidates to be selected but the choices between them would not be necessarily predetermined—in other words, that he did not really care which of the selected candidates win out over other selected candidates."[11]

Hence it did not matter which of the preselected candidates won a seat in parliament so long as the candidates were approved in advance. This is similar in many ways to the Guardian Council's prescreening process. Ultimately, the shah's refusal to share power led to a series of meaningless elections over the course of his time on the throne.

Khomeini initially had reservations about elections. This was due in no small part to the king's manipulation of elections. Khomeini's concerns about the electoral process stemmed from the fact that many of the individuals elected sought to further their own interests and not the interests of the community. It was not elections per se that worried Khomeini but rather the lack of an interest in justice and the common good: "The majority of the people know nothing of representation and its duties and the limits of authority. For this reason, in those provinces which have populations of more than 200,000 not more than 10,000 to 12,000 forms for elections are distributed, and in that case representation is oppression, and its precepts injustice, and therefore cannot be justified. Secondly, there have been fourteen elections in Iran, and everybody has seen that, whether in the period before the dictatorship, or during that disgraceful time, or afterwards, that is, the present, representation has not been a means of spreading justice and freedom."[12]

Finally, Khomeini's distrust of elections and their results stems from the fact that elections are a product of the West. Despite these reservations, the political system Khomeini helped to create in 1979 included elections for a variety of political offices, including the Assembly of Experts, president, and the Parliament.

Before going into detail about the intricacies of presidential and parliamentary elections, it is worth briefly mentioning elections for the Assembly of Experts. As mentioned in chapter 3, the assembly is the political body that selects and oversees the supreme leader. The members of the assembly are elected by the people after being vetted by the Guardian Council. Although the assembly has not been an institution actively engaged in oversight, it is one over which Iranians have some influence.

For much of the last three decades conservatives have controlled the Assembly of Experts. This was demonstrated again in 2006, when conservatives associated with former president Rafsanjani won more than sixty seats in the eighty-six-member assembly. Rafsanjani was also elected that year.[13] This was viewed as a setback for hard-line conservatives associated with Ahmadinejad. Four years later, when elections were again held, Rafsanjani declined to run for a seat in the Assembly of Experts for fear of a disappointing result. When coupled with the 2009 presidential elections and Rafsanjani's criticism of the regime, there have been suggestions that Rafsanjani's star is fading in the political system.

Parliamentary Elections

The first parliamentary elections under the new regime occurred in March 1980. Many of those elected were members of the clergy and shopkeepers.[14] This is not surprising given that bazaar merchants and religious clerics were two of the main elements of the Revolution. The most dominant party in the first Majles was the Islamic Republic Party, which was created as a way for clerics and Khomeini's supporters to influence politics and increase their power. It had a diverse membership, including Mousavi, Khamenei, and Montazeri. It claimed the support of 130 deputies in the first Parliament.[15]

When examining a number of parliamentary elections since the 1980s, one sees some efforts at limiting competition. For example, in the 1984 parliamentary elections the Tudeh Party was prohibited from participating.[16] Despite this limitation these elections were successfully carried out without any violence, as was also the case in the 1980 parliamentary elections.

Parliamentary elections four years later saw significant changes. First, the Islamic Republic Party had been disbanded a year earlier. Because of the absence of this political party, the elections in 1988 were far less predictable than in the past. In fact, a majority of incumbents lost their seats, including many clerics.[17] Robin Wright, a well-respected journalist, noted the changes: "About 150 were new members, according to the Majles public relations office. And only about 27 percent of the members elected in 1988 were clerics, compared with about 45 percent in the previous two parliaments."[18] Further change can be seen from the fact that three women were elected to Parliament.[19]

As the 1990s progressed the Majles changed from a body controlled by conservatives to one in which the reformists held the majority of seats. The members who made up the Sixth Majles in 2000 were dominated by reformists. Reformists took control over the Majles, despite the Guardian Council's efforts to disqualify many of them.[20] Women increased their presence in the Parliament as well. Thirteen women were elected in this round of parliamentary elections. These women would come to form a legislative bloc known as the Women's Faction.[21]

Unfortunately, the efforts of the reformists in the Sixth Majles would be hampered by the more conservative political institutions of the government. Thus legislation to promote women's rights, freedom of the press, and individual rights would be stalled or blocked by the Guardian Council and the judiciary. Some 40 percent of the reformists' parliamentary actions would be overturned by the Guardian Council.[22] By 2004 the hard-line conservatives decided to take a more aggressive approach to blocking the efforts of the reformists. Thus they prevented many reformists from taking part in that year's election.

The Guardian Council, which vets all candidates for office, disqualified some 3,000 candidates from running for Parliament.[23] About a third of the more than 8,000 candidates who wanted to compete in parliamentary elections were unable to do so. In many cases those individuals who were barred from running were associated with the Reform Movement, and some were even sitting members of the Majles. Supreme Leader Khamenei backed the Guardian Council's decision.[24] The result was an election that offered Iranians a choice between conservative candidates.[25] As one scholar noted, this was a rigged election and electoral vandalism.[26]

It also demonstrated the increasingly aggressive approach of the Guardian Council. In the 1980s the Guardian Council never disqualified more than 20 percent of those individuals who wanted to run for political office. However, each parliamentary election since then has resulted in a proportionally greater number of disqualifications. In the parliamentary elections in 1992 some 25 percent of candidates were rejected. Four years later 33 percent were disqualified in the parliamentary elections.[27]

This left the reformists and their followers with a choice. They could boycott the election and have no voice in Parliament. Or they could vote for the lesser of two evils and give legitimacy to the political system and a rigged election. The results of this election for the reformists (and for women in general) were predictable: "A vast majority of eligible voters chose to boycott the 2004 legislative elections. Their view was that nonparticipation in the elections would be the best way to delegitimize the entire process. The result for women's representation was predictable. Thirteen women were elected as members of the Seventh Majlis. However, unlike their reform-minded predecessors, twelve of these women were conservative (and one independent)."[28] Almost half the electorate boycotted the election.[29]

The elections in March 2008 for Parliament proved again that political leaders value elections, especially when given the opportunity to limit the potential threats to their political powers. These elections demonstrated the limitations on reform-minded candidates to compete and showed the growing tensions within the conservative group.

In early 2008 Iranians were again told of the importance of voting. Voting was not simply an obligation of citizenship; it was also a religious obligation. The supreme leader, speaking at a ceremony commemorating the twenty-eighth anniversary of the Islamic Revolution, argued that this religious and patriotic obligation was needed to combat Western efforts to harm Iran through propaganda. He said, "A reviewing of the previous elections helps prove that the hostile propaganda efforts of the global arrogance have revolved around provoking a low turnout in elections, all to no avail nonetheless."[30] The supreme leader's concerns revolved more around the possibility of low voter turnout than specific Western or American interference in the election. Elections only provide legitimacy when voter turnout is high. If only 50 to 60 percent of the electorate votes in an election, the candidate who wins will only be able to speak for 30 percent of the people, depending on the size of the victory. Perhaps more important, low voter turnout shows a lack of support for the regime. When reformists call for a boycott or half the population does not vote because they believe their vote is meaningless or there is no candidate to whom they can relate, this damages the election. It is difficult for Iranian leaders to make the argument that they have the full support of the people when half the population stays home instead of voting. Thus the supreme leader's repeated calls for Iranians to vote indicates his fears about the consequences of low voter turnout. His use of religious rhetoric was merely a means to a political end.

In that same speech the Iranian leader promised an election that would uphold and respect the Constitution. In doing so he assured Iranians that the rule of law would be followed: "I have instructed the authorities in charge of the elections to strictly follow the Constitution. Everyone must respect the rule of law because the Constitution specifies the boundaries of truth and falsehood. It must not be bypassed."[31] What is most significant about this statement is not its point that the rule of law will be vigorously upheld but rather the language that Khamenei is using. His articulation of the importance of the rule of law borrows the language of reformists such as Khatami more than it employs the language of Khomeini.

The eighth parliamentary elections in March 2008 shared some similarities with the previous parliamentary elections in 2004. About 4,500 candidates competed for the 290-seat assembly. More than 2,000 candidates were rejected from competing in this election.[32] The scope of the disqualifications by the Guardian Council surprised some political observers because the Council had not been so aggressive in the past. However, the disqualifications did show how controlled the electoral process has become in Iran. Many reformist candidates were rejected, which prompted former president Khatami to call the disqualifications "disastrous."[33] Former president Rafsanjani also argued for the reinstatement of the reform candidates. Thus the 44 million eligible voters had their political options limited.[34] Competition took take place between some of the more hard-line conservatives affiliated with the president and the more pragmatic conservatives associated with former nuclear negotiator Ali Larjani.

However, in a new approach to influencing the elections, the Guardian Council decided to reinstate a number of candidates from the reformist camp. By the third week in February more than 500 candidates had been reinstated for the March 14 elections, including many reformists.[35] However, this new tactic still hampered those who had been reinstated from campaigning because they had lost time. Additional hurdles that the reformists faced included a media environment that favored conservatives. In many ways the deck was stacked against the reformists.

The final result after two rounds of voting was a victory for the conservatives. The Interior Ministry claimed that voter turnout was 60 percent.[36] Almost 200 of the 290 seats were won by conservatives (both pragmatic and hard-line). Reformists won 47 seats. Independents won the remaining seats.[37] Many of the conservatives elected, such as Ali Larjani, have been critical of President Ahmadinejad. Only about 75 individuals associated with

Ahmadinejad won seats in this election.[38] Larjani was then elected speaker with 76 percent of the members of Parliament.[39]

Noteworthy about these elections is the explicit exclusion of the reformists. As noted by the analyst Abbas Abdi, "The significance of this election lies in the fact that barring political rivals from entering elections has become an established part of political life."[40] It is also worth noting that a prominent theme of the campaign season was the economy. Many candidates promised to deal with the country's economic problems, including inflation and unemployment.[41] Those reformists who were allowed to compete stressed economic grievances as a motivation for voting. As one reformist explained, "the backbreaking inflation is felt by the people and will be a reason to vote."[42]

Presidential Elections

Presidential elections in Iran have proven to be equally challenging for reformers and those within the political regime who want to retain power. In some instances reformers have felt that an election was stolen from them. However, at other times, Iran has had a relatively open and fair presidential election with surprising results, which hard-line conservatives did not foresee. In this section we look at a few important presidential elections and the struggle for power between different political factions.

In the early years of the Islamic Republic presidential elections were marred by violence. The initial presidential contest brought Bani-Sadr to power despite violence from leftists and the fact that Bani-Sadr was not a cleric: "The Mojahedin also tried to disrupt the election. Attempts were made on the lives of two candidates running for parliament and one of the four men running for the presidency. But the opposition was unable to intimidate the mullahs; the turnout was almost 70 percent, almost as high as the poll that brought Bani-Sadr to power."[43] (For the presidents since 1979, see table 3.1 in chapter 3.)

Bani-Sadr's presidency showed the divisions within the revolutionaries. He wanted to create a strong, independent presidency. Khomeini's religious supporters sought a weak president subordinate to the legislative and judicial branches where they had more influence. Bani-Sadr ultimately lost this power struggle. Bani-Sadr fell out of favor with Khomeini and fled the country.

A new round of presidential elections was held, and Prime Minister Raja'i was elected president. Raja'i would engage in an aggressive policy against the Mojahedin and other leftist groups. The new president was trying to consolidate his power and remove the threat from the left. To do so, political freedoms were curtailed and the regime arrested thousands of Iranians.[44] The leftist organizations fought back, and Raja'i would in turn be a victim of the violence that was consuming Iran in the early 1980s.

In October 1981 another round of presidential elections was held, and Khamenei was elected to the presidency. Khomeini had had a change of heart. Initially he did not want religious leaders running for the presidency, but after his disappointment with some secular politicians he turned to someone who was a loyal religious figure. Thus Khamenei became the first cleric to win the presidency.[45]

Khamenei would remain president until Khomeini died in 1989. At that point the regime needed a new supreme leader. Montazeri had lost favor due to his criticisms of the regime. So Rafsanjani orchestrated Khamenei's ascension to the office of supreme leader. Rafsanjani would in turn run for and win the office of the president in 1989 in a landslide. His reelection in 1993 was not as impressive, as only 57 percent of Iranians voted.[46] In the early years of the 1990s Rafsanjani would be the real force behind Iranian politics. He served two terms and stepped down in 1997. It is worth noting that Rafsanjani respected the term limits that exist within the political system and relinquished his office.

The presidential election of 1997 was extraordinary and surprising. Although many candidates, including a number of women, who registered to run were disqualified by the Guardian Council, the outcome was far from what the hard-line conservatives wanted.[47] The speaker of the Majles, Nateq-Nouri, ran for president. He had the support of the supreme leader and was expected to win. However Khatami, the former cultural minister, who had lived in Germany, developed a remarkable campaign. He spoke about the rule of law, women's rights, and the importance of individual liberties. His gentle tone and ease with voters resulted in a landslide victory with more than 90 percent voter turnout. This caught the hard-line conservative off guard. He would be reelected easily in 2001. His efforts to reform the Iranian political system would not be as easy as his victory at the ballot box.

In the summer of 2005, Iranians went to the polls and elected a new president, Mahmoud Ahmadinejad. Some considered the 2005 elections to be a setback for democratic reforms.[48] This election revolved around economic issues and reform. When one looks at the language and themes of the 2005 election, one notices that politicians of various ideological outlooks adopted the language of reform and the need for economic progress.

There were two rounds of voting in the presidential elections. There were a number of disqualifications before the vote took place. More than one thousand individuals registered to run in the election, yet all but six were disqualified. In the first round, a persistent theme employed by reformists and conservatives alike was reform. The discourse of reform stemmed from President Khatami's two terms in office. His previous campaigns had stressed the need to reform the Islamic Republic. Whether some hard-liners wanted to see the Iranian political system reformed is beside the point. They realized the need to use the language of reform.

This was evident when looking at the discussion of women's rights. Typically, efforts at improving the lives of women or efforts at encouraging gender equality have been promoted by reformists and various feminists in Iran. Although it is difficult to believe that many conservative politicians want to usher in the expansion of women's rights, many were forced to address this issue. Some verbalized their support for the gradual expansion of women's rights. This stemmed from the very pragmatic desire to win the women's vote and especially to increase the number of young women voters.[49] This is simply part of the democratic game.

The youth vote is becoming more important in Iranian elections. Given the fact that some 30 percent of the country's 47 million eligible voters are under thirty years of age, this gives the younger generations a significant influence on Iran's political future.[50] Many young people clamor for reforms, especially social reforms. The conservative restrictions on dress and socialization are not appreciated by many who were born after the Revolution in 1979. Thus adjusting to the changing electorate was something that some politicians embraced. One prominent politician who adapted this approach to the election was former president Akbar Hashemi Rafsanjani, who campaigned as a reformer in the runoff election. He offered the image of a moderate politician who would improve relations with the West, especially concerning the nuclear issue.[51]

When candidates feel that they must "talk the talk," we are beginning to see some changes in the system. Even if some rejected the Khatami initiatives, there has been some residual influence.

Economic issues were also a key aspect of this election cycle. Mahmoud Ahmadinejad won the presidency over Akbar Hashemi Rafsanjani in a runoff election by a considerable margin (61.6 percent to 35.9 percent). Ahmadinejad stressed economic issues throughout his campaign.[52] He argued forcefully against the corruption in Iranian society and vowed to fight it.[53] He also promised that he would improve the economy. Iranians responded to this message. Offering a populist message to improve the economic situation of the poor and the middle class was one of the key aspects of his victory. Ahmadinejad, unlike Rafsanjani, was viewed in a favorable light. He was not a wealthy man like Rafsanjani, and he was not known for corruption or rigging elections.[54] His blue-collar background and his simple lifestyle all contributed to the view that he understood the needs of the impoverished in Iran. That he had not received a salary when he was mayor of Tehran added evidence to his trustworthiness and that he was a man of the people. His offer to redistribute oil wealth to those in need and the unemployed only made him more popular.

We should keep in mind that Ahmadinejad is not a cleric. Unlike Khatami and Rafsanjani, Ahmadinejad has not taken religious orders. Although Ahmadinejad is a very religious person, he is not part of the religious establishment. Hence Iranians did not vote for Ahmadinejad due to his religious pronouncements (he did not wear his religion on his sleeve during the election campaign), but rather they voted for him because he promised to improve their economic situation and he was one of the few politicians who were not perceived to be corrupt.

There have been accusations of voter fraud, dirty tricks, and immoral behavior in this election by candidates Mehdi Karroubi, a former speaker of parliament; by Rafsanjani; and by outgoing President Khatami.[55] President Khatami was quoted as saying, "Based on authentic evidence, I will reveal documents on unethical moves taken place in (recent presidential) election." Montazeri also challenged the results, saying that "contrary to the opinions of some of the respected gentlemen, who have presented them as the best and soundest elections, [they] . . . were not good elections."[56] Even if the accusations were true in the first round of voting, the runoff election was not close, with more than 8 million votes separating the two candidates. It is difficult to believe that there were 8 million false ballots cast in an effort to alter the vote. Further complicating matters for Rafsanjani were calls by Akbar Ganji and reformers to boycott the election, and voter turnout was down from 1997 and 2001. Voter turnout has been used by the ruling clerics as evidence of support for the regime.[57]

One thing that scholars did notice during this election was increased competition not between conservatives and reformers but rather within the conservative block. The competition took place between the pragmatic conservatives (Rafsanjani) and the hard-line conservatives (Ahmadinejad). One could argue that any increase in competition is a step in the direction of greater democratization. This has the effect of promoting "competitive politics in conservative ranks."[58]

Criticism of Ahmadinejad after the Election

Winning the presidency has turned out to be easier than running the country for Ahmadinejad. Since assuming office he has been criticized by various individuals across the political spectrum, including the supreme leader. Some of the criticism has been directed at Ahmadinejad's handling of the economy. Many Iranians disapprove of his policies, which have failed to deal with corruption, inflation, and the lack of jobs.

Further criticism has arisen from reform-minded individuals about the president's policies on social issues. Because he favors more social restrictions than his predecessor, some have voiced concerns that he has rolled back the reforms of the Khatami years. However, it is clear that Iranians are more interested in economic progress than in additional social restrictions.

Ahmadinejad's record on social issues has been a mixed bag. He has cracked down on university professors and reformist newspapers such as *Shargh*. However, he also suggested allowing women into football stadiums in segregated sections to allow them to watch the matches. He suggested that "certain prejudices against women have nothing to do with Islam."[59] Thus this would appear to be offering women the ability to be in a public space where they had previously been denied access. He also did not ban New Year's celebrations for Nowruz (associated with Zoroastrianism).

During his first term in office the supreme leader expressed concerns about the president's rhetoric, about the country's economic health, and about Ahmadinejad's inability to address the country's economic woes—high inflation, rising prices for food, and rent—and the possibility of harsh international sanctions.[60] We have seen more public criticism on radio shows such as Goftegoo and in newspapers on these subjects.

As his presidency has worn on, Ahmadinejad has seen an increase in criticism. Students protested his visit to Amir Kabir University. They chanted "death to the dictator" during the president's speech.[61] Former revolutionary leader Ebrahim Yazdi also argued that Iran's government denied its citizens many basic rights and liberties.[62] In addition, various writers, scholars, and politicians have questioned Ahmadinejad's "reckless foreign policy" and harsh rhetoric denying the Holocaust, and more than one hundred and fifty members of parliament have criticized his economic policy.[63] He was also seen as weakened after elections in December of 2006 for the Assembly of Experts. His preferred candidate, Mohammad Taqi Mesbah Yardi, who is considered a hardliner, was beaten decisively. The individual who did well in these elections was former president Rafsanjani, who won almost twice as many votes as Yardi.[64] This did not bode well for Ahmadinejad's reelection campaign in 2009.

Changing the Rules of the Game: The 2009 Presidential Elections

In the tenth election for president of the Islamic Republic, 475 individuals registered to run. But when the Guardian Council announced the candidates in the third week of May 2009, only 4 had been allowed to compete: President Ahmadinejad; former prime minister Mir-Hossein Mousavi; a former speaker of the Parliament, Mehdi Karroubi; and the former head of the Islamic Revolutionary Guards Corps (IRGC) (from 1981–97), Mohsen Rezai. Former president Khatami who had considered running for president again, withdrew his name from consideration to prevent competition among reform-minded candidates.

The presidential elections in 2009 posed a tough challenge for Ahmadinejad. Going into the elections, there was much dissatisfaction with the president's handling of the economy. With rising unemployment and inflation rates, Ahmadinejad's promises to use the country's oil revenue for the poor had gone unfulfilled. When asked about the public's dissatisfaction with the government, Ahmadinejad dismissed the suggestion: "We are always constantly in touch with the people, we live together side by side. I invite you to make the trip with me to Iran, to visit Iran so you can hear what people say. There is a lot of freedom in Iran. They express themselves, they participate in elections, they hold rallies and gatherings. We are not too concerned."[65]

The president declared that he had stood up to the West on the nuclear program while his opponents would weaken the country by compromising with the West. His criticism of Mousavi as weak and willing to cave in to Western pressure sought to project the current president as strong on national security and as willing to stand up to the bellicose West, especially the United States. In stressing the threats from abroad that he has faced, Ahmadinejad invoked the language of Khomeini and the 1979 Revolution. He repeated the populist theme of his earlier campaign. He promised to pour oil revenues into the provinces, and he had the benefit of state television.

Various politicians from both the reformist camp and the conservative camp criticized President Ahmadinejad's handling of the economy. Rezai, a conservative, argued that if Ahmadinejad would continue as president "he would drag the country over a cliff," and he criticized the president for more than $1 billion of missing oil revenue.[66] This demonstrates the fragmented nature of the conservative faction. Although conservatives of different stripes oppose any reform candidate, they did not solidly back the president.

Mir Hussein Mousavi, the former prime minister during the 1980s (the position was abolished under constitutional changes in 1989), criticized the current president over his handling of foreign policy. He accused Ahmadinejad of isolating Iran by denying the Holocaust and leaving Iran with no friends in the region. The former prime minister further criticized Ahmadinejad for acting like a dictator and for his disastrous economic policies.

Mousavi's emergence as the face of the reformists was a surprising aspect of the campaign. Far from the charismatic speeches of Khatami, he is a calm, soft-spoken individual. The former prime minister had been a hard-liner along with revolutionaries such as Rafsanjani and Khamenei in the 1980s. Reformists rallied to him because he was the anti-Ahmadinejad.

Women's issues were part of this election campaign as well. Women had campaigned for the abolishment of discriminatory laws based on gender for years. As part of this campaign, women's rights groups organized numerous activities, including seminars advocating gender equality. They advocated for the reform of constitutional articles that allow gender discrimination.[67] It is also the case that the candidates realize the importance of the women's vote. When Zahra Rahnavard campaigned with her husband, Mousavi, this was the first time a candidate had incorporated his wife into his political campaign, and it was an element that helped him win many women's votes.

Mousavi also had significant support from young people in this election. Students expressed frustration at the country's economic situation and the lack of jobs that awaited them after graduation. They also complained about the lack of freedom in society. One student, Rassool Zarehee, explained his frustration: "I will do my share so that he [Mousavi] gets elected. We have been like prisoners at [the] university for the past four years. . . . We want to become free and be progressive in the world."[68] Student organizations, including the Office for Consolidating Unity, articulated a set of demands that included freedom of expression and association, as well as academic freedom and gender equality.[69]

Debates

The debates between candidates in the weeks before the presidential election also offered the Iranian public something novel. These lively and frank debates offered Iranians very different priorities for governing. Furthermore, the debates engaged in a type of direct criticism rarely witnessed in the Islamic Republic. In the first debate between President Ahmadinejad and former prime minister Mousavi, the current president accused former president Rafsanjani of corruption and of supporting Mousavi. Although Rafsanjani is widely believed to have been corrupt, it is rare in the Islamic Republic of Iran to hear this criticism offered in a public forum. The supreme leader often chastised politicians who sowed the seeds of disunity in Iran.

During the campaign before the election, the supreme leader warned the candidates about proper campaign etiquette. In a warning against foreign threats, to which he has frequently alluded, Khamenei added this admonishment: "The enemies of Iran and Iranians do not welcome taking pride in Islam and Islamic values. Thus, all officials including election candidates should be alert not to utter words which delight the enemies."[70]

In other words, the criticism of other presidential contenders should not cross certain boundaries and engage in criticism that was too harsh. And yet this is exactly what President Ahmadinejad did when, in a televised debate, he accused political elites of corruption. Exposing the Islamic Republic's dirty laundry is not exactly what the supreme leader wanted. So why did the supreme leader come out almost immediately and support Ahmadinejad's victory? First, there was the threat from the reformists. Many conservatives, including the supreme leader, understood the threat from the reformists associated with the Green Movement. Materially and ideologically, there was much at stake. Losing control of the presidency to Mousavi would have weakened some hard-line conservatives who had benefited from Ahmadinejad's policies. Furthermore, it would have given Mousavi and the reformists a platform to challenge or criticize neoconservatives associated with the IRGC and Khamenei. This threat was significant: "In this light, a Mousavi victory in the 2009 presidential election would have in many ways realized the principlists' [hard-line conservatives'] worst nightmare, because it would have paired a reformist's presidency with the pragmatic conservative Rafsanjani's control of the Assembly of Experts and the Expediency Council. Indeed, Rafsanjani's decision to side with Mousavi and the reformists in the election's aftermath may have been motivated by political expediency (after all, Rafsanjani had been the bane of the reformist movement during Khatami's presidency)."[71]

In addition, many hard-line conservatives in the IRGC would have limited political and economic opportunities under a Mousavi presidency. If reformists associated with Mousavi and the Green Movement were able to take over government ministries, this would have had a financial impact on Ahmadinejad's supporters.

The Election Results according to the Government

When the results of the election were released by the Interior Ministry, President Ahmadinejad had won reelection with 62.6 percent of the vote. Mousavi received 33.8 percent, and the other two challengers received about 1 percent each.[72] These results surprised many in Iran and abroad. Voter turnout was more than 80 percent, and in the past a large turnout tended to favor the reformists. Further, the 2 to 1 victory by Ahmadinejad went against the results of previous polling. In the third week of May a poll suggested that Ahmadinejad would get about 55 percent of the vote.[73] A later poll the week before the election even showed Mousavi in the lead. Various questions have been raised about the legitimacy of the election: How did the Interior Ministry count some 40 million votes so quickly? Two hours after the polls had closed, it announced the results. Why did some polling stations run out of ballots? Why did the votes counted exceed the number of registered voters in so many polling places? Equally puzzling was the question of why the regime would allow foreign journalists to cover the election if they were going to manipulate the results afterward. Whether or not there was widespread voter fraud is difficult to verify precisely. Equally important is the perception of electoral manipulation. Millions of Iranians believe their votes were stolen.

The Immediate Response to the Election

A few hours after the polls had closed throughout Iran, the Interior Ministry announced that President Ahmadinejad had been reelected with more than 60 percent of the vote. In response Mousavi declared that the results were a fraud. One confidential report from the American Embassy in Ashgabat suggested that Mousavi had won 26 million votes (roughly 61 percent) and that Karroubi had received some 10 million votes. Ahmadinejad had gotten approximately 4 to 5 million votes. The electoral fraud was carried out by the IRGC, which altered the votes from each precinct.[74] This led to massive protests on the streets of Tehran and in other cities across Iran.

Protests continued in the week after the election results. A rally on Monday, June 15, in Tehran was estimated at 3 million people.[75] The protesters, mostly supporters of Mousavi, engaged in largely peaceful, silent protests.[76] In response to the large demonstrations (anywhere between 70,000 and 500,000) the regime responded with a heavy hand.[77] Many individuals associated with the security forces beat protesters with batons and others were shot. On June 14, 7 students from the University of Tehran were killed by members of the Basij.[78] Another 15 protesters were killed on the following day.[79] Neda Agha Soltan was shot on June 20. The crackdown was in full force by Sunday, June 21. Force was used primarily by the Basij, which accounts for many of the deaths and injuries reported. In response to those deaths, Mousavi called for additional protests to mourn those who lost their lives. This is important in Shia Iran, where mourning rituals typically occur over a few weeks.[80] However, the police prevented Mousavi and others from attending these mourning rituals for fear that they would lead to more political protests, as they had done in 1978. By the middle of July close to 200 people had died during the protests.[81] These daily protests show the frustration of many Iranians. Not only were many in Iran, especially the young, frustrated by the lack of jobs and opportunities, but they were also angry that their votes had not been counted. These demonstrations are some of the largest since the Revolution thirty years ago. The protesters chanted "Death to the Dictator," "God Is Great," and even "Death to Khamenei."

In addition, censorship of the media increased. Foreign journalists were prohibited from recording or reporting on any demonstration that did not have authorization.[82] The organization Reporters Without Borders criticized the government for its heavy-handed approach. In the first four months after the presidential election, "at least 100 journalists and cyber-dissidents [were] arrested," and many left the country due to harassment.[83]

Many foreign journalists were forced to leave the country when their press credentials were revoked. Besides the media crackdown, various public figures were arrested, including Saeed Laylaz (a newspaper editor and political commentator), and other reformists and intellectuals such as Mohseri Aminzadeh (director of Mousavi campaign, who served in the Foreign Ministry under Khatami) and Mostafa Tajzadeh, the deputy interior minister under Khatami to name just a few.[84]

The clerical regime appeared during the first week to be groping for an appropriate response to the demonstrations. Supreme Leader Khamenei endorsed the results shortly after they were announced. However, a few days after the election, the Guardian Council announced its willingness to allow a partial recount in an effort to quell the protests.[85] Despite this effort to appease the demonstrators, the protests continued into the weekend (June 19–21). The Guardian Council refused to hold a new election.

There has also been an ongoing effort to limit Internet access, block Web pages associated with the Green Movement, and cut off access to Facebook and other social networking sites. There were also efforts to limit the activities of the main opposition figures. Mousavi said he was ready for martyrdom.[86] His movements were being restricted. In a statement on his Web page, he complained that pressure was applied in an effort to give up his election demands. He complained that his access to the people was limited.[87] He and Karroubi were eventually placed under house arrest in February 2011.

The supreme leader made his views clear in Friday Prayers on June 19. He demanded an end to the rallies and protests. He denied that this was a rigged affair by saying, "There is 11 million votes difference. How can one rig 11 million votes?"[88] Thus he denied voter fraud. He used the language of the rule of law and democracy when he said, "The Islamic State would not cheat and would not betray the vote of the people. The legal mechanism for elections would not allow any cheating." And he went further: He issued a challenge and a warning, and he told the demonstrators to stay off the streets lest there be violence. He warned the reformist leaders that if they continued to encourage protests, the bloodshed would be on their hands.[89] He refused to compromise with those on the streets who were demanding a new election. He also claimed that the reformists were working for foreign powers. This is consistent with some of the fears of the hard-line conservatives and members of the IRGC of a velvet or color revolution from within.[90]

The election also showed the divide among the revolutionaries. Former president Rafsanjani supported Mousavi, whereas the supreme leader supported Ahmadinejad. Both Rafsanjani and Khamenei were key figures in the Revolution of 1979. This was clearly demonstrated when five relatives of Rafsanjani, including his outspoken daughter, Faezeh Hashemi, were arrested on Saturday, June 20. Additional fissures in the government were evident when only 105 out of 290 members of Parliament showed up for Ahmadinejad's victory party. Ali Larjani, the speaker of the Majles, did not attend.[91]

The fact that the supreme leader had to make his speech at Friday prayers after he had already accepted the election results was already a sign of weakness. Unfortunately, all these events make the West's efforts at engagement on the nuclear issue more difficult. A divided regime desperately trying to hold on to power is not a regime that can make a political deal or engage in negotiations.

Aftermath of the Election

In the months after the contested presidential election, Iran witnessed protests, violence, trials, more demonstrations, and more violence. In June more than 30 people were killed and more than 4,000 protesters were arrested.[92] Protests continued at various times from August to December 2009. The Green Movement, which includes many reformists, used traditional holidays to mobilize their supporters. In August 2009, Mousavi and Khatami attempted to use Quds Day (Jerusalem Day in support of the Palestinians) to criticize the government and its handling of the election. While marching with their supporters, they were physically attacked. Despite being physically threatened, Mousavi issued a statement that paid homage to Khomeini and criticized the oppression of the regime: "Al-Quds day is one such assembly. With such a ritual, one cannot distance the people from the events. With such an invite, one cannot protest against injustice in far away [lands] without providing and spreading justice inside [the country]. He [Imam Khomeini] dedicated this day not only to Palestine, but also to the oppressed and to Islam, so as not to leave any place for the slightest speculation. Now, the true value of his emphasis on the need for the continued participation of the people in their millions has become apparent."[93]

In December 2009 supporters of the Green Movement/reformists took to the streets to protest on the religious holiday of Ashura. The authorities used violence to quash the demonstrations. At least 13 people were killed and another 1,500 were arrested. Some of those arrested have ties to Mousavi and the opposition. Mousavi's nephew, Seyed Ali Mousavi, was among those who were shot.[94]

Criticism of the Regime's Handling of the Election

Reformists associated with the Green Movement—including Karroubi, Mousavi, and Khatami—have called for free and fair elections, freedom of association and the ability to protest peacefully, the release of political prisoners, and a free media. A number of senior clerics have also criticized the regime's handling of the elections. Ayatollahs Sanei, Safi, Montazeri, and Taheri all voiced criticisms of the fraudulent nature of the elections. Ayatollah Taheri claimed the election results were "void and false."[95] Ayatollah Zanjani called the election results a "gross injustice."[96] Thus there were many clerics who strongly opposed the regime's response to the election.

Criticism from Conservatives

Presidential candidate and former leader of the IRGC Rezai also criticized the way the government handled the election and the aftermath of the election. He stated his belief that ballots had been tampered with.[97] Former president Rafsanjani was also critical of how the election was handled. This is not surprising because he supported Mousavi during the campaign. In a speech during Friday prayers he emphasized that the people's will should be respected and used the language of freedom and democracy.[98] He called on the government to release the protesters from jail, allow for greater freedom of the press (he criticized the Islamic Republic of Iran Broadcasting for its biased coverage), and resolve the doubt and perception of fraud concerning the election.[99] He did not challenge Khamenei directly but expressed his fears that the Iranian people had lost their trust in the government.

Detention and Trials

Many demonstrators and individuals associated with the Green Movement have been detained and jailed. One report suggested in the six months following the election more than 2,000 people (reformists, journalists, student leaders, human rights activists, etc.) were detained.[100] A year after the contested elections the numbers were even higher. Thousands of people have been jailed, and the opposition claims that at least 72 people were killed.[101] There have been numerous accounts of torture and rape while in custody. Former speaker of Parliament and presidential candidate Mehdi Karroubi publicly condemned the rape and torture of protesters.[102] The reports of prisoner abuse have been widespread. Some protesters were beaten. Others have reported witnessing prisoners being beaten to death.[103] Supreme Leader Khamenei dismissed the allegations of rape as false, and a judicial committee that was set up to investigate the allegations said that the allegations were baseless.[104] This is further evidence of the loss of the regime's legitimacy.

The trials have fallen far below any reasonable standard of justice. Many reformists have appeared in court to "confess" to their crimes again to the regime. These confessions are widely believed to be the result of coercion and physical abuse. For example, the August 2009 televised confession of a former vice president under Khatami, Muhammad Ali Abtahi, was immediately dismissed by his wife and other opposition figures as the result of intimidation.[105]

In the first few months after the presidential election, the regime put more than a hundred opposition figures on trial for threatening the regime through a "velvet revolution." The show trials, the brutality committed against those detained, and the treatment of women have cost the regime its veneer of piety and legitimacy. Even after death sentences were handed down in increasing numbers and word had gotten out of the torture and death of detainees at the Kahrizak detention center (which ultimately led to its closure by the supreme leader), individuals continued to voice their dissent.[106]

Larger Consequences of This Election

The supreme leader's direct insertion into election politics may have large consequences for the future of Iranian politics. By siding so clearly with Ahmadinejad (out of fear that the reformists would hold the presidency and this would be a material and ideological threat to the hard-line conservatives including the supreme leader), he put himself in the political fray as opposed to the role of the supreme leader as a guardian of Iran who is above politics. Furthermore, by telling the protesters to end their demonstrations, he also put himself in the direct line of fire. That many street demonstrations continued represented a direct rejection of the supreme leader.

An additional consequence of this election is the impact on the factional divisions within the polity. For more than a decade Iranians watched as conservatives (both pragmatic and hard-line) vied for power with the reformists. However, the regime's handling of the election and its aftermath demonstrated that conservatives—especially those associated with the supreme leader and the IRGC—would no longer tolerate the reformists. It was not that the reformists would not be tolerated on the ballots; they would no longer have a political presence. The threat from the reformists in the Green Movement was significant enough that hard-line elements in the regime would seek to dismantle the reformists altogether. Some scholars have suggested that the election was a watermark for the regime:

> The 2009 election was transformative for Iran. The unspoken contract between the government and the people—in which Iranians were permitted some political participation and limited personal space in return for acquiescence to the status quo—was shattered. The Islamist Left political grouping was effectively pushed out of the political system. The Revolutionary Guards emerged as the dominant political and economic institution in the country. Deep fractures among long-standing members of Iran's leadership and clergy, traditionally addressed in the Islamic Republic behind closed doors, were uncharacteristically aired

in public, as key figures openly expressed their dismay at the government's handling of the election and subsequent protests. The country had taken an irrevocable turn.[107]

Trends for Future Elections

Scholars have observed a number of themes during the last four or five elections (both presidential and parliamentary). The first is the exclusion of the reformists. The vetting by the Guardian Council has severely limited the reformists' ability to compete in the electoral process and hence in political institutions. Reformists are not only hampered in their ability to get on the ballot; they are also hampered by a media environment that favors the conservatives. Various newspapers such as *Kayhan* and *Ansar News* forcefully attack politicians associated with the reform movement.[108] Reformists' treatment by the Islamic Republic of Iran Broadcasting was not much better. Much of the coverage of reformists has been negative. And given the number of reformist newspapers that have been closed, they are at a disadvantage and must rely on the internet to get their message across to voters.

Another trend of recent elections has been the growing competition and antagonism between conservatives. This was evident in the 2005 presidential campaign between Rafsanjani and Ahmadinejad. It was also apparent in the parliamentary elections in 2012.

On March 2, 2012, Iranians went to the polls to select the members of the Majles. This was the first nationwide election since the controversial presidential election in 2009. Ayatollah Khamenei traveled around the country urging Iranians to vote. He argued that Iranians needed to send a strong message of unity to the world and especially to the West. The increasing threats from the West (sanctions) and the possibility of an Israeli attack on Iran's nuclear facilities were part of Khamenei's argument that Iranians need to stand united against the belligerence of the West: "With the grace of God, the Iranian nation will give the global arrogance (forces of imperialism) a slap in the face in Friday's election, which will be harder than the one (they received) on Bahman 22, and will flaunt their resolve and strong determination in the face of the enemy so that the hegemonistic bloc will realize that they will not be able to make progress in their confrontation with the (Iranian) nation."[109]

A large turnout would suggest support for the regime. As Khamenei noted on the eve of the election: "In every corner of the world, vibrant elections are a symbol of the vitality of a nation and their indomitable will. Therefore, in every country, a high turnout for elections shows the people's vigilance and their support for the system."[110]

The election was a competition and power struggle between those conservatives associated with the supreme leader and those who were allies of President Ahmadinejad. Reformists associated with the Green Movement did not play a significant role in this election for a variety of reasons. Many have been largely silenced since the 2009 presidential election. Their supporters are either in jail or under house arrest (Mousavi and Karroubi). Newspapers and websites associated with the Green Movement have been shut down, and many reporters are behind bars.[111] Many opposition figures, including Karroubi and Ebadi, urged their followers to boycott the elections because they are meaningless. However, former president Khatami was reported to have voted in Vadan.[112]

More than 5,000 candidates registered to run; however, the Guardian Council only permitted roughly 3,400 to compete in this election. Some of the individuals who were rejected were reformists; however, some were individuals associated with Ahmadinejad. The Guardian Council reported that the turnout for the 2012 election was 9 percent higher than that in the last parliamentary election in 2008.[113] However, foreign journalists in Iran noted that there were few voters at polling stations.[114] Some have suggested that regardless of the turnout, the regime will claim that a high percentage of the population voted. The election strengthened the hand of the supreme leader because most of his supporters won seats in Parliament. Khamenei wants a malleable and docile parliament. This not only allows him to run the country according to his dictates but also enables him to hide behind others.

An additional trend that scholars have seen in recent elections is the growing role of the IRGC in the electoral process. The IRGC, along with the Basij, has been dispersed throughout the country to provide security. Many reformists fear that their presence at polling stations has less to do with security and more with electoral manipulation (of people and voter tallies). The presence of the IRGC and Basij has no constitutional foundation.[115]

Scholars have also seen a decline in the number of clerics elected to political office, and this is especially true of the Parliament. In 1980 and 1984 clerics were close to 50 percent of the members of the Majles. By 2004 and 2008 they made up only 15 percent of the members of Parliament.[116] Given the recent elections and the problems associated with them, will Iranians bother to vote in the future?

Conclusion

Some have criticized Iran's political system for the limits placed on who can run for office. Critics focus on the large numbers of people who have been prevented from running for office by the Guardian Council. Although these are valid criticisms that prevent Iran from becoming a consolidated democracy, they only tell half the story. Since the Revolution Iran has held numerous elections for both the presidency and Parliament. And while the competition has been limited due to disqualifications, there has been some competition for political office. This was most evident in the victories of Khatami in 1997 and 2001. Furthermore, it is worth noting that Khatami, like Rafsanjani before him, turned over power in a peaceful succession. Equally important is the fact that no elected president has refused to leave office at the end of his term. Thus the democratic disposition of turning over power at the end of a term of office has been institutionalized in the Iranian political system. Iran is in sharp contrast to its Arab neighbors in the Middle East, which rarely relinquish power via elections (consider Assad's Syria or Mubarak's Egypt before 2011).

Elections, even controlled affairs such as these, can give the veneer of a democratic political system. Thus the supreme leader can claim to have the support of the people, and the theocracy can give the pretense of living up to the international norm of democracy in an Islamic form. However, despite the regime's efforts, the elections in 2009 and 2012 further eroded the legitimacy of the regime.

Some electoral progress in the past cannot undo the electoral manipulations associated with the 2009 presidential election. The regime demonstrated that it was willing to jettison the democratic parts of the political system. When coupled with the human rights violations that are discussed in the next chapter, this situation shows that Iran still has a long way to go before it becomes a fully democratic system.

Notes

1. "Supreme Leader Meets Executive Officials," August 23, 2012, www.leader.ir/langs/EN/print.php?id=3777.

2. Ayatollah Khamenei, "High Turnout in Parliamentary Elections Showed That People Trust Islamic Republic," March 8, 2012, www.english.khamenei.ir//index.php?option=com_content&task=view. . . .

3. Thus one can argue that we already see norms of democracy in effect. Ladan Boroumand, "The Role of Ideology," *Journal of Democracy* 16, no. 4 (October 2005): 52–63.

4. Kaveh-Cyrus Sanandaji, "The Eighth Majles Elections in the Islamic Republic of Iran: A Division in Conservative Ranks and the Politics of Moderation," *Iranian Studies* 42, no. 4 (September 2009): 621–48, at 623.

5. There are also local elections in cities and provinces throughout Iran. Space limitations do not allow for a full treatment here.

6. "The Guardian Council has the responsibility of supervising elections of the Assembly of Experts for leadership, the President of the Republic, the Islamic Consultative Assembly, and the direct recourse to popular opinion and referenda." The Iranian Constitution can be found at www.servat.unibe.ch/icl/ir00000_.html.

7. Shahrough Akhavi, "The Thought and Role of Ayatollah Hossein' ali Montazeri in the Politics of Post-1979 Iran," *Iranian Studies* 41, no. 5 (December 2008): 645–66, at 655.

8. "Iran Vetoes Candidates," *New York Times*, February 7, 2008, www.nytimes.com/2008/02/07/world/middleeast/07tehran.html?ref=world&pagewant. . . . He was later reinstated but refused given the lack of democratic protections.

9. Ali Ansari, *Modern Iran Since 1921: The Pahlavis and After* (London: Pearson Education, 2003), 118.

10. Ibid., 145; Ervand Abrahamian, *A History of Modern Iran* (Cambridge: Cambridge University Press, 2008), 117.

11. Martin Hers, "Counselor of Embassy, Confidential Memorandum of Conversation, November 26, 1966," RG 59 General Records of the Bureau of Near Eastern and South Asian Affairs, US Department of State, box 18.

12. Vanessa Martin, *Creating an Islamic State: Khomeini and the Making of a New Iran* (New York: I. B. Tauris, 2000), 107.

13. Nazila Fathi, "Election Seen as Setback for Iran's President," *New York Times*, December 18, 2006, www.nytimes.com/2006/12/18/world/middleast/19irancnd.html?ei=5094&en=e96. . . .

14. Cyrus Vakili-Zad, "Continuity and Change: The Structure of Power in Iran," in *Modern Capitalism and Islamic Ideology in Iran*, edited by Cyrus Bina and Hamid Zangeneh (New York: St. Martin's Press, 1992), 13–48, at 37.

15. Ibid., 37.

16. Robin Wright, *In the Name of God* (New York: Simon & Schuster, 1989), 125.

17. Ibid., 180.

18. Ibid.

19. Ibid., 181.

20. Kasra Naji, *Ahmadinejad: The Secret History of Iran's Radical Leader* (Berkeley: University of California Press, 2008), 44.

21. Rebecca Barlow and Shahram Akbarzadeh, "Prospects for Feminism in the Islamic Republic of Iran," *Human Rights Quarterly* 30 (2008): 21–40, at 27.

22. Yonah Alexander and Milton Hoenig, *The New Iranian Leadership* (Westport, CT: Praeger Security International, 2008), 16.

23. Bernd Kaussler, "European Union Constructive Engagement with Iran (2000–2004): An Exercise in Conditional Human Rights Diplomacy," *Iranian Studies* 41, no. 3 (June 2008): 269–95, at 289.

24. Nazila Fathi, "Iran's Leader Said to Refuse Delay in Vote," *New York Times*, February 4, 2004.

25. "43 percent of the registered candidates (3,500 of 8,172) were disqualified." Akbar Ganji, "The Latter-Day Sultan," *Foreign Affairs* 87 (November–December 2008): 45–66, at 47. See also Barlow and Akbarzadeh, "Prospects for Feminism," 34.

26. Ali Ansari, *Confronting Iran* (New York: Basic Books, 2006), 210.

27. Said Amir Arjomand, "Constitutional Implications of Current Political Debates in Iran," in *Contemporary Iran: Economy, Society, Politics*, edited by Ali Gheissari (Oxford: Oxford University Press, 2009), 247–76, at 250.

28. Barlow and Akbarzadeh, "Prospects for Feminism," 35.

29. Naji, *Ahmadinejad*, 53.

30. Ayatollah Khamenei, "Iran Found New Identity after the Revolution," February 8, 2008, www.leader.ir/langs/EN/index.php?pnews&id=3852.

31. Ibid.

32. According to the BBC, almost 40 percent of the candidates were disqualified. "Iranians Vote in General Election," BBC, March 14, 2008, http://news.bbc.co.uk/go/pr/fr/-/2/hi/middle_east/7295732.stm. Sanandaji also notes that more than 40 percent were disqualified in 2004 and 2008. Sanandaji, "Eighth Majles Elections," 629.

33. Nazila Fathi, "Iran Celebrates Revolution and Muzzles Reformers," *New York Times*, February 12, 2008, www.nytimes.com/2008/02/12/world/middleeast/12tehran .html?ei=5070&en=325a2.

34. "Iranians Vote for a New Parliament," *Tehran Times*, March 15, 2008, www.tehran times.com/NCms/2007.asp?code=165090.

35. Fardad Pouladi, "Iran Reinstates More Reformist Candidates for Election," Agence France-Presse, February 16, 2008, news.yahoo.com/s/afp/20080216/w/_mideast/afp/iran polticsvote_080216141906&. . . .

36. Nazila Fathi, "Reformers Gain in Iran Vote Despite Being Barred," *New York Times*, March 16, 2008, www.nytimes.com/2008/03/16/world/middleeast/16iran.html?ei=5070 &en=a255aaa. . . .

37. Nazila Fathi, "Conservatives Prevail in Iran Vote, but Opposition Scores, Too," *New York Times*, April 27, 2008.

38. Sanandaji, "Eighth Majles Elections," 622.

39. Ibid., 638.

40. Nazila Fathi, "Iran's Religious Conservatives Are Expected to Solidify Power at Polls," *New York Times*, March 6, 2008, www.nytimes.com/2008/03/06/world/middle east/06iran.htmlref=world&pagewanted. . . .

41. "Iranians Vote for a New Parliament," *Tehran Times*, March 15, 2008, www.tehran times.com/NCms/2007.asp?code=165090.

42. Sanandaji, "Eighth Majles Elections," 626.

43. Wright, *In the Name of God*, 99.

44. Ibid.

45. Ibid., 101.

46. Robin Wright, *The Last Great Revolution: Turmoil and Transformation in Iran* (New York: Alfred A. Knopf, 2000), 23.

47. Ibid., 25.

48. Elections in Iran have been criticized by various Bush administration officials as well as nongovernmental organizations. The Guardian Council excluded women, religious minorities, and other candidates who have been critical of the regime. These criticisms have also been voiced about the recent presidential elections in June. Human Rights Watch, www.hrw.org/English/docs/2005/06/12/iran/1114/htm.

49. Barbara Ann Rieffer-Flanagan, "Improving Democracy in Religious Nation-States: Norms of Moderation and Cooperation in Ireland and Iran," *Muslim Journal of Human Rights* 4, no. 2 (2007).

50. The Iranian government stated that there were 46.7 million eligible voters, with more than 30 percent under thirty years of age. Michael Slackman, "No Candidate Wins Majority in Iranian Presidential Election, Forcing a Second Round," *New York Times*, June 18, 2005, www.nytimes.com/2005/06/18/international/middleeast/18iran.html.

51. He did not, however, offer to give up the country's nuclear ambitions. He offered a means of verifying that the country was enriching uranium for peaceful purposes, but he also asserted the right of Iran to develop nuclear technology. In general, Iranians believe that it is their national right to develop nuclear technology. Ali Mohammadi, "The Sixth Majles Election and the Prospects for Democracy in Iran," in *Iran Encountering Globalization: Problems and Prospects*, edited by Ali Mohammadi (New York: RoutledgeCurzon, 2003), 38.

52. Acting as his campaign manager was Mujtaba Khamenei, the Supreme Leader's oldest son. Amir Taheri, "Winners and Losers Turn the Fate of Iran," *Gulf News*, June 29, 2005, www.gulfnews.com/opinion.NF.asp?articleID=170841. Ahmadinejad's webpage is www.mardomyar.ir.

53. Scott Peterson, "Iran's New Hard-Liner Maps Path," *Christian Science Monitor*, June 27, 2005, www.csmonitor.com/2005/0627/p01s04-wome.htm.

54. Kenneth Pollack, *The Persian Puzzle: The Conflict between Iran and America* (New York: Random House, 2004), 249.

55. Naji, *Ahmadinejad*, 73–89.

56. Akhavi, "Thought and Role of Ayatollah Hossein' ali Montazeri," 655.

57. "President Khatami: I Would Reveal Documents on Unethical Moves in Election," Payvand Iran News, www.payvand.com/news/05/jun/1226.html. See also Michael Slackman, "Iran Moderate Says Hard Liners Rigged Election," *New York Times*, June 19, 2005; www.newsvote.bbc.co.uk/mpapps/print/news.bbc.co.uk/1/hi/world/middle_east/. . . .

58. Vali Nasr, "The Conservative Wave Rolls On," *Journal of Democracy* 16, no. 4 (October 2005): 9–22. It also demonstrates the divisions within conservative ranks.

59. Nazila Fathi, "Iran Lifts Ban Barring Women from Attending Sporting Events," *New York Times*, May 1, 2006, www.nytimes.com/2006/05/01/world/middleeast/01iran.html. His proposal was ultimately rejected by a number of ayatollahs and the Supreme Leader Ayatollah Khamenei as being un-Islamic. The clerics were opposed to women looking at men's legs during the match.

60. Nazila Fathi, "A President's Defender Keeps His Distance," *New York Times*, January 8, 2008, www.nytimes.com/2008/01/08/world/middleeast/08iran.html.

61. Nazila Fathi, "Student Cry 'Death to the Dictator' as Iranian Leader Speaks," *New York Times*, December 12, 2006.

62. Michael Slackman, "An Iranian Revolutionary, Dismayed but Unbowed," *New York Times*, February 16, 2008, www.nytimes.com/2008/02/16/world/asia/16yazdi.html?ei=5070&en=61e4bde678. . . .

63. Nazila Fathi, "Iranian Scholars Denounce Conference That Denied Holocaust," *New York Times*, February 27, 2007. Laura Secor, "Whose Iran?" *New York Times*, January 28, 2007, www.nytimes.com/2007/01/28/magazine/28iran.t.html?ref=magazine&pagewanted. . . .

64. Nazila Fathi, "Election Seen as a Setback for Iran's President," *New York Times,* December 18, 2006.

65. "An Interview with President Mahmoud Ahmadinejad," *New York Times,* September 26, 2008, www.nytimes.com/2008/09/26/world/middleeast/26iran-transcript.html?ref =world&. . . .

66. Nazila Fathi, "Many Try to Run for President in Iran, but Few Will Be Allowed," *New York Times,* May 11, 2009, www.nytimes.com/2009/05/11/world/middleeast/11iran .html?ref=wor. . . .

67. Ladan Boroumand, "Civil Society's Choice," *Journal of Democracy* 20, no. 4 (October 2009): 16–20, at 18.

68. Nazila Fathi, "Iranian Candidate Taps Student Woes," *New York Times,* May 31, 2009, www.nytimes.com/2009/05/31/world/middleeast/31iran.html?_r=1&e. . . .

69. Boroumand, "Civil Society's Choice," 18.

70. "Leader Advises Presidential Candidates Not to Delight Enemies," *Tehran Times,* May 25, 2009, www.tehrantimes.com/NCms/2007.asp?code=195367.

71. Ali Reza Nader, David E. Thaler, and S. R. Bohandy, *The Next Supreme Leader: Succession in the Islamic Republic of Iran* (Santa Monica, CA: RAND Corporation, 2011), 50–51.

72. "Crowds Join Ahmadinejad Victory Rally," BBC, June 14, 2009.

73. "Mousavi Vows to Defend Women's Rights," *Tehran Times,* May 19, 2009, www .tehrantimes.com/NCms/2007.asp?code=194903. This is not a reformist paper. Said Amir Arjomand, *After Khomeini: Iran under His Successors* (Oxford: Oxford University Press, 2009), 166.

74. American Embassy Ashgabat, "Iran Post-Election," classified cable, June 15, 2009, reference ID- 09ASHGABAT757, Cablegate.wikileaks.org/cable/2009/06/09ASHGABAT757 .html. . . .

75. Nazila Fathi and Michael Slackman, "As Confrontation Deepens, Iran's Path Is Unclear," *New York Times,* June 19, 2009, www.nytimes.com/2009/06/19/world/middleast/ 19iran.htm?_r=1&e . . .

76. There were some reports of violence.

77. BBC, "Fresh Rally Takes Place in Tehran," June 17, 2009, http://news.bbc.co.uk/2/ hi/midd. . . .

78. The Basij are an arm of the IRGC.

79. Arjomand, *After Khomeini,* 170.

80. It was mourning rituals that helped the grassroots movement in 1979.

81. Arjomand, *After Khomeini,* 170.

82. BBC, "Iran to Hold Election Recount," June 16, 2009, http://news.bbc.co.uk/go/ pr/fr/-/2/hi/middle_east/8102400.stm.

83. Reporters Without Borders, "Arrest of Journalists since Disputed June Election Now Top 100," www.rsf.org/spip.php?page=impression&id_article=34918.

84. Michael Slackman and Sharon Otterman, "Clerical Council in Iran Rejects Plea to Annul the Vote," *New York Times,* June 24, 2009, www.nytimes.com/2009/06/24/world/ middleeast/24iran.htm?hp=&pa. . . .

85. BBC, "Iran to Hold Election Recount."

86. "Violence Grips Tehran Amid Crackdown," *New York Times,* June 21, 2009, www .nytimes.com/2009/06/21/world/middleeast/21iran.html?emc=et. . . .

87. Thus, formally, he was not under house arrest, but he does not have freedom of movement or speech. BBC, "Iran's Mousavi Defies Crackdown," June 15, 2009, www.news .bbc.co.uk/go/pr/fr/-/2/hi/middle_east/8118783.stm.

88. BBC, "Ayatollah Demands End to Protests," June 19, 2009, http://news.bbc .co.uk/go/pr/fr/-/2/hi/middle_east/8108661.stm.

89. Nazila Fathi and Alan Cowell, "Iran's Ruling Cleric Warns of Bloodshed If Protests Persists," *New York Times*, June 20, 2009, www.nytimes.com/2009/06/20/world/ middleast/20iran.html?hp=pa. . . .

90. Michael Slackman, "Iran Opposition Calls for End to Crackdown," *New York Times*, July 8, 2009, www.nytimes.com/2009/07/08/world/middleast/08iran.html?hp =&page. . . .

91. BBC, "Iran's Mousavi Defies Crackdown," June 25, 2009, www.news.bbc.co.uk/ go/pr/fr/-/2/hi/middle_east/8118783.stm.

92. BBC, "Clashes Erupt at Iran Mass Rally," September 18, 2009, http://news.bbc .co.uk.go/pr/fr/-/2/hi/middle_east/8262273.stm.

93. Mousavi, "Mousavi Issues 13th Statement," http://english.mowjcamp.com/article/ id/38750.

94. Nazila Fathi, "Tehran Protesters Defy Ban and Clash with Police," *New York Times*, December 27, 2009, www.nytimes.com/2009/12/27/world/middleast/27iran.html?_r=1 &emc=eta1&pa. . . . ; Robert Worth, "Iran Arrests Dissidents, Cites Report," *New York Times*, December 29, 2009, www.nytimes.com/2009/12/29/world/middleast/29iran.html ?emc=eta1&pagewant. . . . ; BBC, "Iran Arrests Opposition Figures," December 28, 2009, http://news.bbc.co.uk/go/pr/fr/-/2/hi/middle_east/8432297.stm.

95. Nader, Thaler, and Bohandy, *Next Supreme Leader*, 86.

96. There have been some clerics who have sided with the government. Ayatollah Ahmad Khatami said the protesters should be "savagely punished." Radio Free Europe/ Radio Liberty, "Many Religious Figures Critical of Iran Election Results," July 2, 2009, www.payand.com/news/09/jul/1017.html. Neil MacFarquhar, "Clerics May Be Key to Outcome of Unrest," *New York Times*, June 18, 2009, www.nytimes.com/2009.06/18/ world/middleast/18clerics.html?emc=. . . .

97. Robert Worth, "Candidate Declares Iran May Face 'Disintegration,'" *New York Times*, July 13, 2009, www.nytimes.com/2009/07/13/world/middleeast/13iran.html?ref =wor. . . .

98. Given his harsh response to student demonstrations in 1999 and his efforts to remain central to political power, his speech in July may say more about his political ambition than about his deep-seated beliefs about democracy.

99. Elaine Sciolino, "Iranian Critic Quotes Khomeini Principles," *New York Times*, July 19, 2009, www.nytimes.com/2009/07/19/world/middleeast/19assess.html?_r=1. . . .

100. "Classified Cable from Dubai to Secretary of State, Subject: Iran Domestic Politics," January 13, 2010, reference ID 10RPODUBAI15, cablegate.wikileaks.org/cable/ 2010/01/10RPODUBAI15.html.

101. Agence France-Press, "Rafsanjani Boosts Pressure on Iran Regime before Anniversary," May 29, 2010, http://news.yahoo.com/s/afp/20100529/ts_afp/iranpolitics oppositionra. . . .

102. Nazila Fathi, "Reformist Details Evidence of Abuse in Iran's Prisons," *New York Times*, September 15, 2009, www.nytimes.com/2009/09/15/world/middleeast/15iran.html.

103. Robert Worth, "Reports of Prison Abuse and Deaths Anger Iranians," *New York Times*, July 30, 2009, www.nytimes.com/2009/07/30/world/middleeast/30iran.html?ref =wor. . . .

104. Nazila Fathi, "Iran's Supreme Leader Issues New Warning," *New York Times*, September 12, 2009, www.nytimes.com/2009/09/12/world/middleeast/12iran.html?emc=et. Nazila Fathi, "Iran Opposition Leader's Aide Is Freed," *New York Times*, September 14, 2009, www.nytimes.com/2009/09/14/world/middleeast/14iran.html?_r=1&e. . . .

105. Robert Worth and Nazila Fathi, "Iran Broadcasts Confessions by 2 Opposition Figures on Trial," *New York Times*, August 3, 2009, www.nytimes.com/2009/08/03/world/middleeast/03iran.html?emc=eta. . . .

106. Robert F. Worth, "Accused Spies Offer Apologies at Iran Trial," *New York Times*, August 9, 2009, www.nytimes.com/2009/08/09/world/middleeast/09iran.html; Nazila Fathi, "Iranian Court Shuts Down 3 Pro-Reform Newspapers as Dissent Continues to Simmer," *New York Times*, October 7, 2009, www.nytimes.com/2009/10/07/world/middleeast/07iran.html; Michael Slackman, "Iranian Site Reports a Protester's Death Sentence," *New York Times*, October 9, 2009, www.nytimes.com/2009/10/09/world/middleeast/09tehran.html; Michael Slackman, "Iran's Death Penalty Is Seen as a Political Tactic," *New York Times*, November 23, 2009, www.nytimes.com/2009/11/23/world/middleeast/23iran.html.

107. Nader, Thaler, and Bohandy, *Next Supreme Leader*, 2.

108. Sanandaji, "Eighth Majles Elections," 627.

109. "Iranian Voters Will Deal a Blow to Enemies on Election Day," *Tehran Times*, February 29, 2012, www.tehrantimes.com/politics/95933-hegmons-to-receve-a-sla. . . .

110. Ibid.

111. Robert Worth, "Iran Invokes the West to Motivate Voters," *New York Times*, February 29, 2012, www.nytimes.com/2012/03/01/world/middleeast/iran-invokes-w. . . .

112. "High Turnout for Election," *Tehran Times*, March 2, 2012, www.tehrantimes.com/politics/95976-iranians-vote-in-parliamen. . . .

113. Ibid.

114. Laura Secor, "Election, Monitored," *New Yorker*, May 7, 2012, 48–59; Robert Worth, "Iran's Government Declares Huge Turnout in First National Vote since '09 Protests," *New York Times*, March 2, 2012, www.nytimes.com/2012/03/03/world/middleeast/iran-election-pa. . . .

115. Sanandaji, "Eighth Majles Elections," 627.

116. Arjomand, *After Khomeini*, 113.

CHAPTER 5

Pressuring the Islamic Republic to Promote Human Rights

> We must bear in mind that in their attempt to take societies to a uto-
> pian future, free from any suffering, radical social and political projects
> tend to inflict great suffering on living individuals.
> —Akbar Ganji, *The Road to Democracy in Iran*

For decades scholars have discussed the value and broad appeal of human rights.[1] Richard Rorty described the elevated status of human rights: "Some have argued that a human rights culture is persuasive throughout the world. This human rights culture refers to the fact that human rights have reached iconic status in modern culture such that the belief in human rights, at least in the importance of the concept, is near universal."[2]

Understanding the status of human rights in the thirty-plus years since the Islamic Revolution is a major undertaking. However, in these brief remarks it is worth recalling that despite the shah's rhetorical support for international human rights and the holding of a major conference on human rights in Tehran in 1968, the monarch's regime during his twenty-eight years on the Peacock Throne engaged in numerous human rights violations. The lack of democracy and free speech, along with SAVAK's brutal treatment of Iranians, are evidence of the fact that Iran had a poor record on human rights before the Revolution. The Islamic Revolution did little to significantly improve Iran's human rights record on many issues. The lack of personal and political freedoms is a significant concern.

The human rights violations that have occurred since the Revolution are serious and demand explanation. Why have various basic rights, as outlined in the International Bill of Human Rights, been denied during the last three decades? In addition, are there any indications that these violations will cease to occur in the future? Or alternatively put, can Iran improve its record on human rights in the future? Some scholars have suggested that states can be socialized to improve their protection of human rights.[3] The issue at the heart of this chapter is whether Iran, given its political evolution, will be able to improve its human rights record via international norms, pressure, and socialization. Therefore, this chapter explores the evolution of human rights by looking at the interplay between Islamic tenets, perceived threats, international norms, and factional politics.

This exploration of human rights begins with a brief discussion of those rights that have been violated, including the right to life and personal integrity, women's political rights, and those civil and political rights necessary for meaningful political participation.[4] The chapter offers two explanations for these human rights violations: perceived threats to the regime, and a specific interpretation of Islam.

Next, the chapter examines improvements in human rights since the Revolution—namely, the improvement of some socioeconomic rights, including education and health care. Improving education, especially for girls, and efforts to improve access to health care services are not perceived as a threat to the regime and are consistent with the Islamic themes that Khomeini used before the Revolution.

Finally, the chapter considers what steps are needed to improve human rights in Iran in the coming years. Although the nuclear issue and energy resources hinder efforts by the international community to pressure Iran on human rights, the situation is not hopeless. We have already seen some limited steps in Iran's socialization concerning human rights. Although these are small steps, they suggest that some international norms of human rights have had an effect on political leaders in Iran. To see further progress, the international community, and especially the United States, must refrain from threats (i.e., regime change). One should not expect the Islamic Republic to emerge in the near term as a liberal democracy that protects a wide range of human rights. However, one should not be completely pessimistic about the potential for progress. Since the end of the Pahlavi regime, Iran has improved its protection of human rights (basic needs, health care, and education), and it has incorporated the language of international human rights into its discourse. This suggests that Iran has internalized some international norms concerning human rights.

Identifying the Extensive Violations of Fundamental Human Rights

The human rights situation in Iran has been an ongoing concern for many individuals and organizations throughout the world. Whether the voices are Iranians complaining about the lack of human rights or international nongovernmental organizations (NGOs) or international governmental organizations such as the United Nations, admonishing the Islamic regime for violating the basic dignity and rights of its peoples, the critiques are unfortunately similar. Akbar Ganji, an Iranian journalist and former supporter of the regime, complained about a series of human rights violations:

> We strongly oppose the current laws and policies in Iran, because they do not recognize freedom of thought, freedom of expression, or freedom of religion and assembly. We oppose them because they still sanction the death penalty for an infidel; because they imprison dissidents and those who live differently; because in the last eight years, they have closed more than a hundred magazines and newspapers. We oppose them because according to their version of Islamic law, they have allowed individuals to kill others deemed *mahdour-al dam*, or deserving of death. We oppose them because they have denied the citizens of Iran the right to determine their own fate. They deny the people the right to replace the current rulers in a peaceful manner. They have blocked all democratic methods of reform, and they have deprived our women of many of their civic and political rights.[5]

Other noted human rights activists, such as the Nobel Prize winner Shirin Ebadi, have voiced similar complaints.

Many in the international community have also expressed their frustration at the lack of basic freedoms in Iran.[6] Amnesty International complained on the thirtieth anniversary of the Revolution that Iran's protection of human rights has receded in recent years: "Despite promises made by Ayatollah Khomeini that all Iranians would be free, the past thirty years has been characterized by persistent human rights violations. The vast scope and scale of those violations of the early years of the Islamic Republic did decline somewhat with time. Limited relaxation of restrictions on freedom of expression during the period of reform under former President Khatami raised hopes of a sustained improvement in the human rights situation, although the situation remained poor. However, these hopes have been firmly crushed since accession to power of President Ahmadinejad."

Freedom House, another human rights NGO that analyzes progress or backsliding on civil and political rights, has consistently rated the theocracy in Iran as "not free," with scores of 5, 6, and 7.[7] The World Bank's Worldwide Governance Indicators project also gives Iran low marks.[8] Many NGOs, such as Human Rights Watch and Reporters Without Borders, have lamented the limitations of basic rights and freedoms. Due to the concerns about human rights violations in Iran, the UN Human Rights Council created a special rapporteur in March 2011 to address these violations.[9] The UN special rapporteur on human rights in Iran, Ahmed Shaheed, expressed concerns about the "pattern of systematic violations of . . . fundamental human rights," including "practices that amount to torture, cruel, or degrading treatment of detainees, the imposition of the death penalty in the absence of proper judicial safeguards, the status of women, the persecution of religious and ethnic minorities, and the erosion of civil and political rights, in particular, the harassment and intimidation of human rights defenders and civil society actors."[10]

Various Western countries have issued numerous reports on the violations of human rights. A recent US State Department report on human rights criticized a wide range of violations:

> The government severely limited citizens' right to peacefully change their government through free and fair elections, and it continued a campaign of postelection violence and intimidation. The government committed extrajudicial killings and executed persons for criminal convictions as juveniles and through unfair trials, sometimes in group executions. Security forces under the government's control committed acts of politically motivated violence and repression, including torture, beatings, and rape. The government administered severe officially sanctioned punishments, including amputation and flogging. Vigilante groups with ties to the government, such as Basij militia, also committed acts of violence. Prison conditions remained poor. Security forces arbitrarily arrested and detained individuals, often holding them incommunicado. Authorities held political prisoners and continued to crack down on women's rights activists, ethnic minority rights activists, student activists, and religious minorities. There was little judicial independence and few fair public trials. The government severely restricted the right to privacy and civil liberties including freedoms of

speech and the press, assembly, association, and movement; it placed severe restrictions on freedom of religion.[11]

Much of this condemnation focuses on first generation rights concerning civil and political rights.[12] The next section explains how human rights violations are related to perceived threats to the regime.

The Right to Life and Personal Integrity in the Islamic Republic of Iran

If one examines the three decades that have passed since the Islamic Revolution overthrew the shah, one notices an escalation of human rights at specific periods, especially those rights that revolve around personal and physical integrity. This can be understood in relation to perceived threats to the religious establishment. For individuals who did not demonstrate their loyalty to Khomeini's vision for the Islamic Republic, there were harsh punishments and much loss of life. When looking at the early years of the 1980s, one sees numerous purges and deaths specifically of those individuals who were thought to be loyal to the shah. These purges included many high-ranking military officials, as well as members of Parliament. Robin Wright, a journalist who has written about Iran for more than two decades, estimated that "almost six hundred Iranians faced the firing squad" in the nine months between February 1979 and November 1979.[13] Many individuals who supported the monarchy went into exile to avoid these political executions. Those who did not escape were often imprisoned.

After the revolutionaries eliminated most of the shah's supporters, secular intellectuals became the next target. As noted in chapter 3, Khomeini's Revolution brought together a diverse mix of individuals who were frustrated with the monarchy. This eclectic group included Islamic clerics and secular intellectuals as well as Marxists. Although they all shared the common goal of ousting the shah from power, they did not all agree on what should replace the monarchy. Thus a power struggle between these various groups followed in the aftermath of the Revolution.

Many of the secular leaders expected and believed that the clerics would return to their religious seminaries after the Revolution. The Iranian political system would be Islamic (laws would not violate shari'a), but the government would be run by secular individuals with technical experience. Bazargan, Iran's first prime minister, and Bani-Sadr, its first president, both thought that they could increase their power and direct the political system. Both ultimately failed. Khomeini's supporters refused to share power with any secular leader who threatened their control over the political system. The resulting power struggle resulted in many deaths.

Beyond the executions at the hand of the newly created republic, there were additional human rights violations committed by *komitehs* (neighborhood committees). These groups were created, outside the constitutional process, to protect the new political system from moral vice and a potential counterrevolution. These *komitehs* punished individuals engaged in un-Islamic behavior such as consuming alcohol. Unfortunately, this alternative police force was not under the control of the political institutions created by the Constitution. Prime Minister Bazargan complained, "The committees are everywhere and no one knows how many exist, not even the imam himself."[14]

The Constitution, with its emphasis on Islamic values and also on the brutal treatment of the *komitehs* for un-Islamic activities, infuriated some of the leftists who had supported the Revolution. Many of the clerical types were skeptical of the leftists and their Marxist doctrines. In response to the repression, some in the leftist camp used violence in retaliation. Thus factional fighting took a very bloody turn. The Mojahedin (MEK) engaged in assassinations to weaken the clerical regime. For example, numerous bombs killed clerics and other individuals associated with the political system. Supreme Court Chief Justice Mohammad Beheshti was killed along with seventy other political figures in June 1981. In that same month a bomb went off in Tehran during Friday prayers. Its victim, Ali Khamenei, was seriously injured.[15] Two months later President Raja'i and Prime Minister Bahonar were assassinated.

The government's response was quick and brutal. The reign of terror, which included numerous executions, took hundreds of lives. In September 1981 close to 150 individuals were executed in a single day. The following week saw more bloodshed, with 110 people killed on one day.[16] The theocracy sought revenge for the attacks on its supporters, but it also wanted to quell the secular threat that could bring down the regime. The killings ended in late 1982 when Khomeini criticized the government for "deviating from Islamic behavior and exceeding their mandates" and instructed the government to end the bloodshed.[17]

Torture

Beyond the violation of the fundamental right to life that the reign of terror ushered in, there were numerous reports of torture committed by the regime.

Political opponents of the regime, students, as well as religious minorities have recounted the harsh treatment, beatings, and humiliations that they were forced to endure while in jail.[18] Some individuals did not survive their interrogations. Zahra Kazemi, a Canadian-Iranian journalist, died in Evin Prison in 2003.[19] One student demonstrator recalled the threats and beatings that he received while in custody. Ahmad Batebi explained how in addition to sleep deprivation, he was hung from the ceiling with his arms tied behind his back.[20] Marina Nemat, another citizen who criticized the government, also describes the beatings and harassment she received while incarcerated. Individual testimonials such as these are often included in reports by Western governments and human rights NGOs. The US State Department's annual report echoed the torture of individuals in prison: "Common methods of torture and abuse in prisons included prolonged solitary confinement with extreme sensory deprivation (sometimes called "white torture"), beatings, rape and sexual humiliation, long confinement in contorted positions, kicking detainees with military boots, hanging detainees by the arms and legs, threats of execution, burning with cigarettes, pulling out toenails, sleep deprivation, and severe and repeated beatings with cables or other instruments on the back and on the soles of the feet."[21]

Beyond the reports from members of the international community, individuals within the government have also expressed concerns about torture in Iranian prisons. Reformists tried to protect individuals being interrogated from being subjected to physical abuse. Although a bill was passed in 2002 by the reformist-controlled parliament to prohibit torture, the Guardian Council rejected the bill claiming that it "was un-Islamic and unconstitutional" and that torture may be necessary "in some exceptional circumstances."[22] This decision by the Guardian Council contradicts Article 38 of the Constitution, which states, "All forms of torture for the purpose of extracting confession or acquiring information are forbidden." Despite the action taken by the Guardian Council, other individuals within the government have acknowledged the problem of torture. In 2009 the head of the judiciary, Ayatollah Shahroudi, criticized the abuse of four men, saying: "The interrogators and prosecutors committed a serious negligent and careless acts in this case that lead to the abuse of the detainees' words and writings in producing confession letters."[23] By acknowledging these human rights violations, and in his refusal to justify these actions as necessary for national security, Shahroudi was invoking some of the international norms surrounding the human right to be free from torture.

Political Rights

Protecting basic political rights such as freedom of speech and association is key not only to a democratic polity but also for the basic dignity of individuals. These fundamental political rights must be protected for all groups, including minorities. Without basic rights for all citizens regardless of religion, gender, or ethnicity, one will often see repression and discrimination. Unfortunately, that has often been the case in Iran.

Freedom of Expression

Many of the basic political rights outlined in the International Bill of Human Rights are not protected in the Islamic Republic. One right essential to human dignity is freedom of expression, whether in written or spoken form. Individuals in Iran are not guaranteed the right to freely speak their mind, despite claims to the contrary by political leaders.[24] Although Article 26 of the Constitution guarantees freedom of speech, it is limited within an Islamic context. What this limitation means in reality is that individuals who disagree with or criticize the government have been harassed, censored, and arrested. The denial of freedom of expression has occurred since the Revolution, and is consistent with the teachings of Khomeini.

Khomeini consistently expressed concerns about the negative influence of Western ideas, which were un-Islamic and detrimental to society. In *Islamic Government*, he outlined these fears: "Although all things contrary to the Shari'a must be forbidden, emphasis has been placed on sinful talk and consumption of what is forbidden, implying that these two evils are more dangerous than all others and must therefore be more diligently combated. Sometimes the statements and propaganda put forth by oppressive regimes are more harmful to Islam and the Muslims than their actions and policy."[25]

To protect against these fears, limitations were placed on freedom of expression in the Constitution. Furthermore, Khomeini and his supporters understood that internal dissent and criticism could undermine the theocratic system that they had created. Thus the religious revolutionaries tolerated very little dissent or criticism, which led to purges and repression.[26]

After the early years of the Islamic Republic, and well into the 1990s, restrictions on freedom of expression continued. Numerous individuals who criticized the government, challenged its interpretation of Islam, or called for changes in the political system have been harassed, detained, and tortured. One such influential individual is Abdolkarim Soroush, who is a threat to the regime because he developed an alternative interpretation to the Islam of Khomeini. Soroush argued in numerous venues that because humans are imperfect, we can revise and improve on our interpretation of religious works. Although the Qur'an does not change, our understanding of religious texts may change as we become more enlightened. Hence, we can reinterpret a religious text: "Nothing is sacred in human society. All of us are fallible human beings. Though religion itself is sacred, its interpretation is not sacred and therefore it can be criticized, modified, refined and redefined."[27]

Reinterpreting religious texts such as the Qur'an is a threat to the regime because it challenges Khomeini's religious interpretation, which is the basis of the system. Furthermore, that Soroush, a lay person who is willing to interpret religious texts is a challenge to the religious clerics that are in positions of power. Khomeini's justification for clerical rule was due to the cleric's intimate knowledge of religious texts. If their religious interpretations are challenged, then the entire political system is also open to challenge.

Soroush has further challenged the regime with his discussion of Islamic democracy: "I give two bases for Islamic democracy. The first pillar is this: In order to be a true believer, one must be free. To become a believer under pressure or coercion won't be true belief. . . . Thus freedom is the basis of democracy."[28]

This version of democracy offers fewer restrictions on individual freedom than one finds in the Islamic Republic. For his challenge to the foundation of the political system, Soroush has been fired from various university positions, physically threatened, and prohibited from teaching and at times from traveling outside the country.[29]

Pressure has been brought on other outspoken critics of the regime. Very few can openly criticize the president without fear of criminal prosecution or harassment.[30] Shirin Ebadi, a winner of the Nobel Peace Prize, has also been harassed. In December 2008 she was faced with intimidation from the police, who shut down her office, Defenders of Human Rights Center (DHRC). Human Rights Watch's executive director criticized the raid as an attempt by the government to intimidate human rights defenders throughout the country: "The closure of DHRC is not just an attack on Shirin Ebadi and her Iranian colleagues, but on the entire international human rights community of which she is an influential and important member."[31]

Akbar Ganji has faced similar harassment. Ganji, who was an early supporter of the Revolution and served in the Islamic Revolutionary Guard, has been jailed for his investigative journalism. His exposure of corruption (including among family members of Rafsanjani) and a series of high-profile murders, along with his passionate defense of human rights, landed him in solitary confinement in Evin Prison.[32]

The Islamic Republic tried to silence Ganji because he, like Soroush, challenges the government's views on Islam. Human rights are also mutable according to Ganji, and this poses a direct challenge to some of the religious doctrine argued by clerical leaders. Some clerics in Iran confine religion to Islamic laws, which they view as unchanging and infallible. In contrast, Ganji argues: "The concept of human rights remains open to change: New rights might develop, or old rights might lose their relevance. This mutability has two sources: as humans gain more knowledge about their condition, their self-perception evolves and expands. New understandings of causes of suffering may emerge and require new rights. In addition, as life becomes more developed and more complex, new problems arise."[33]

Other high-profile denials of freedom of expression include the famous fatwa against Salman Rushdie. It was on February 14, 1989, that Supreme Leader Khomeini issued a fatwa because *The Satanic Verses* was deemed an affront to Islam due to its description of the prophet. The fatwa demanded a response for this insult to Islam:

> In the name of God Almighty; there is only one God, to whom we shall all return; I would like to inform all the intrepid Muslims in the world that the author of the book entitled *The Satanic Verses* which has been compiled, printed and published in opposition to Islam, the Prophet and the Qur'an, as well as those publishers who were aware of its contents, have been sentenced to death. I call on all zealous Muslims to execute them quickly, wherever they find them, so that no one will dare to insult the Islamic sanctions. Whoever is killed on this path will be regarded as a martyr, God willing.[34]

Many in the West criticized Khomeini's call for Rushdie's execution and the denial of freedom of expression that accompanied the threat.

Beyond high-profile cases of individuals with an international reputation, various persons have been subjected to persecution and detention for their ideas. Evin Prison has had numerous university students as residents for complaining about government policies. Students protested against the closure of newspapers (the closure of *Salam*—a pro-Khatami, reformist paper—led to student protests in the summer of 1999) and the lack of academic freedom. Student protesters were beaten and killed in the summer of 1999 by

Ansar-e-Hezbollah.[35] Student protests at Shiraz University also resulted in a harsh crackdown with many arrests. In 2009, students at the Amir Kabir University in Tehran who protested the lack of academic freedom and the burial of war veterans from the Iran–Iraq War on campus grounds were arrested.[36] Dozens of students were also arrested in December 2010 for their political activities and criticism of the government.[37]

The reason why political opponents have been silenced stems from the fear of both domestic and foreign threats. Threats from abroad have increased the insecurity of the political elite: "At the same time, the Bush administration's efforts to promote democracy and threats of military action against Iran—made more vivid by the presence of tens of thousands of American troops in neighboring countries—have given Tehran's hard-liners a pretext to silence dissent and reverse political and social freedoms secured during the Khatami era."[38]

Khatami and the reformists, unlike some of the hard-line conservatives, spoke favorably about encouraging human rights in Iran. He wanted to promote a greater democratization of the Iranian political system. He also encouraged more cultural freedoms and freedom of the press.[39] Khatami created a supervisory committee in Parliament to follow up on allegations of human rights violations.[40] However, many of the reformists' efforts were blocked by the conservatives on the Guardian Council, judiciary, and other aspects of the government. This was due to the fact that reformers were perceived to be a threat to the power of some of the hard-line conservatives. Thus the regime's response to the elections in 2009, echoing the Khatami years, demonstrated once again when the regime faced a threat to its political security, it responded in a harsh manner.

The aftermath of the June election has proven to be one of the greatest challenges the clerical regime has faced. Various seats of power (Revolutionary Guards, president, parliament, supreme leader) have struggled to find the right response to the protests. At times there have been conciliatory gestures— Khamenei denied that reformists such as Mousavi and Karrubi had worked with foreign powers[41]—however, mostly the government has responded with brutality and oppression. Protests, gatherings, and other displays of criticism of the regime were suppressed. Mousavi and Karroubi, along with their wives, were placed under house arrest in February 2011 and held for more than a year.[42] In the months following the disputed election, protesters were beaten with batons, doused with tear gas, and prohibited from mourning those killed in the aftermath of the election. Hundreds, including many university students, have been detained, raped in prison, and put on trial. More than 6,000 individuals were arrested in the seven months following the election.[43] These show trials have often involved coerced confessions and apologies and have resulted in long prison sentences. Besides the arrests there have been numerous reports of death sentences handed down by the judiciary for a variety of offenses. One report suggested that in the first five months of 2011, at least 135 individuals were killed by the government, often without access to a lawyer or due process.[44] Another report noted that more than 600 individuals were executed by the government.[45] Reformist newspapers and websites have been shut down. These efforts are all part of a campaign to intimidate the opposition.[46]

Women's Rights

The issue of women's rights in Iran is a polarizing one for politicians on various sides of the political divide. Ganji compared the situation with South Africa, and referred to the circumstances of Iranian women as "gender apartheid."[47] Others have suggested that Iran be used as an example to other countries in the Middle East. The situation for women in Iran incorporates elements of both political freedom and gender inequality. How much freedom women have in Iran fluctuates with the political winds and factional politics. When reformist-led governments have been in charge, there have been attempts to improve women's rights, albeit with limited success. In the June 2009 presidential election women were active in the campaign, including Mousavi's wife, Zahra Rahnavard, who campaigned with her husband and energized the women's vote. In response, some of the candidates promised to address women's rights. When hard-line conservatives have occupied positions of power, greater limits were placed on women. These mixed messages are tied to factional politics and the inconsistency in Khomeini's thinking. Khomeini's views on gender evolved. However, some of his earlier writings are still used to limit women to a traditional domestic role.

If one examines some of Khomeini's early writings in the 1960s, one sees his concerns about gender equality and the dangers of offering women excessive freedom. He criticized the White Revolution for the policies that would allow women to be corrupted: "The court of the oppressor (illegitimate ruler) wants to give equal rights to women and men, and trample on the precepts of the Qur'an and the shari'a, and to take eighteen-year-old girls into compulsory military service."[48]

The opportunities that the shah offered to women, the same opportunities that women in the West had, were a confusion of proper gender roles. Khomeini initially did not believe that women ought to have political or social equality.

By the late 1970s his views began to evolve toward greater equality for women. He encouraged women to participate in the Revolution. By 1978 Khomeini offered a different vision for women: "In the Islamic system a woman is a human being who can be equally active as a man in the building of a new society."[49] In March 1979 he praised the political involvement of women during the Revolution: "One of the blessings of this movement is that women have become involved in the matters of the day and in political matters. . . . Now all the people, whether women or men, are involved in the destiny of their country."[50]

Thus Khomeini's thinking on women evolved from a limited domestic role to greater political equality. Khomeini did not offer full political equality for women, as demonstrated by the fact that there are some positions in the government that are not open to women (e.g., supreme leader). What Khomeini did offer was a greater political space that many other women in the Middle East enjoy (save Israel, Kuwait, and Turkey).

Although women are able to vote and can run for Parliament, they are still second-class citizens in the political system. Although the Constitution guarantees the equal rights of women in Articles 3 and 20, there are also limiting clauses. Article 20 places this within the criteria of Islam: "All citizens of the country, both men and women, equally enjoy the protection of the law and enjoy all human, political, economic, social, and cultural rights, in conformity with Islamic criteria."

These Islamic criteria have prevented women from full equality. Many political elites, especially hard-line conservatives, have argued that women should play the traditional role of nurturing mother and dutiful wife.[51] Although women were allowed to vote after the Revolution, they were not always welcomed in the legal profession. Women who were judges before the Revolution were replaced by men, and some women were dissuaded from practicing law.[52] Further inequality between the genders is evidenced by the fact that a woman's testimony in a court of law is "valued at half that of a man's."[53]

Aside from discrimination in the court system, there is also discrimination seen in social settings. Women are also segregated in many public places including in classrooms, and they have been prohibited from attending sporting events.[54] Additional restrictions on women include their choice of attire. All women are required to wear a veil in public regardless of their faith. A woman must have her head covered because it is a means to protect her chastity and purity. As Ayatollah Khamenei noted, "Any hijab removal would lead to the removal of chastity from society and the destruction of the family."[55] (It is worth noting that the veil was not required immediately after the Revolution.

Khomeini encouraged women to wear a veil, but he did not impose it initially.[56])
Women who do not wear their veil properly (their veil does not cover their hair)
can be brought into police custody and fined by the authorities. There have been
various crackdowns on women who do not completely cover their hair.[57]

According to Rebecca Barlow and Shahram Akbarzadeh, these discriminatory practices stems from "a culture of patriarchy" and the fundamental belief
of many of Iran's conservative elite that "women are inferior to men in terms
of rationality and their ability to live autonomous lives."[58] Some have argued
that women are not as capable as men. Mohammad Taghi Rahbar, a member
of Parliament, stated: "There are religious doubts over the abilities of women
when it comes to management."[59]

Since the Revolution in 1979, many women have challenged the notion
that they are second-class citizens. Women have protested against the discriminatory laws that leave them vulnerable to domestic violence and limit their
custodial rights.[60] The response from the government has often been violent
and harsh. Security forces arrested many women engaged in peaceful protests
against discriminatory laws (including stoning for adultery). Many women
were charged with acting against national security by participating in an illegal
gathering, even though Article 27 of the Iranian Constitution and Article 21
of the International Covenant on Civil and Political Rights recognize the right
to peaceful assembly.[61] Some of the peaceful protesters were also beaten before
being taken to Evin Prison.

The One Million Signatures Campaign has been a movement in Iran to
end gender discrimination, especially in the area of family law. Many of the
individuals involved in the campaign have been harassed and arrested for their
work on gender equality. In March 2006 Nasrin Afzali, Nahid Jafari, and
Minoo Mortazi were arrested and convicted of "acting against national security, disrupting public order, and refusing to follow police orders." They
received suspended sentences of lashings and prison time.[62] Another thirty-
three women were arrested after a public demonstration in June 2006.[63] Additional efforts by the campaign to ratify the Convention on the Elimination
of All Forms of Discrimination Against Women have not been successful. The
Guardian Council refused to approve the convention; it argued that it was
unconstitutional and un-Islamic.

Minority Groups in Iran

The Islamic Republic has produced a mixed record on religious minorities.[64]
The republic recognizes those religious groups that had a sizable presence

in the Arabian Peninsula in the seventh century and were mentioned in the Qur'an. The most protected of these groups are the People of the Book (Jews and Christians). In the Constitution, the People of the Book are guaranteed the freedom to worship in private gatherings, and they are allotted their own representatives in the Majles. Religious minorities are allowed to practice their religion under the Constitution. They can hold religious services and ceremonies, so long as the government is notified before the event. Despite these constitutional protections, some discrimination exists in Iran.

Although the People of the Book are guaranteed rights by the Constitution, they faced hardships in society and in political institutions, especially in the first five years of the republic. They have been denied jobs and government promotions. They are forbidden from consuming alcohol, and the sexes are segregated in society. The most significant limitation, especially on the Christian churches, is that proselytizing is forbidden. Additionally, there is discrimination in the legal system, especially in sentencing. Non-Muslims sometimes receive harsher sentences than Shia Muslims for the same crime. Furthermore, they do not enjoy equality in education.

Although the People of the Book do not enjoy equal status in Iran, they enjoy more rights than the Baha'is, which have suffered considerably since the Revolution in 1979. The Baha'is do not enjoy legal protection or the status of a religious minority because they are not perceived as a People of the Book, and they are viewed as a threat to Shia Islam. They do not share the belief that Muhammad was the last of the prophets and are therefore considered heretics. Furthermore, there is a widespread perception that the Baha'is enjoyed a privileged status before the Revolution.[65] This has translated into religious discrimination and human rights violations. They are prohibited from practicing their religion or engaging in communal worship. Private worship is also subject to prosecution by the authorities. In addition, they have lost jobs and have been denied employment and access to higher education due to their religious beliefs. The Baha'i community had more than 300,000 members before 1979. Since then the number of Baha'is in Iran has decreased due to persecution at the hands of the government.[66]

Ethnic and sexual minorities have also faced discrimination and harassment. Many in the lesbian, gay, bisexual, and transgender (LGBT) community have been detained, beaten, and abused. The legal code in Iran criminalizes sexual relations between two men or two women with punishments as severe as death.[67] Ethnic minorities such as the Kurds, Azeris, and Arabs have not fared much better with the Iranian authorities. The Constitution specifically states the equality of all citizens regardless of ethnic affiliation in Article 19: "All people of Iran, whatever the ethnic group or tribe to which they belong, enjoy equal rights; color, race, language, and the like do not bestow any privilege." Despite this constitutional protection, ethnic minorities are discriminated against: "In practice minorities did not have equal rights, and the government consistently denied their right to use their language in school. The government disproportionately targeted minority groups—including Kurds, Arabs, Azeris, and Baluch—for arbitrary arrest, prolonged detention, and physical abuse. These groups reported political and economic discrimination, particularly in their access to economic aid, business licenses, university admissions, permission to publish books, and housing and land rights. The government blamed foreign entities, including a number of governments, for instigating some of the ethnic unrest."[68] The government fears an ethnic uprising that could result in the loss of land and a threat to the political stability of the regime.

In sum, one can also see many human rights violations occurring as a result of perceived threats to those who control the levers of power. Whether this was a foreign threat (e.g., the Iran–Iraq War 1980–88) or a domestic threat (reformist, secular types, MEK), Tehran often responded with crackdowns and repression at home.[69] Additional violations of human rights have been a result of Khomeini's interpretation of Islamic concepts and values. Despite the various violations of human rights in the Islamic theocracy, we have also seen some limited improvements in a few second-generation rights.

Progress on Human Rights

Although much media and scholarly attention has focused on the lack of basic political freedoms and rights in Iran, much less attention has been paid to economic rights. Iranians, especially those in rural areas, have experienced some improvements in basic rights, including access to water, health care, and education.[70] These rights, necessary for surviving and prospering in society, are not viewed as threatening by many in the regime. In fact, providing these basic rights to Iranians is consistent with the rhetoric used by Khomeini in the 1970s.

Since 1979 the Iranian government has improved some aspects of the lives of the poor. Access to water and electricity has improved in rural areas.[71] In addition, political leaders in Tehran have improved access to health care. Improving access to medical services in Iran has resulted in a decrease in child mortality rates.[72] The religious orientation of the government has facilitated these medical endeavors. For example, in some parts of southern Iran, families did not trust foreign medical practices, including the use of vaccinations. However, after Khomeini established the theocracy and had gained control of the government, vaccinations at health clinics became more acceptable to rural Iranians.[73] Health clinics have also offered a needle-exchange program for drug users to decrease the transmission of AIDS and other diseases. According to a UNAIDS report this program is working, as evidenced by a decrease in new infections.[74] The government also increased access to birth control. In the late 1980s the government developed a policy called the National Birth Control Policy, which "provided free contraceptives (to married couples) through the primary health care system."[75] This policy was developed to help with family planning and encourage women to have fewer children. These initiatives demonstrate that pragmatic policies have been adopted by the theocratic regime.

Educational Progress

Iranian women have also benefited from the government's efforts in education. They have enjoyed greater access and opportunities via the education policies since the Islamic Revolution. For some conservative Iranians, the segregation of education by gender and the classes offered at mosques facilitated the ability of girls to get an education.[76] The improvement in literacy rates has been remarkable. Between 1976 and 1996, women's literacy doubled (in 1976, 36 percent of Iranian women were considered literate; and by 1996, the figure rose to 72 percent). By 2006, the literacy rates for girls ten years and older was 80 percent.[77] Furthermore, women were also attending universities in much greater numbers.[78] More than 60 percent of university students were women.[79]

Women have used their increasing educational opportunities to enhance their work opportunities. More women have entered the workforce in the last thirty years, and many are working in the service sector. By 2006, close to 50 percent of women were employed in education, health care, and social services.[80] Thus the increase in women working outside the home has not been limited to cheap jobs in manufacturing or the textile industry. Rather, many were using their education to secure higher-paying jobs.[81]

Women's Political Rights

Although women enjoy some basic political rights in Iran, such as the right to vote and to hold positions in government (women have been elected to Parliament), they do not enjoy complete political equality with their male counterparts.[82] Although women in Iran enjoy more basic social rights (e.g., driving) and political rights than women in other parts of the Middle East (Iran has more female members elected to Parliament than some other countries in the region), it is far from ideal. Despite these shortcomings, some have suggested that Iran is a model for other Muslim countries.[83] In some areas where there has been progress (education, birth control), it is worth noting that these are not viewed as threatening to political elites. Ultimately, though women enjoy some rights and some limited progress has been made, women do not enjoy full equality in many areas. Even Supreme Leader Khamenei acknowledged that "many efforts have been made in the Islamic system to (help) women regain their rightful position, but women are still facing many problems, especially in their family life, and these problems should be resolved through making the necessary laws and taking practical measures."[84]

In sum, one can explain the lack of political freedom and personal integrity rights stem from perceived domestic and international threats to the regime, and a specific and narrow interpretation of Islam. The role of threats can also explain the improvement in some second-generation rights. The progress we see in the areas of health care and education is available because they can be seen as nonthreatening to the regime. Therefore, beyond a commitment to Islamic purity, the self-interest of political leaders in Tehran and their desire to remain in control of the levers of power can explain many of the human rights violations in Iran during the last thirty years. Having examined the progress and limitations on human rights in Iran, the next section explores the role of international norms and the discourse of human rights in Iran.

Can Iran Be Socialized to Protect Human Rights?

Given the human rights violations noted above, can Iran become a regime that is more protective of human rights? Some countries with egregious human rights records have, over time, improved the protection of basic rights. Spain, South Africa, Argentina, and Turkey are examples of states that changed their policies and improved their record on human rights. Iran has, at times, taken some small steps along this path.

Norms

How does a state evolve from a flagrant abuser of human rights to one where the rule of law protects the basic human rights of its citizens? Some scholars have argued that states can be socialized to improve their protection of human rights.[85] Although a regime such as Iran will ignore many domestic complaints about human rights, international condemnation can have an impact. When international NGOs and other states criticize the regime's record on human rights, the regime's first response is typically to assert state sovereignty and to deny the charges: " 'Denial' means that the norm-violating government refuses to accept the validity of international norms themselves and it opposes the suggestion that its national practices in this area are subject to international jurisdiction. Thus, denial goes further than simply objecting to particular accusations. The norm-violating government charges that the criticism constitutes an illegitimate intervention in the internal affairs of the country. The government may even succeed in mobilizing some nationalist sentiment against foreign intervention and criticism."[86]

In some instances international pressure can have a limited impact. The regime backpedals and offers minor concessions as a demonstration that it cares about human rights. The regime may offer to release some political prisoners, open some media outlets, and change some domestic laws all in an attempt to pacify the international criticism that it faces. However, if the regime starts to use the language of freedom of the press, freedom of speech, and political justice for prisoners, it may become entrapped by the human rights rhetoric it uses. If the regime starts to "talk the talk," it may be challenged to "walk the walk."

After these first limited steps toward improving human rights, some states are pushed further toward the protection of basic rights. When the regime regularly invokes human rights norms, this suggests that the international norms surrounding human rights are no longer controversial.[87] This can usher in further progress on human rights, including becoming a signatory to a human rights treaty or greater adherence to human rights norms. By this point the regime has made significant progress on human rights. If this progress continues, albeit with bumps in the road, the regime will have moved significantly away from its past history of violating human rights.

The remainder of this chapter argues that Iran has made some limited progress on human rights, as evidenced by the changing discourse in Iran. However, I also want to suggest that in order to see greater improvements in Iran, we will need to see a reduction in threats from the international community and especially the United States. The focus on threat reduction stems from the fact, as noted in the first section, that human rights violations can be partially explained in relation to real and perceived threats. The less the regime feels threatened, the greater opening there is for improvement in human rights (i.e., education). Therefore, reducing threats is essential to see further progress on human rights. This is not the only step that is necessary to improve human rights in Iran, but it is an important one.

Decreasing threats (real and perceived) from abroad can provide an opening for the gradual improvement of human rights. Iran has often responded to Western criticism with harsh rhetoric about the sins of the West. The West is viewed by some of the political elite as a threat that must be dealt with for the political survival of the regime. This is especially true of Iran's relationship with the United States.[88] The benefit of reducing foreign threats is that it stifles attempts by the regime to engage in a rally-around-the-flag propaganda effort. In Iran's case, removing threats would include avoiding any rhetoric about regime change and discouraging the threat from Israel.[89] President Obama's efforts to reach out to Iran and negotiate are steps in this direction. Further international cooperation on the nuclear issue, including economic incentives, would be helpful. Reducing threats would allow the regime to focus less on survival (will the United States invade and overthrow the clerical rulers? will Israel bomb various nuclear and military facilities?) and more on domestic improvements.

Ultimately, improvement in human rights in Iran will involve significant political changes, including allowing elected bodies (the president and Parliament) to exercise more power. This may in the short term require some power-sharing agreement (as seen in Chile) to allow political elites to feel protected legally and financially before they relinquish some power. Although the road may be bumpy, as was evident in places such as Chile, gradual change, including the establishment of the rule of law, will take time and require patience.

As this process unfolds it is important that domestic groups and NGOs continue to put pressure on the regime to protect human rights. If domestic pressure incorporates Islamic elements, the process may see substantial results. If domestic groups and individuals make the case for a reinterpretation of Islam in a manner that is more friendly to human rights, this may facilitate the political transition. Thus the efforts by Soroush and others who work within an Islamic framework to improve human rights protections in Iran are instructive. This is less threatening than a Western approach, because it incorporates elements that are consistent with the culture and history of the people.

Ultimately, the transition from a regime that violates human rights to one that consistently upholds human rights will take time to develop. However, in the meantime, while political elites are negotiating, progress can still occur on socioeconomic rights, such as education or health care, because they are not viewed as threatening as political rights.

The Evolution of the Discourse on Human Rights

In the past, Iranian leaders have denied the applicability and the worth of international human rights. Human rights were a product of the West; they were inferior to the duties and obligations laid out in the Qur'an. However, in more recent years, we have seen various Iranian leaders, including hard-line conservatives, using the language of international human rights. This linguistic transition demonstrates that international norms concerning human rights have had an impact on the Islamic Republic.

Some of the animosity toward international human rights stems from Ayatollah Khomeini. The leader of the Revolution believed that Islam and Islamic law were superior to anything that the West had produced, including international law. Human rights treaties, such as the International Covenant on Civil and Political Rights, were likewise inferior to shari'a. (Khomeini had a general disregard for many aspects of international law. This was demonstrated by the violation of diplomatic immunity during the hostage crisis in 1979.) So it should come as no surprise that Khomeini was not moved by international treaties on human rights. On February 19, 1978, Khomeini gave a speech in which he articulated the hypocrisy of the West and the Universal Declaration of Human Rights:

> All the miseries that we have suffered, still suffer, and are about to suffer soon are caused by the heads of those countries that have signed the Declaration of Human Rights, but that at all times have denied man his freedom. Freedom of the individual is the most important part of the Declaration of Human Rights. Individual human beings must all be equal before the law, and they must be free. They must be free in their choice of residence and occupation. But we see the Iranian nation, together with many others, suffering at the hands of those states that have signed and ratified the Declaration.[90]

Khomeini went on to add that "the Declaration of Human Rights exists only to deceive the nations; it is the opium of the masses."[91] At another time he asserted, "What they call human rights is nothing but a collection of corrupt rules worked out by Zionists to destroy all true religions."[92] Taking Khomeini's lead, various political leaders would also criticize international human rights at various times since the Revolution. Khomenei also stressed that international law was inferior to Islamic law: "Changing some absolute Islamic decrees to correspond to certain international conventions is quite wrong."[93]

Despite the fact that some prominent political elites denied the value of international human rights and the covenants that established their parameters, we have seen an evolution in the language and rhetoric relating to human rights. Some political leaders have suggested that not only are human rights valid, but that Iran protects these rights. For example, in his remarks on June 19, 2009, Supreme Leader Khamenei said that the Islamic Republic is a strong supporter of human rights, especially of the oppressed.[94] Former president Rafsanjani (not known for his passionate support of human rights) also used the language of human rights in the aftermath of the 2009 election, when he said that a resolution to this crisis requires respect for the law and a free and open debate. His support for the rule of law and freedom of speech echoes the norms of the international community.[95] Mohamad Larijani told the UN Human Rights Council in 2010 that Iran was "in full compliance with the relevant international commitments it has taken on in a genuine and long-term approach to safeguard human rights."[96] Although it is a stretch to suggest that Iran is at the forefront of protecting human rights, especially in the aftermath of the presidential elections in 2009, the linguistic transition is important. Some regimes become entrapped by the human rights language they employ.

Some have denied that the Islamic Republic violates human rights by insisting that the issue at hand is not a human rights issue. For example, Mohamad Larijani who is on Iran's Human Rights Committee (which was established by the supreme leader), argued that stoning is not torture and hence not a violation of a person's rights. The use of stoning as a punishment for adultery is neither "torture nor disproportionate punishment."[97] Despite this comment, international outrage in 2010 and 2011 in the case of Sakineh Mohammadi-Ashtiani resulted in the suspension of a death by stoning sentence.[98]

Although Iran's protection of human rights has been flawed in many areas, as noted above, the regime has voiced concerns about the violation of human rights abroad, especially concerning the Palestinians. Many in Iran have criticized the lack of many fundamental rights and freedoms for Palestinians living in Israel and the occupied territories.

Khomeini often voiced concern for Palestinians. In February 1971, he urged Muslims to help liberate "the Islamic land of Palestine from the grasp of Zionism."[99] After the Revolution he continued to argue for the plight of the Palestinians in a message to pilgrims in September 1979: "Today the first *qibla* of the Muslims has fallen into the grasp of Israel, that cancerous growth in the Middle East. They are battering and slaughtering our dear Palestinian and Lebanese brothers with all their might."[100]

Although the concern for the Palestinians is consistent with the founder's message, it has also evolved in recent years to incorporate aspects of international law and international human rights documents. In 2009, Ahmadinejad submitted a bill to Parliament that would allow the prosecution of any individuals in the world who committed a crime against humanity or war crimes. This international war crimes bill echoed aspects of established international law, including the Genocide Convention and the Geneva Conventions. Specifically, this includes denying a civilian population humanitarian assistance, attempts to exterminate a group of people, rape, and using toxic weapons.[101] This bill is aimed specifically at Israel, and it was drafted in response to the war in the Gaza Strip in 2008. Two months later, Tehran announced that it would host an international conference to examine war crimes during the war in Gaza. The statement from the prosecutor's office said, "With the rise in war crimes and human rights violations in many parts of the world, all countries and international organizations have a responsibility to prevent such incidents."[102] In 2010, Ayatollah Khamenei condemned the Israeli response to the Turkish Aid Flotilla: "What does the three-year blockade of food and medicine imposed on 1.5 million Palestinian men, women, and children actually mean? How are the massacre, imprisonment, and daily torture of young Palestinians in Gaza and the West Bank justified? Palestine is no longer an Arab issue. It is not even an Islamic issue any more. Rather, it is the most important human rights issue of the modern world."[103]

Although these actions are politically motivated, it is important to note that Iran is using the tools and language of the international human rights community. This can also be used against Iran itself.

An additional example of the clerical regime using the tools of international human rights occurred in November 2009. The Majles approved a bill that would allocate $20 million to expose human rights violations by the United States and Great Britain.[104] The bill is intended to inform the international community of the crimes of these two Western powers. Although clearly political in nature, this again demonstrates how the government is using the discourse of international human rights.

The point to emphasize here is that during the past few years, scholars have noticed that the language that various political elites are using is similar to the language employed by human rights activists in the West. By using the language of international human rights to criticize other countries, even for political purposes, one can see the influence of the norms and values of human rights on Tehran. Most important is the fact that international human rights evolved from being rejected as a product of the West to being employed as a legitimate tool of political leaders.

Improving Human Rights in the Future

Although some of the findings in this chapter are grim, we have also seen some limited areas of improvement (education). This allows for some guarded optimism for future progress on human rights in Iran. Although the nuclear issue will distract from the issue of human rights (because the West perceives it to be a bigger threat to international relations), one should not dismiss the fact that political leaders in Iran, including conservatives, are using the language of human rights. They are "talking the talk." Even if selectively applied, this still suggests a use of the language of international human rights, which is a large step from Khomeini's rejection of human rights and a step toward the protection of human rights.

In addition, scholars continue to see efforts on the part of domestic NGOs to promote human rights. Whether it is the One Million Signatures Campaign or religiously based efforts, these grassroots initiatives are essential to see improvement in the future. The religiously based efforts to reinterpret Islamic texts in a manner that is more protective of rights may prove to have a large impact because they use the cultural and religious tools of Iranian society.[105] Some Islamic feminists in Iran have specifically argued that women's rights can be protected in an Islamic state if a proper reading of the Qur'an is undertaken.[106] For example, many Iranian women participate in Qur'anic meetings in which they discuss various Qur'anic verses. As one scholar noted, these meetings allow women to explore their rights in the context of Islamic thought and this offers them a means to use Islamic concepts to enhance their status in the Islamic Republic:

> The women at the meetings engage in their own personalized *ijtihad,* as one woman conveyed it to me, by reappropriating a community space where they subvert the existing rational methodology for exegesis, and finding the basis for it within the very texts of Islam itself. Nanaz's explanation of the methodology of exegesis—"according to the laws of interpretation, community can read and reach an agreement on the sections of the Qur'an that are unclear"—breathes local agency into the process. Using Islamic principles to legitimize their work, the women at the meetings seek and find paths to individual

agency, which leads to a discourse of empowerment and rights that is based on ideas that are expressed in terms like individual liberty, free will, and personal responsibility.[107]

In this sense, they do not challenge the religious foundations of the political system. They are seeking to reform—not overturn—the present political system.[108] When Shirin Ebadi, a prominent human rights lawyer, won the Nobel Peace Prize in 2003, she specifically stressed the compatibility of Islam and internationally recognized human rights.[109]

Conclusion

Many of the human rights violations witnessed in Iran stem from a specific interpretation of Islam and perceived threats to the regime. This suggests that these elements must be addressed to see further progress. Limitations on political rights, including freedom of expression, occur to limit political opposition to the regime and especially the hard-line conservatives in power. Human rights violations that occur in the name of Islam (requiring women to wear a veil or punishing an individual accused of adultery by stoning) may offer hope for progress under a reinterpretation of Islamic texts. However, even a reinterpretation of religious doctrine is not a guarantee of greater protection of human rights. Islam will go only so far when the political elites feel they are threatened.

Although Iran has a long way to go before it guarantees every citizen the basic protections articulated by the International Bill of Human Rights, one should not forget the limited progress that has been made in areas of health care and education. Further progress is more likely to occur in an atmosphere of reduced threats. Although Iran has improved some aspects of its human rights record, it still has much work to do. Although the road is not guaranteed, the less threatened the regime feels the greater chance there is for improved human rights protections in Iran.

Notes

1. "The idea of international human rights has proved broadly appealing. Even those like Stalin, who denied most human rights in practice, wrote liberal constitutions and organized elections so as to pretend to recognize human rights." David Forsythe, *Human Rights in International Relations,* 2nd ed. (Cambridge: Cambridge University Press, 2006), 11. See also Richard Falk, *Achieving Human Rights* (New York: Routledge, 2008), 27: "In these

contexts the language and pursuit of rights provides a moral motivation for initiatives that aim both to resist oppressive moves emanating from the established order and to transform the status quo in accord with goals associated with equity, equality and human solidarity." Despite the broad appeal of human rights, many governments have not found it appealing to protect the human rights of its citizens.

2. Richard Rorty, "Human Rights, Rationality, and Sentimentality," in *The Philosophy of Human Rights*, edited by Patrick Hayden (Saint Paul: Paragon House, 2001), 241–57, at 245.

3. Thomas Risse and Kathryn Sikkink, "The Socialization of International Human Rights Norms into Domestic Practices: Introduction," in *The Power of Human Rights: International Norms and Domestic Change*, edited by Thomas Risse, Stephen C. Ropp, and Kathryn Sikkink (Cambridge: Cambridge University Press, 1999), 1.

4. One cannot do justice to all of the civil and political rights articulated in the Covenant on Civil and Political Rights or even in the Universal Declaration of Human Rights, so I have selected specific civil and political rights that are representative of the situation of human rights in Iran.

5. Akbar Ganji, *The Road to Democracy in Iran* (Cambridge, MA: MIT Press, 2008), 21–22.

6. Human Rights Council, "Report of UN Secretary General on the Situation of Human Rights in Iran at the Human Rights Council in Geneva," Document: A/HRC/16/75, March 28, 2011.

7. In the 1980s (1980–91) Iran consistently received scores of 5 and 6. The five years from 1992 to 1997 saw a deterioration in rights, according to Freedom House: 6 and 7. Between 1998 and 2012 the number has remained relatively stable at 6.

8. Worldwide Governance Indicators for 2009 (1996–2008), percentile rank: voice and accountability, 8.2; political stability, 14.4; government effectiveness, 24.6; regulatory quality, 2.9; rule of law, 23.0; control of corruption, 28.5; of these statistics have deteriorated since 2003; see http://infor.worldbank.org/governance.

9. Ahmed Shaheed submitted a report on the human rights violations in the country. The government of Iran did not cooperate with Shaheed.

10. UN General Assembly, "The Situation of Human Rights in the Islamic Republic of Iran," Document A/66/374, September 23, 2011.

11. Bureau of Democracy, Human Rights, and Labor, US Department of State, "2010 Country Reports on Human Rights Practices," April 8, 2011, www.state.gov/g/drl/rls/hrrpt/2010/nea/154461.htm.

12. It is worth noting that Iran is a party to the International Covenant on Civil and Political Rights, which it ratified in 1975.

13. Robin Wright, *In the Name of God* (New York: Simon & Schuster, 1989), 69.

14. Ibid., 67–68.

15. Ibid., 98.

16. Ibid., 100–101.

17. Ibid., 107.

18. Zarah Ghahramani with Robert Hillman, *My Life as a Traitor* (New York: Farrar, Straus & Giroux, 2008); Marina Nemat, *Prisoner of Tehran* (New York: Free Press, 2007). Human Rights Watch has repeatedly condemned the torture in Iranian prisons. See Human Rights Watch, "Torture Used to Obtain Confessions," December 6, 2004;

and Human Rights Watch, "Judiciary Uses Coercion to Cover Up Torture," December 20, 2004. Also see Campaign for Equality, "Statement by the Women's Movement in Protest of the Recent Escalation of Violence against Women in Iran," July 26, 2011.

19. Haleh Esfandiari, *My Prison, My Home: One Woman's Story of Captivity in Iran* (New York: HarperCollins, 2009), 75. No investigation was seriously undertaken to punish those responsible for her death.

20. Scott Shane and Michael R. Gordon, "Dissident's Tale of Epic Escape from Iran's Vise," *New York Times*, July 13, 2008, www.nytimes.com/2008/07/13/world/middleeast/13dissident.html. See also Afsin Molavi, *The Soul of Iran* (New York: W. W. Norton, 2002), 206–7.

21. See Bureau of Democracy, Human Rights, and Labor, US State Department, "2010 Country Reports on Human Rights Practices," April 8, 2011, http://www.state.gov/g/drl/rls/hrrpt/2010/nea/154461.htm.

22. Ali Ansari, *Confronting Iran* (New York: Basic Books, 2006), 207.

23. Ayatollah Shahroudi is not known for his reformist leanings or sympathy for liberal causes. Human Rights Watch, "Iran: Four Journalists Sentence to Prison, Floggings," February 10, 2009, www.hrw.org/en/news/2009/02/10/iran-four-journalists-sentenced-prison-floggings? . . .

24. In September 2008, in an interview with the *New York Times*, President Ahmadinejad said, "Iran is a free country for people to express their opinions. . . . Everyone is free to express what he or she wants whether for or against the government and there are in fact hundreds of opinions that in fact speak in favor of our policies." The interview can be found at www.nytimes.com/2008/09/26/world/middleeast/26iran-transcript.html?ref=world& . . .

25. Khomeini, *Islam and Revolution: Writings and Declarations of Imam Khomeini,* translated and annotated by Hamid Algar (Berkeley, CA: Mizan Press, 1981), 113.

26. John Esposito and John Voll, *Islam and Democracy* (Oxford: Oxford University Press, 1996), 66.

27. Quoted by Robin Wright, *The Last Great Revolution: Turmoil and Transformation in Iran* (New York: Alfred A. Knopf, 2000), 42.

28. Quoted in ibid., 41.

29. Mahmoud Sadri and Ahmad Sadri, "Introduction," in *Reason, Freedom, and Democracy in Islam: Essential Writings of Abdolkarim Soroush* (New York: Oxford University Press, 2000), xi.

30. One of the few individuals to criticize Ahmadinejad in an open and direct manner is former president Khatami, who in December 2007 criticized the president's economic policy and crackdown on political activists. Nazila Fathi, "Former Iranian President Publicly Assails Ahmadinejad," *New York Times*, December 12, 2007, www.nytimes.com/2007/12/12/world/middleeast/12iran.html.

31. Human Rights Watch, "Iran: Reverse Closure of Nobel Laureate's Rights Group," press release, December 21, 2008, available at www.hrw.org. See also "Iranian Police Shut Down Rights Office," December 22, 2008, www.nytimes.com/2008/12/22/world/middleeast/22tehran.html.

32. Ganji, *Road to Democracy*, xvii. Ganji's defense of human rights is based on the capacity for suffering: "The common experience of pain is thus the foundation for human rights. We believe that any human being who has the capacity to suffer is entitled to certain

rights. . . . Supporters of universal rights, including signatories to the International Declaration of Human Rights, believe that human beings suffer from common sources, and that we must find ways to spare people these experiences" (6–7).

33. Ibid., 7.

34. Mehdi Mozaffari, "Rushdie Affair," in *The Oxford Encyclopedia of the Modern Islamic World*, edited by John L. Esposito (New York: Oxford University Press, 1995), 443.

35. Molavi, *Soul of Iran*, 201–2; Jean-Daniel Lafond and Fred A. Reed, *Conversations in Tehran* (Vancouver: Talon Books, 2006), 55.

36. Human Rights Watch, "Iran: Release Students Detained for Peaceful Protests," February 24, 2009. See also BBC, "Arrests after Protest in Tehran," news.bbc.co.uk/go/pr/fr/-/2/hi/middle_east/7907276.stm. Amnesty International, "Iran's Presidential Election Amid Unrest and Ongoing Human Rights Violations," June 5, 2009, available at www.amnesty.org.

37. Human Rights Watch, "Iran: Escalating Repression of University Students," December 7, 2010.

38. Karim Sadjadpour, *Reading Khamenei: The World View of Iran's Most Powerful Leader* (Washington, DC: Carnegie Endowment for International Peace, 2008), 2.

39. Ali Ansari, *Confronting Iran* (New York: Basic Books, 2006), 158.

40. Bernd Kaussler, "European Union Constructive Engagement with Iran (2000–2004): An Exercise in Conditional Human Rights Diplomacy," *Iranian Studies* 41, no. 3 (June 2008): 269–95, at 282.

41. Michael Slackman, "Panel in Iran Will Oversee Investigations into Unrest," *New York Times*, August 31, 2009, www.nytimes.com/2009/08/31/world/middleeast/31iran.html.

42. International Campaign for Human Rights in Iran, "Supreme Leader Directly Responsible for Illegal Detentions of Opposition Leaders," February 8, 2012, www.iranhumanrights.org/2012/02/home-arrest-anniversary.

43. Amnesty International believes the number is even higher. Amnesty International, "Iran Dire Human Rights Situation Persists 2 Years after Disputed Elections," AI Index: 13/057/2011, June 9, 2011.

44. Michael Posner, "Human Rights and Democratic Reform in Iran, Testimony before the Senate Foreign Relations Committee," May 11, 2011, Washington, DC.

45. International Campaign for Human Rights in Iran, "Secret Executions: Findings Challenge Judiciary's False Narrative," January 5, 2012, www.iranhumanrights.org/2012/01/vakilabad-101/.

46. Robert F. Worth and Nazila Fathi, "Iran Gathering Is Broken Up," *New York Times*, July 31, 2009, www.nytimes.com/2009/07/31/world/middleeast/31iran.html; Robert F. Worth, "Accused Spies Offer Apologies at Iran Trial," *New York Times*, August 9, 2009, www.nytimes.com/2009/08/09/world/middleeast/09iran.html; Nazila Fathi, "Authorities in Iran Arrest 18 Students," *New York Times*, October 3, 2009, www.nytimes.com/2009/10/03/world/middleeast/03iran.html; Nazila Fathi, "Iranian Court Shuts Down 3 Pro-Reform Newspapers as Dissent Continues to Simmer," *New York Times*, October 7, 2009, www.nytimes.com/2009/10/07/world/middleeast/07iran.html.

47. Ganji, *Road to Democracy*, 33.

48. Vanessa Martin, *Creating an Islamic State: Khomeini and the Making of a New Iran* (New York: I. B. Tauris, 2000), 61.

49. Ibid., 155.

50. Ibid., 156.

51. Azar Nafisi, *Reading Lolita in Tehran* (New York: Random House, 2003). See also Mahmood Monshipouri, *Islamism, Secularism, and Human Rights in the Middle East* (Boulder, CO: Lynne Rienner, 1998), 188. The legal age for girls to marry was raised from nine to thirteen years. Rebecca Barlow and Shahram Akbarzadeh, "Prospects for Feminism in the Islamic Republic of Iran," *Human Rights Quarterly* 30 (2008): 21–40, at 27.

52. Valentine M. Moghadam, "Islamic Feminism and Its Discontents: Towards a Resolution of the Debate," *Signs* 27, no. 4 (Summer 2002): 1135–71.

53. Barlow and Akbarzadeh, "Prospects for Feminism," 23; Monshipouri, *Islamism*, 189.

54. In June 2005, hundreds of women demonstrated against the gender discrimination that exists in Iran. Nazila Fathi, "Hundreds of Women Protest Sex Discrimination in Iran," *New York Times*, June 12, 2005, www.nytimes.com/2005/06/12/international/middleast/13womencnd.html?ei=5094. . . . Some women have also complained of the practice of temporary marriage. A temporary marriage is "a religiously sanctioned marriage with contractual obligations but for a finite period of time." Vali Nasr, *The Shia Revival* (New York: W. W. Norton, 2007), 69.

55. "Nation Must Develop Insight Prior to Ballot," Office of the Supreme Leader, January 23, 2008, www.leader.ir/langs/EN/print.php?id=3816. Women during the Pahlavi monarchy were courageous and stood up to the shah's pressures to remove the hijab. The hijab covers the head and the neck. Some Iranian women wear a chador, which is a cloak that covers the entire body. A burka covers not only the entire body but a woman's face as well.

56. Ali Ansari, *Modern Iran since 1921: The Pahlavis and After* (London: Pearson Education, 2003), 224.

57. Foreign journalists have noted the limited effects of these government actions. BBC, "New Iranian Dress Code Crackdown," June 17, 2008, news.bbc.co.uk/go/pr/fr/-/2/hi/middle_east/7457212.stm.

58. "Prospects for Feminism in the Islamic Republic of Iran," *Human Rights Quarterly* 30 (2008): 21–40, at 23.

59. He was voicing his concerns about women ministers in Ahmadinejad's cabinet. BBC, "Row of Iran's Women Ministers," August 22, 2009, news.bbc.co.uk.go/pr/fr/-/2/hi/middle_east/8215880.stm.

60. More women are also getting divorced. William Yong, "Iran's Divorce Rate Stirs Fears of Society in Crisis," *New York Times*, December 6, 2010, www.nytimes.com/2010/12/07/world/middleeast/07divorce.html.

61. Those charged were Nusheen Ahmadi Khorasani, Parvin Ardalan, Sussan Tahmasebi, Shahla Entesari, and Fariba Davoodi Mohayer. Barbara Ann Rieffer-Flanagan, "Improving Democracy in Religious Nation-States: Norms of Moderation and Cooperation in Ireland and Iran," *Muslim World Journal of Human Rights* 4, no. 2 (2007). Human Rights Watch, "Iran: Women on Trial for Peaceful Demonstration: Activists Arrested for Protesting Discriminatory Laws," February 27, 2007; Kasra Naji, *Ahmadinejad: The Secret History of Iran's Radical Leader* (Berkeley: University of California Press, 2008), 252.

62. Payvand, "Iran: Women's Rights Activists Get Suspended Lashing Sentences," April 24, 2008.

63. Human Rights Watch, "Iran: Women on Trial for Peaceful Demonstration. Activists Arrested for Protesting Discriminatory Laws," February 27, 2007; Nazila Fathi,

"Iranian Women Are Arrested after Protests Outside of Court," *New York Times*, March 6, 2007, www.nytimes.com/2007/03/06/world/middleeast/06iran.html.

64. For a detailed discussion of the human rights violations experienced by the Baha'i, Protestants, Sunni Muslims, and Jews, see US State Department, "International Religious Freedom Report," www.state.gov/g/drl/irf/rpt. See also John Esposito and John Voll, *Islam and Democracy* (Oxford: Oxford University Press, 1996), chap. 3.

65. This may be a misperception as Mohammad Reza Shah promoted an Anti-Baha'i campaign, which included the physical destruction of Baha'i property in Tehran.

66. Monshipouri, *Islamism*, 193. Richard Cottam, *Nationalism in Iran* (Pittsburgh: University of Pittsburgh Press, 1979), 87.

67. LGBT refers to lesbian, gay, bisexual, and transgender. Sexual relations between any two people who are not married is punishable under Iranian law. Human Rights Watch, "Iran: Discrimination and Violence against Sexual Minorities," December 15, 2010.

68. US State Department report, 2010.

69. This is consistent with Davenport's findings on threat perception and an increase in repression. Christian Davenport, "Multi-Dimensional Threat Perception and State Repression: An Inquiry into Why States Apply Negative Sanctions," *American Journal of Political Science* 38, no. 3 (1995): 683–713.

70. A more detailed discussion of economic rights is included in chapter 7.

71. Electricity: 16.2 percent (1977) to 98.3 percent (2004); piped water: 11.7 percent (1977) to 89.0 percent (2004). Statistical Center of Iran, 1984–2005, Household Income and Expenditure Surveys.

72. In 1960 there were 281 deaths per 1,000 births versus 42 deaths per 1,000 births in 2001. World Bank, "World Development Indicators," 2003, Washington, DC.

73. Janet Afary, *Sexual Politics in Modern Iran* (Cambridge: Cambridge University Press, 2009), 150.

74. Tina Rosenberg, "An Enlightened Needle Exchange in Iran," *New York Times*, November 29, 2010, http://opinionator.blogs.nytimes.com/2010/11/29/an-enlightened -exchange-in-iran/.

75. Pardis Mahdavi, "Who Will Catch Me if I Fall? Health and the Infrastructure of Risk for Urban Young Iranians," in *Contemporary Iran: Economy, Society, Politics*, edited by Ali Gheissari (Oxford: Oxford University Press, 2009), 165.

76. Roksana Bahramitash and Hadi Salehi Esfahani, "Nimble Fingers No Longer! Women's Employment in Iran," in *Contemporary Iran*, ed. Ali Gheissari, 92.

77. See the Statistical Center of Iran, www.sci.org.

78. Jane Howard, *Inside Iran: Women's Lives* (Washington, DC: Mage, 2002), 85, 79.

79. It is worth noting that education can be a double-edged sword for the regime. Improvements in women's literacy and education can create more productive citizens for the workforce. It can also create citizens who are more willing to question the regime's legitimacy and founding ideology.

80. See the Statistical Center of Iran.

81. As Bahramitash and Saleshi Esfahani note, this is contrary to the female workforce in other parts of the global south: "The trend has been the opposite: Women have increasingly left nimble-finger jobs in the carpet industry to go to school so as to take on clerical, technical and professional positions" (p. 79).

82. Ahmadinejad selected Marzien Vahid Dastjerdi as health minister. She is the first female cabinet minister since 1979. BBC, "Iran Backs First Woman Minister," September 10, 2009, newsvote.bbc.co.uk/mpapps/pagetools/print/news.bbc.co.uk/2/hi/midd.

83. Hassan Hanizadeh, "Women's Rights in Iran," *Tehran Times,* July 8, 2007.

84. *Tehran Times,* "Islamic Republic Has Elevated Status of Women: Leader," May 23, 2011, www.tehrantimes.com/index_View.asp?code=241201

85. For the description of Risse and Sikkink's five-phase spiral model, see Risse and Sikkink, "Socialization," 22–35.

86. Ibid., 23.

87. Ibid., 29.

88. Tehran is particularly concerned with the rhetoric of regime change that was used during the George W. Bush administration. Criticisms from Western NGOs, though inconvenient, do not pose the same threat as Washington does.

89. Although the United States does not control Israeli foreign policy, Washington can apply pressure to Tel Aviv to avoid threats to Tehran and especially a strike on Iranian territory. Toward the end of George W. Bush's presidency, Israel sought permission to fly in Iraqi airspace for a mission over Iran. This request was denied, and despite various hawkish statements from Israel's prime minister Netanyahu, Israel has not, at the time of writing, engaged in provocative military actions against Tehran.

90. *Islam and Revolution: Writings and Declarations of Iman Khomeini*, translated and annotated by Hamid Algar (Berkeley, CA: Mizan Press, 1981), 213.

91. Ibid., 214.

92. Ann Elizabeth Mayer, *Islam and Human Rights* (Boulder, CO: Westview Press, 2007), 35. Khomenei, while president, expressed similar sentiments: "When we want to find out what is right and wrong, we do not go to the United Nations, we go to the Holy Koran. For us the Universal Declaration of Human Rights is nothing but a collection of mumbo-jumbo by disciples of Satan."

93. "Leader: No Conflict between Women's Social and Family Roles," *Tehran Times,* July 5, 2007.

94. His remarks from Friday prayers can be found at www.leader.ir/langs/EN/index.php.

95. Robert Worth, "Tehran Losing Iranian's Trust, Ex Leader Says," *New York Times,* July 18, 2009, www.nytimes.com/2009/07/18/world/middleeast/18iran.html.

96. Nick Cumming Bruce, "Iran Defends Human Rights Record before UN Council," *New York Times,* February 16, 2010, www.nytimes.com/2010/02/16/world/middleeast/16geneva.html.

97. October 1, 2007, *Tehran Times,*"West's Criticism of Iran's Human Rights Record Is Politically Motivated: IPM Director."

98. William Yong, "Iran May Drop Stoning Sentence," *New York Times,* January 2, 2011, www.nytimes.com/2011/01/04/world/middleeast/04iran.html. The suspension of her death sentence continued throughout 2011.

99. *Islam and Revolution*, trans. and ann. Hamid Algar, 195.

100. Ibid., 276.

101. "Ahmadinejad Submits International War Crimes Bill," *Tehran Times,* February 23, 2009, www.tehrantimes.com/index_View.asp?code=189890.

102. "Tehran to Host Conference Calling for Prosecution of Zionist War Criminals," April 14, 2009, www.tehrantimes.com/index_View.asp?code=192197.

103. "Zionist Regime Is the New Face of Fascism: Leader" June 2, 2010, www.tehran times.com/index_View.asp?code=220586.

104. *Tehran Times*, "Majlis Allocates $20 Million to Reveal Rights Violations by US, UK," November 11, 2009.

105. Abdullahi Ahmed An-Na'im has argued for both an internal dialogue within Islam and a cross-cultural dialogue between the Islamic world and the West that would alleviate any conflicts between Islam and international human rights. He specifically suggests that this can happen in the controversial area of family law: "A clear acknowledgment of this reality will open the door for more innovative approaches to family law reform that may be guided by Islamic principles, without being confined to outdated understandings of Shari' a." Abdullahi Ahmed An-Na'im, "Shari' a and Islamic Family Law: Transition and Transformation," *Ahfad Journal* 23, no. 2 (December 2006): 2–30, at 5. See also Abdullahi Ahmed An-Na'im, *Toward an Islamic Revolution: Civil Liberties, Human Rights, and International Law* (Syracuse, NY: Syracuse University Press, 1990).

106. It is worth noting that some Iranian women believe the notion of Islamic feminism is "a contradictory notion" and thus is implausible. Nafisi, *Reading Lolita*, 262.

107. Arzoo Osanloo, *The Politics of Women's Rights in Iran* (Princeton, NJ: Princeton University Press, 2009), 84.

108. Barlow and Akbarzadeh, "Prospects for Feminism," 26.

109. Shirin Ebadi, *Iran Awakening: A Memoir of Revolution and Hope* (New York: Random House, 2006), 191. See also Barlow and Akbarzadeh, "Prospects for Feminism," 38.

CHAPTER 6

Assessing Iranian Foreign Policy since the Revolution
Islamic Realpolitik

President Ahmadinejad captured a lot of media attention with his remark that Israel should be "wiped off the map." Comments by other policymakers in Iran concerning Iran's legal rights under the Nuclear Non-Proliferation Treaty, or their support for Hezbollah, have caused concern in many capitals around the world. These statements make it difficult for makers of foreign policy to discern the orientation of Iranian foreign policy. Does Tehran want to build nuclear weapons, or is it merely seeking nuclear energy to supplement its natural energy reserves? Should Israel be concerned about an imminent attack from the theocratic regime if Iran goes nuclear? Or are these statements merely rhetoric meant largely for domestic consumption?[1]

Sorting through the language and actions of Iran's leaders presents a complicated picture for anyone trying to understand Iranian foreign policy. A number of scholars, including Ray Takeyh, have noted that many in the West have misunderstood Iranian foreign policy: "From the original 1979 Revolution that launched the Islamic Republic to the more recent confrontation over Iran's nuclear intentions, the United States has persistently misjudged Iran's clerical oligarchs."[2] Former secretary of state Condoleezza Rice confessed that the George W. Bush administration did not understand Iran.[3] Despite a history of misunderstandings and hostile confrontations, improving relations with the Islamic Republic is possible if one understands that realism often drives Tehran's foreign policy. In numerous instances, Iran demonstrated that Islamic principles are secondary to power politics and the survival of the state.

When trying to formulate foreign policy toward the Islamic Republic, political leaders need to distinguish two levels: the level of domestic politics, and the level of international politics. Almost all states must deal with the complicated interactions of global politics. However, most political leaders cannot completely ignore their domestic constituents and the pressures that arise from domestic politics. Regrettably, many policymakers around the world have allowed the religious rhetoric offered for domestic consumption in Tehran to cloud the realist policies that have often been practiced by Iran at the international level.

To understand Iranian foreign policy, one must separate statements geared toward Iran's domestic audience from those policy decisions in the global arena. Given the prominence of realism in many foreign policy decisions made during the last thirty years, this chapter argues that religious radicalism does not guide Iranian foreign policy. Thus foreign leaders should give less attention to the religious rhetoric aimed at Iran's domestic politics. Although the international community did see an emphasis on Shia Islam in the 1980s, this was part of an effort to consolidate domestic power in the aftermath of the Revolution. The more one moved away from the Revolution, the more one noticed the emphasis on realpolitik.

Understanding the realism at the heart of Iranian foreign policy leads to a number of policy goals. First, the United States and other countries should primarily approach Iran as a rational actor with national interests, instead of as an irrational radical state. Forgoing any grand bargain, makers of foreign policy should try to find limited, shared interests upon which to cooperate with Tehran. Cooperation on those areas of common interest would allow for some trust to develop, and ultimately it would help to reduce tensions. Although religious rhetoric often billows from Friday sermons, foreign policy in Iran is often determined by pragmatic policies based on realism. If the international community understands that realism is the foundation of Tehran's foreign policy, this can help to prevent a recurrence of the failed policies of the past.

Domestic Politics

When developing a state's foreign policy, political leaders will be influenced by domestic policies. This is most obvious when public opinion forces a president or prime minister to change course in a democracy, as was the case in Vietnam in the 1970s and in Somalia in the early 1990s. Domestic factors can have an impact in nondemocratic states. Even in Iran's authoritarian political system, internal disputes between political factors and the political climate within a state can have an impact on foreign policy decisions. Thus understanding the internal political dynamics can help us comprehend decisions related to global politics.

Factional Politics

Foreign policy in Iran is developed and implemented by a number of actors under the direction of the supreme leader. Besides setting the overall course of foreign policy, the supreme leader is the commander in chief. Under Iran's Constitution, he has the power to declare war or peace (Article 110), and he has control over the armed forces.[4] Aside from a few brief articles, the Iranian Constitution is largely silent on how foreign policy should be developed and implemented. Although Article 52 rejects imperialism and foreign influence, there are few specific powers designated by the Constitution concerning foreign policy.[5] Given the lack of specificity in the Constitution, it is not surprising that a variety of actors have tried to influence foreign policy.

Besides efforts by the Supreme National Security Council and the Majles to sway policy decisions, various presidents also had their hand in foreign policy.[6] Presidents such as Rafsanjani and Khatami took a conciliatory approach to global politics and specifically tried to improve relations with the West. President Ahmadinejad, conversely, adopted a rhetorically confrontational approach to the United States and Europe.

Aside from individual policymakers, there are ideological divisions within the country between reformists, conservatives, and neoconservatives that shape debates on foreign policy. Some conservatives, such as Rafsanjani, tried to improve economic relations with the West in order to attract much-needed foreign investment into the country. Neoconservatives or hard-line conservatives are opposed to cooperating with the West, and especially the United States. As Sandra Mackey notes, "In their view, Iranian foreign policy centers on the export of the revolution, even by subversion and terrorism," which is more in line with the views of Ayatollah Khomeini.[7] Beyond the ideological foundations, hostility toward the United States allows hard-line conservatives to deflect blame. Neoconservatives denounce the United States for the economic problems in Iran due to the sanctions regime. Furthermore, hostility toward the United States can be used as an excuse to suppress dissent and unify supporters.[8]

In contrast to the neoconservatives, reformists aligned with Khatami and Mousavi also argue for improving relations with other countries. Khatami specifically put this policy into action by denouncing terrorism and encouraging a dialogue among civilizations.[9]

Realism can be seen most clearly in the policies of conservatives and re-formists. Structural realism stresses the importance of state power, the survival of the state, and the insecure nature of global politics due to the anarchy of international relations.[10] Although efforts to specify a state's national interests are always difficult, many in Tehran have concluded that the survival of the Islamic Republic of Iran is fundamental to the country's national interests. Rafsanjani and Khatami believed that improving Iran's economy was also essential to Iran's national interests.

One conclusion that should be reached from Tehran's realism is that pursuit of a "grand bargain" is impractical. Some policymakers, such as Flynt Leverett, have argued that a grand bargain is the best solution to improving relations with Tehran: "The United States needs to pursue a 'grand bargain' with the Islamic Republic—that is, a broad based strategic understanding in which all of the outstanding bilateral differences between the two countries would be resolved as a package."[11] Leverett suggests that this agreement would include cooperation and compromise on Iran's nuclear program, support for terrorist organizations, security guarantees for Iran, and the lifting of sanctions on Iran. However, a grand bargain is unrealistic given Iran's history of realism, as well as Tehran's regional insecurity. In contrast to a grand bargain, a confidence-building approach that gradually builds trust between Tehran and other countries is a better course when dealing with the Islamic Republic.

The Early Years of the Revolution: Consolidating Domestic Power via Foreign Policy

The hostage crisis. On November 4, 1979, Americans working at the US embassy in Tehran were taken hostage and held for 444 days.[12] The hostage crisis had a dramatic impact on US–Iranian relations. Each day that the hostage crisis dragged on, with Americans being paraded around in blindfolds, was another day that the United States was being humiliated by Iran. President Carter's efforts to secure the release of the hostages all failed. Despite freezing Iranian assets in the United States, breaking diplomatic relations with Iran (a policy that largely continues to this day), imposing economic sanctions on Tehran, and authorizing a failed rescue attempt, the hostages remained in captivity.[13]

The Muslim Student Followers of the Imam's Line who took over the American embassy did so to keep Washington from restoring the shah to the throne. The students wanted to prevent a repeat of 1953.[14] The students clearly were not prepared for a prolonged crisis of more than a year. They had provisions for only three days.[15] These university students were also quickly entangled in a chaotic domestic situation. As Mark Bowden notes in his study of the hostage crisis, the students were swept up in a political storm: "The take-over of the US Embassy had ignited a great storm of anti-Americanism and anti-secularism, which swept aside any prospect of a conventional, Western-style nation. Religious conservatives were going to shape Iran's future, not the secular nationalists, socialists, and communists who had dominated the move-ment's educated class. The young leftist cleric who had 'advised' the students, Mousavi Khoeniha, had foreseen the possibility of this happening but had never guessed that it might work so well, so fast."[16]

The hostage crisis developed a political life of its own and one that the students quickly lost control over. The hostage crisis was hampered by misunder-standings and misguided policies in Washington. The Carter administration believed that it was "dealing with a religious fanatic."[17] Its inability to see that Khomeini had manipulated the situation for domestic purposes contributed to the crisis. Khomeini's reaction to the situation was to praise the hostage takers: "I have said repeatedly that the taking of hostages by our militant, committed Muslim students was a natural reaction to the blows our nation suffered at the hands of America."[18] Despite Khomeini's revulsion for "the Great Satan," his primary interest was in strengthening the hand of his domestic supporters.[19] As Takeyh notes, "Khomeini exploited them [the hostages] as a means of radi-calizing the populace, claiming that the Revolution was in danger from the manipulations of America and its internal accomplices."[20] Khomeni's support for the students contributed to the status of religious groups vying for power with the leftists in the aftermath of the Revolution. Thus taking Americans hostage was not motivated by fidelity to Islamic principles (it actually violated Islamic traditions of protecting visitors), but was based on domestic politics. In the hostage crisis we see that a domestic power struggle trumped Islam. Although holding Americans hostage at the embassy may have enhanced Khomeini's position domestically, it would have significant consequences in-ternationally. Tehran's hostility to the United States, and its willingness to ignore international law (diplomatic immunity) and international norms would have severe repercussions in its war with Iraq.

War with Iraq in the 1980s. In September 1980 Saddam Hussein attacked the nascent theocracy in Iran. A victory over the religious leaders in Tehran would not only increase his material wealth; it would enhance his status as a regional leader. The president of Iraq saw the Iranian Revolution as an oppor-tunity to take advantage of the inexperience of the clerics in Tehran. The revo-lutionaries had little military training, and they had killed or eliminated many uniformed officers perceived to be loyal to the deposed monarch. Given these perceived weaknesses in Tehran, Saddam Hussein did not envision a long or difficult conflict. He was mistaken in both of these assumptions.

The war with Iraq was the most threatening challenge that the Islamic Republic faced in its early years, and it demonstrated the realism at work in Tehran's foreign policy. In the first few years Tehran would encourage Iranians to rally around the religious flag. Ayatollah Khomeini encouraged Iranians to understand the war in religious terms: "It is not a question of a fight between one government and another. . . . This is a rebellion by blasphemy against Islam."[21] Khomeini constructed this conflict as a war between good and evil, and Islam and Saddam's secular Baath Party. Thus Iranians who fought and died for Allah and Islam would be martyrs: "We should all sacrifice our loved ones for the sake of Islam. If we are killed, we have performed our duty."[22]

The religious motivation helped to encourage many Iranians to sacrifice themselves for the theocracy. Their willingness to die for their religiously defined nation was one of the few advantages that Iran had over its neighbor. Iraq enjoyed the financial assistance of many states in the region, and it also had greater access to weapons in the fight against Iran. This initially resulted in Iraq's capture of thousands of miles of land within Iran. But the Islamic Republic would eventually recapture much of this land.[23] Many Western states, including Great Britain and the United States, offered military and intelligence support to Iraq because they did not want to see the Islamic Revolution spread throughout the region. Furthermore, there was lingering resentment from the hostage crisis, and Khomeini's hostility toward the international community.[24] Washington specifically helped Saddam Hussein to develop his military strategy with satellite photographs of Iranian troop movements. In addition, the United States made sure that Iraq had access to economic resources needed to continue the war.[25] Thus Tehran faced an enemy that had access to far greater resources and international support than it had.

Despite these disadvantages, Iran managed to recapture territory lost in the early years of the conflict, and it fought to a stalemate. After eight bloody years of war, Tehran agreed to a cease-fire negotiated by the United Nations. Although Khomeini did not want to compromise with Saddam Hussein, he eventually accepted this "poisoned chalice." Despite the difficulty of squaring compromise with the supreme leader's religious rhetoric, Khomeini understood the weakness of Iran's military. Furthermore, Baghdad's use of chemical weapons had a devastating effect on morale. The Iranian people had grown tired of religious martyrdom and the devastation of war. Thus Khomeini understood that the country's national interests required an end to the war. Although religion played a role in motivating the population, as the war labored on, the goal of spreading the Islamic Revolution took a backseat to the survival of the state.

Despite the military stalemate, the war did help Khomeini and his supporters to consolidate their power. In the fog of a religiously defined war, Khomeini's supporters removed those domestic critics and secular opposition figures who challenged their hold on power.[26]

International Politics

Because there is no global police force or world government to maintain stability in international relations, many states have adopted a realist approach to foreign policy. A realist approach to global politics includes pursuing a state's national interests, which are often defined in terms of national security and independence. Iran's fervent anti-Western rhetoric has led some makers of foreign policy in the West to mistakenly believe that Tehran is pursuing an irrational and radical religious foreign policy. However, this section argues that for much of the last three decades realism has dominated many foreign policy decisions.

US–Iranian Relations

Since the Islamic Revolution, Washington and Tehran have had a hostile relationship. As noted in chapter 2, for many Iranians this dates back to 1953, when the United States engineered the coup against Mossadeq, and gave military and economic support to an authoritarian monarch. Although there have been brief moments of cooperation, for the most part these two states have spent much of the last three decades criticizing each other. Despite the animosity, many of Tehran's policy decisions toward the United States have been rooted in realism.

Cooperation with the United States. The Iran–Contra scandal, as it was known in the United States, was a complicated set of policies in the Middle East and Latin America. The Reagan administration wanted to secure the release of Americans held hostage by Shia groups in Lebanon. In the 1980s a number of Western nationals had been taken hostage in Lebanon (including Terry Anderson).[27] The United States wanted Tehran to apply pressure to these Lebanese groups to secure the release of the American hostages.

To do so, the United States agreed to sell arms to Iran, using Israel as an intermediary. As the war with Iraq dragged on, much of Iran's military equipment was destroyed. Iran had a difficult time purchasing weapons because many states sided with Iraq. Khomeini's desire to spread the Islamic Revolution around the world, and his harsh comments about the West, hindered Iran's ability to purchase new military supplies from the West. Thus Tehran needed to work with Washington to fight Saddam Hussein's regime. The money from these arms sales was then used to support the Contras in Nicaragua.

Tehran's willingness to cooperate with two enemies, the "Great Satan" and Israel, demonstrates that realism would trump Islam if the national security needs of the state required it. Ultimately, Supreme Leader Khomeini would be forced to terminate this embarrassing relationship when it became public in November 1986.[28]

After Khomeini's death Ali Akbar Hashemi Rafsanjani was the most influential political leader in the country. Although a cleric, his primary interest as president was economic reform. As Ansari notes, "He was a shrewd politician and a merchant, with little time for Islamic austerity."[29] Rafsanjani's desire to improve Iran's economy motivated him to improve diplomatic relations with the United States. In an interview in 1994 he explained his reasoning: "I have always been opposed to completely breaking our ties with the United States, they provide us with much needed spare parts and we sell them petrol. Therefore, our economic ties have never been completely halted and some kind of dialogue must always exist. Although we pursue pragmatism in foreign policy, we will not be the first to initiate further dialogue with the Americans. They must first show goodwill by unfreezing our assets in America."[30]

Rafsanjani hoped to slowly improve relations with Washington through economic cooperation. The offer to Conoco, an American oil company, for a $1 billion contract was a step in this direction.[31] Beyond improved relations, it would have increased investment in Iran. This olive branch was rejected by the Clinton administration. President Clinton went further in March 1995, when he issued Executive Order 12957, which included "comprehensive sanctions" to "deal with the unusual and extraordinary threat to the national security, foreign policy, and economy of the United States constituted by the actions and policies of the Government of Iran." This was followed by the Iran-Libya Sanctions Act in 1996, which put sanctions on companies that invested more than $40 million in Iran's (or Libya's) energy industry.[32]

When Khatami, also a cleric, succeeded Rafsanjani, he continued the policy of engagement with the West. Khatami saw no difficulties with increasing economic ties: "From our point of view there are no obstacles preventing economic cooperation with the US."[33] He took a number of steps to lessen the tensions between the two countries. Khatami not only rejected terrorism; he also offered regret for the hostage crisis.[34] This was consistent with his views on realism and national interest. As one scholar notes, Khatami "insists that Iran's foreign policy is based on the principles and values of national interest, and in his speeches in the countryside has been known to say 'first comes Iran, then Islam.'"[35]

His efforts to improve relations with the United States echoed the wishes of many Iranian citizens. A poll taken in 2002 suggested that 74 percent of Iranians living in Tehran approved of opening a dialogue with Washington.[36] In 2008 a World Public Opinion Poll showed that 69 percent of Iranians favored talks with the United States.[37]

Many in the Clinton administration were unsure of how to deal with the new, soft-spoken president of Iran. The George W. Bush administration ignored Khatami's conciliatory gestures. Khatami's cooperation in Afghanistan after the terror attacks on September 11, 2001, did not result in better US–Iranian relations.[38] Iran accepted millions of Afghan refugees and agreed to assist US pilots if they went down in Iranian territory. This did not have an effect on the Bush administration. Bush's inclusion of Iran in the "Axis of Evil" with Iraq and North Korea in his 2002 State of the Union Address created problems in Tehran. Many Iranians resented the comparison with Saddam Hussein's Iraq. Not only did it weaken Khatami and the reformists who had gambled by trying to improve relations with the United States, but it also allowed other politicians to harden their position toward the United States. President Ahmadinejad's statement offers an example of this: "I have said many times that we would like to have good relations with everyone, including the United States. But these relations must be based on justice, fairness and mutual respect. . . . One can embark on a new period of talks. I've said that our absolute principle for these talks are fairness and mutual respect. We helped in Afghanistan. The result of that assistance was Mr. Bush directly threatening us with a military attack. For six years he has been engaged in similar talk against us."[39] Thus efforts by Iranian leaders to improve relations with Washington yielded few tangible results for Tehran.

Iranian Attempts to Improve Relations with Europe

As president, Rafsanjani tried to mend relations with Europe in an attempt to bolster the economy and decrease Iran's isolation. His efforts to reach out to Europe led some European states to normalize relations with Iran, and France and Germany sent their foreign ministers to Tehran.[40] However the killing of

Iranian exiles—including Shapour Bakhtiar in Paris, and Kurdish dissidents in Berlin—quashed this diplomatic outreach.[41]

President Khatami's efforts at engagement also went beyond the United States. He also tried to improve relations with many European states. While president, he embarked on a series of diplomatic visits to European countries, including Germany, France, and Italy.[42] This rapprochement was necessary after the assassinations in Europe. The European Union tried to strengthen Khatami, and the moderate reformists around him, through a policy of constructive dialogue in the late 1990s. Although Tehran saw improved economic relations with Europe during Khatami's presidency, President Ahmadinejad stepped back from some of Khatami's efforts. He placed more emphasis on the non-Western world, and concentrated more efforts on Latin and South America, including Venezuela, Brazil, and China.[43]

Iranian Foreign Policy in the Region: Islamic Support When Convenient

Although political elites in Tehran often spoke of assisting their Islamic brethren, support for Muslims in the Middle East did not always materialize. Ayatollah Khomeini spoke of spreading the Islamic Revolution: "Until the cry 'There is no God but God' resounds over the whole world, there will be a struggle."[44] Efforts to spread the Revolution were not always successful, nor were they a priority when other national interests were evident. Tehran's continuing support for Hamas and Hezbollah has not resulted in theocratic governments in those territories.

Furthermore, in the aftermath of Khomeini's death in 1989, many influential political leaders walked away from his rhetoric. Supreme Leader Khameini downplayed talk of exporting the Iranian Revolution when he said: "The export of the Revolution did not mean that we would rise up and throw our weight and power around and begin wars, forcing people to revolt and carry out revolutions. That was not the Imam's intention at all. This is not part of our policies and in fact it is against them. . . . This is what exporting the Revolution means: to enable all nations in the world to see that they are capable of standing on their own feet, resisting submission with all of their strength by relying on their own will and determination and by replacing their trust in God."[45]

Beyond the fact that Iranian leaders have not tried to export the Revolution in the aftermath of Khomeini's death, there were also significant efforts to improve relations with neighbors in the region, with the exception of Israel.

Khatami made special efforts to improve relations with Saudi Arabia, although this was particularly difficult. Both Saudi Arabia and Iran viewed themselves as religious rivals leading distinct religious sects. The Saudis did not appreciate Khomeini's harsh rhetoric, or his encouragement to Shiites living in Saudi Arabia to rebel. [46] Khatami's efforts in Saudi Arabia and in the Persian Gulf, as noted by Takeyh, were an example of the realism in Iranian foreign policy: "An entire range of trade, diplomatic, and security agreements were signed between the Islamic Republic and the Gulf Sheikdoms. In this way, Khatami managed finally to transcend Khomeini's legacy and to displace his ideological antagonism with policies rooted in pragmatism and self-interest."[47] And it is worth noting that Ahmadinejad has not reversed this policy.

Although Iran has tried to mend fences and improve relations with neighboring countries this has not always been a smooth process. Iran has had long, complicated relationships with some of its neighbors, especially Russia. Iranians have long resented Russian interference in Iranian politics in the twentieth century. More recently, Moscow has expressed concern about Iran's nuclear program, and supported some UN Security Council resolutions that include economic sanctions. President Medvedev also canceled the delivery of S-300 missiles to Tehran.[48] Despite the concern over Iran's nuclear program and its missiles, which are capable of hitting Moscow, Russia still has an economic interest in good relations with Tehran.[49] By one estimate Moscow exports to Iran totaled more than $3 billion in 2008.[50]

A number of Arab states also have difficult relations with Iran despite Khatami's efforts. Much of this stems from the fear of Iran's nuclear program. Political leaders in Oman, Bahrain, and Saudi Arabia have privately voiced their concerns about the nuclear program. According to one diplomatic cable, the king of Bahrain argued that Iran's nuclear program must be stopped: "The danger of letting it go on is greater than the danger of stopping it."[51]

Iran's policies, though not as threatening as Khomeini's calls to spread the Revolution, still have the ability to unnerve its neighbors. Protests across the Arab world in 2011, also known as the Arab Awakening, disquieted some of the monarchies in the Middle East to begin with and Iran's behavior did not help. At Friday prayers in February, Ayatollah Khamenei claimed that the Iranian Revolution had inspired the developments in Tunisia and Egypt: "Today's events in North Africa, Egypt and Tunisia and certain other countries have another sense for the Iranian nation. They have special meaning for the Iranian nation. This is the same as 'Islamic Awakening,' which is the result of the victory of the big revolution of the Iranian nation."[52]

Despite Khamenei's claim that Arab protesters were imitating the Iranian Revolution, many protesters throughout the Arab world have not invoked the Islamic Revolution of 1979, nor have they demanded a theocratic polity.[53] Iran tried to use these protests in Tunis, Cairo, and elsewhere to enhance its position as a regional power. Iran has already benefited from the political revolutions in Tunisia and Egypt because these countries' respective now-deposed leaders, Ben Ali and Hosni Mubarak, were American allies. The future leadership, including Islamic organizations, may be less deferential to Washington. Further, Iran has criticized Bahrain's use of force against protesters (largely Shiites) demanding greater freedom. The decision by the Sunni monarch, Hamad bin Isa al-Khalifa, to use lethal force and allow Saudi troops in the country only intensifies the proxy war going on between Saudi Arabia and Iran for influence in the region. The only country where protests specifically threaten an Arab ally is Syria. The Assad regime has had a long, productive relationship with Tehran. The demise of Bashir Assad's regime could produce a less friendly government in Damascus. Beyond the possible development of a new Sunni government with ties to Saudi Arabia, Tehran has other concerns about the future of Syria. The longer the conflict in Syria drags on, the weaker the Syrian regime will be. A greatly weakened Syria, even if Assad manages to hold on to power, would be unable to play a supportive role in regional politics. For all these reasons, Tehran has provided assistance to Assad's regime. As one US official noted, Iran has given Syria "weapons and teams of experts that have flown to Damascus to provide intelligence and eavesdropping capabilities to locate and suppress opposition networks."[54]

Ultimately, Iranian foreign policy offers support to Islamic groups in the region only when it is consistent with Iran's national interests. Thus financial and military support for Hezbollah was not done merely for the sake of Islamic solidarity. Rather, strengthening Hezbollah allowed Iran to enhance its status in the region. The State Department estimated that the Iranian government had used Bank Saderat to transfer at least $50 million to Hezbollah between 2001 and 2006.[55] Some estimates suggest that Iran spends anywhere from $25 million to $200 million in annual funding to Hezbollah.[56] By extension, Iran's political stock rose in the region when Hezbollah was able to hold off Israel during the war in the summer of 2006. That Hezbollah was able to stand up to the most powerful military force in the Middle East was a public relations victory, even if not a military victory.[57] This policy appears unlikely to change in the immediate future.[58]

Tehran's support for Shia groups in Iraq, such as Supreme Council for the Islamic Revolution in Iraq, is also an investment in Iran's national interests. Iran allowed prominent members of Iraq's Shia community to live in Iran during Baath Party rule under Saddam Hussein.[59] This was not merely generosity toward fellow Shiites; it was also a political investment in Iraqi politics. After the United States removed Saddam Hussein from power in 2003, elections were held in 2005 that saw various Shia groups come to power, including the Supreme Islamic Iraqi Council and Dawa.[60] Furthermore, Tehran could now be confident that there would no longer be a military threat from Iraq.

Tehran also demonstrated a willingness to ignore or neglect their Shia brethren when national security demands it. One sees realism at work in Iranian foreign policy toward Azerbaijan. Iran chose to support Christian Armenia over Shia Azerbaijan in the conflict over the territory of Nagorno-Karabakh. In a similar fashion Tehran did not actively assist the Chechens in their conflict against Russia. Although some of the Chechen fighters argued for an Islamic state as they sought to gain independence from Russia, Iran did not side with their Muslim brethren. More often than not, Tehran watched from the sidelines, claiming that this was a domestic matter for the parties to sort out. Iran opted not to confront the Russian bear in the north in spite of calls for Islamic solidarity.

In a similar fashion Tehran has opted for economic cooperation with China over support for China's Muslim citizens. China sells a number of products to Iran, including oil, arms, and electronics.[61] Iran needs these economic transactions not only because China "provides up to a third of Iran's petrol imports" but also because Chinese investments demonstrates financial commitments in the face of sanctions.[62] These economic opportunities outweigh any Islamic solidarity with Chinese Muslims. Even in Afghanistan, Iran appears more concerned with stability for their neighbor than in promoting a theocratic state.

When Religious Rhetoric Coincides with Realism

There were times when the religious rhetoric billowing from Friday prayers was consistent with the realism at the heart of Tehran's foreign policy. Although political rhetoric is often difficult to discern, when makers of foreign policy see this congruence, they should understand the commitment the regime is making to a policy. In examining Tehran's hostility toward Israel, concerns about the Palestinians, and the nuclear issue, one can see how realism and religious ideology reinforce each other.

Iran's Relationship with Israel

Although Tehran has long expressed its hostility toward Israel, its actions, often supported by religious themes, are consistent with realism. Furthermore, the Islamic Republic has been careful not to allow the religious rhetoric to push the country into radical policies that would threaten its national interests or its existence as an independent state. Although some scholars—Takeyh, for example—have suggested that Tehran's policies toward Israel exhibit a radical Islamic approach to foreign policy, I believe that most of the foreign policy decisions regarding Israel demonstrate more realpolitik than religious radicalism.[63] Iran's willingness to work with Israel, to acquire much-needed weapons in its war with Iraq, is just one example of the realism that has driven Iranian foreign policy. Assistance to religious groups in the region, both Hamas (Sunni) and Hezbollah (Shia), also demonstrate the overlap between religious rhetoric and realism.

The support that Iran has provided to Islamic groups, such as Hezbollah in Lebanon and Hamas in the Gaza Strip, is consistent with its religious ideology and realism. Although many religious leaders have issued verbal assaults on Israel, Tehran has not allowed the religious rhetoric to draw the state into a direct confrontation with Israel's superior military power.[64] For example, in June 2010, Hossein Salami, the deputy commander of the Islamic Revolutionary Guards Corps (IRGC), said that the IRGC had "no plan to escort humanitarian aid ships to Gaza."[65] Thus Iran was unwilling to confront Israel as the Turkish humanitarian ships had done a week before. In addition, there is no evidence that Iran has transferred chemical weapons to either Hamas or Hezbollah.

Material and verbal support for these groups allows Tehran to use its religious ideology to enhance its regional reputation. Iran's support has not crossed a critical threshold to jeopardize its national security by provoking a direct attack from Israel. In examining the conflict between Hamas and Israel at the end of 2008, one can see verbal support in public settings coupled with a cautious approach. Supreme Leader Khamenei prevented Iranians from becoming directly involved in the fighting. In January 2009 he said, "I thank the pious and devoted youth who have asked to go to Gaza, . . . but it must be noted that our hands are tied in this arena." Although he criticized countries such as Saudi Arabia or Egypt, the supreme leader made sure not to get drawn into the conflict.[66]

Harsh statements such as President Ahmadinejad's call to wipe Israel off the map can be viewed in a similar fashion. Severe rhetoric toward Israel is popular throughout many countries in the Middle East, and it allows Iranian leaders to demonstrate common cause with Arabs in the region. Criticism of the Zionist regime in Israel and support for the Palestinians has support in Iran and in the Arab world.[67] Thus support for groups such as Hamas and Hezbollah, along with harsh criticisms of Israel, demonstrate a powerful combination of realism and religious rhetoric in foreign policy.

Nuclear Policies in Iran

Developing nuclear energy has been a goal of Iran's leadership since the time of the shah. The shah sought to develop twenty-three nuclear power plants that could produce nuclear energy for the country. With the help of the French and Germans, and with the approval of the United States, Iran embarked on this nuclear project.[68] This project was shelved after the Revolution because the Islamic revolutionary leaders decided that Iran had other priorities that were more pressing. By the 1990s this view changed and Iran again began moving down the nuclear path.

One can understand the motivation to master the science of nuclear energy and potentially nuclear weapons. Possessing a nuclear weapon would reassure some in Iran that they would not be attacked by the United States or any other country. Washington's willingness to attack Afghanistan and Iraq has made some Iranian leaders understand their own vulnerability. At the same time, despite much provocation, the United States has not attacked a nuclear-armed North Korea. Thus it is not surprising that some in Tehran might see nuclear weapons as the true means of deterring an American attack or attempt at regime change.

Officially, Tehran has argued that it is only pursuing nuclear energy and not nuclear weapons. Nuclear energy is necessary, because Iran's oil and gas reserves are not unlimited. Even the supreme leader, who ultimately controls nuclear policy in Iran, has insisted that Iran is not interested in nuclear weapons. Khameini stated: "The Islamic Republic of Iran has repeatedly announced that in principle, based on Shari'a, it is opposed to the production and use of nuclear weapons."[69] Other Iranian leaders have echoed these remarks, including the mayor of Tehran—Mohammad Baqer Ghalibaf—saying that nuclear weapons are un-Islamic: "We don't need any atomic weapons or unconventional weapons. In our Islamic belief, these kinds of things are forbidden."[70]

Many in the international community have expressed skepticism that Iran is simply interested in nuclear energy. Various political leaders have voiced their apprehensions over a nuclear-armed Iran. Some have suggested that it would lead to nuclear proliferation, and a nuclear arms race in the Middle East. Ahmadinejad's offer to share its nuclear capabilities with other Islamic states was particularly alarming to many in the West. President Ahmadinejad's generous offer to the prime minister of Turkey that "with respect to the needs of Islamic countries, we are ready to transfer nuclear know-how to these countries" sent a chill down the spine of many diplomats in Europe, especially those within the reach of Iran's ballistic missiles.[71]

As a result of these nuclear efforts, regional adversaries such as Saudi Arabia and Jordan may try to develop their own nuclear capability to defend themselves against Iran. There is much instability in the region already (Iraq, fragile state of Lebanon, Israeli-Palestinian conflict, Arab Awakening, etc.), and a nuclear arms race would only complicate matters further. Former Secretary of State Hillary Clinton expressed this concern, saying that if Iran had nuclear weapons the results would be disastrous because other Middle Eastern leaders would say, "If Iran has a nuclear weapon, I better get one, too, to protect my people."[72]

The country that is most concerned about Iran's nuclear program may be Israel. Israel warned the United States and others that it will not allow Iran's nuclear program to cross certain lines. Given its willingness in the past to strike at other potential nuclear plants in the region (Osirak in Iraq in 1981), this is not a meaningless threat. Throughout 2012 Prime Minister Netanyahu stated that Israel would not allow Iran to have the capability of producing nuclear weapons because he views that as an existential threat to his country. Some scholars have also voiced concerns about regional allies or a confrontation between Iran and Israel:

> It seems more likely that Iran would become increasingly aggressive once it acquired a nuclear capability, that the United States' allies in the Middle East would feel greatly threatened and so would increasingly accommodate Tehran, that the United States' ability to promote and defend its interests in the region would be diminished, and that further nuclear proliferation, with all the dangers that entails, would occur. The greatest concern in the near term would be that an unstable Iranian-Israeli nuclear contest would emerge, with a significant risk that either side would launch a first strike on the other despite the enormous risks and costs involved.[73]

An Israeli attack would encounter a number of problems, including the fact that Iran's nuclear facilities are spread out throughout the country and would not be as easy to eliminate. Some in Israel's intelligence community have also warned that attacking Iran would not be wise.[74] Former American military leaders, including General David Petraeus and Admiral Mike Mullen, also voiced concerns about an Israeli attack on Iran. They argued that it would destabilize the region.[75] Furthermore, an Israeli attack would likely create a rally around the flag response from many Iranians.

Despite Iran's efforts to master nuclear technology, their nuclear program has experienced a number of setbacks in recent years. A number of Iranian nuclear scientists have been assassinated. In addition, a malicious software program—Stuxnet—disrupted Iran's nuclear centrifuges. This computer attack is believed to have set Iran's nuclear program back a few years. Some computer security experts suspect that the Stuxnet worm was created by a Western government, possibly the United States or Israel, to sabotage Iran's nuclear program.[76] In 2011, Iran reported a problem at the Bushehr nuclear reactor that required Tehran to unload nuclear fuel.[77] Although this will not result in a cessation of Iran's nuclear program, it does suggest that Iran is still trying to master the scientific knowledge required to develop nuclear energy and possibly nuclear weapons. It is reasonable to assume that Iran is, if not currently developing nuclear weapons, holding out the potential for their development at a later point in time.[78]

It is worth mentioning that for all the difficulties associated with Iran's nuclear program, Tehran has preserved a working, albeit strained relationship with the International Atomic Energy Agency (IAEA), the organization that monitors the worldwide development of nuclear energy under the Nuclear Non-Proliferation Treaty. Iran signed the Nuclear Non-Proliferation Treaty in 1968 and thus has the legal right to develop a peaceful nuclear energy program. Despite these legal rights, the IAEA has complained about the lack of full cooperation from the Islamic Republic.

In the spring of 2006, the IAEA concluded that Iran had not suspended its uranium enrichment program, and in the fall of that same year, it concluded that Tehran had expanded the program. Iran has repeatedly rejected any halt to its uranium enrichment. In addition, the IAEA has complained that Iran has violated its legal obligations under the treaty by not fully disclosing its nuclear activities.[79] Two years later the IAEA again voiced concerns about Iran's nuclear program.[80] The report in May 2008 noted "that the Agency currently has no information—apart from the uranium metal document— on the actual design or manufacture by Iran of nuclear material components of a nuclear weapon." Thus the IAEA had found no evidence that Iran was pursuing nuclear weapons. Four months later the IAEA again complained of a lack of complete cooperation concerning information on the production of nuclear warheads.[81] In 2011, the IAEA issued its most critical report to date. The report expressed concerns about "the possible military dimension" to Iran's nuclear program. It specifically stated the following concerns:

> The information indicates that Iran has carried out the following activities that are relevant to the development of a nuclear explosive device:
> —Efforts, some successful, to procure nuclear related and dual use equipment and materials by military related individuals and entities;
> —Efforts to develop undeclared pathways for the production of nuclear materials;
> —The acquisition of nuclear weapons development information and documentation from a clandestine nuclear supply network; and
> —Work on the development of indigenous design of a nuclear weapon including the testing of components.[82]

Although the IAEA did not produce a smoking gun, it did conclude by saying "while the Agency continues to verify the non-diversion of declared nuclear materials at the nuclear facilities and LOFs (locations outside facilities) declared by Iran under its safeguards agreement, as Iran is not providing the necessary cooperation, including by not implementing its additional protocol, the Agency is unable to provide credible assurance about the absence of undeclared nuclear material and activities in Iran, and therefore to conclude that all nuclear material in Iran is in peaceful activities."

Iran has engaged in activities relevant to the development of a nuclear weapon; however, there is no evidence that Iran has mastered all the scientific and technical aspects of a nuclear weapon. Immediately after the report's publication, numerous leaders throughout Iran denounced it as inaccurate and biased. Given Tehran's lack of transparency in the past, international distrust is understandable.[83]

Beyond Iran's relationship with the IAEA, there also have been a couple of confidence-building measures to prevent Iran from using nuclear fuel for a nuclear weapon. In October 2009, the IAEA had negotiated a deal where Iran would send 75 percent of its nuclear fuel to Russia for further enrichment and return to Iran in the form of fuel rods. This would prevent Iran from building a nuclear weapon because it would have too little fuel on hand.[84] Some conservatives, such as Ali Larjani, criticized the nuclear swap as a trick by the West. Ahmadinejad made some positive statements about the deal, suggesting divisions within the conservative movement.[85] Another deal Iran negotiated with Brazil and Turkey would have sent Iran's nuclear fuel to Turkey as part of a fuel swap. Both these efforts failed.[86]

Given the lack of full cooperation from Tehran and the persistent questions concerning its enrichment of uranium, the West has sought to place economic sanctions on Iran. The purpose of the sanctions is to discourage Iran from developing nuclear weapons. Washington has led the way by placing sanctions on a number of entities in Iran, including Bank Mellat and the IRGC, due to their involvement in the nuclear program.[87] The sanctions regime has not been universally endorsed even within the United States. The nonpartisan US Government Accountability Office (GAO) issued a report in 2008 questioning the efficacy of the sanctions program. The report stated, "US officials and experts report that US sanctions have specific impacts on Iran; however, the extent of such impacts is difficult to determine."[88] The GAO specifically referred to $20 billion in contracts that Iran signed with foreign firms. Many in Iran, including Ahmadinejad, also dismissed the sanctions regime as ineffective and irrelevant. It is also worth noting that Tehran has suffered from economic sanctions since the revolution. Thus many in the Islamic Republic believe they can weather the latest phase of the economic sanctions storm.

The Obama administration strongly disputed this claim and argued for the efficacy of the sanctions region. It notes that Iran's oil fields have suffered due to sanctions and lack of investment especially from the West. In testimony before Congress, Robert Einhorn, special adviser for nonproliferation and arms control, explained that "at least $50–60 billion in oil and gas development deals have either been put on hold or have been discontinued in the last few years—due in part to our conversations with companies about the threat of ISA [Iran Sanctions Act] sanctions." He went on to add that Tehran had engaged in various diplomatic efforts (threats and incentives) with other states to vote against United Nations Security Council Resolution 1929.[89] If sanctions were not hurting the regime, Tehran would not need to engage in diplomatic efforts to undermine the sanctions.

Despite the question concerning the efficacy of sanctions, the Obama administration has continued to strengthen the sanctions regime against Iran. These more stringent sanctions can be seen in UN Security Council Resolution 1929 (passed in June 2010) and the Comprehensive Iran Sanctions Accountability and Divestment Act (passed in July 2010).[90] These sanctions were described by William Burns, undersecretary for political affairs at the State Department, as "the strongest and most comprehensive set of sanctions that the Islamic Republic of Iran has ever faced."[91] Burns went on to describe the most critical elements of Resolution 1929: "Targeting the central role of the IRGC in Iran's proliferation efforts; banning for the first time all Iran activities related to ballistic missiles that could deliver a nuclear weapon; sharply limiting Iran's ability to use the international financial system to fund and facilitate nuclear and missile proliferation; and for the first time highlighting formally potential links between Iran's energy sector and its nuclear ambitions. Russia's partnership was particularly crucial to passage of such an effective resolution, which led directly to its enormously important cancellation of the S-300 surface to air missile sale to Iran."[92]

The State Department estimates that Iran could be losing more than $50 billion in energy investments.[93] Burns went on to state that a number of multinational corporations have already pulled out of Iran or limited their economic transactions with Iran, including Daimler, Toyota, Deutsche Bank, HSBC, Royal Dutch Shell, Reliance, and Lukoil.[94] The French energy company Total decided against an investment project in Iran's South Pars gas field, saying that the project was politically too risky.[95] This hurts Iran's energy development, which could have increased Iran's gas exports and the economic profit that comes with it. The European Union, Canada, Japan, South Korea, Norway, and Australia also have all announced economic sanctions on Iran. Russia voted for Resolution 1929 and even canceled the S-300 air defense system.[96] Even China has tentatively supported the sanctions, including decreasing its crude oil imports from Iran in 2010.[97]

Given Iran's continuing defiance, the Obama administration took the sanctions regime a step further. The National Defense Authorization Act of 2012 put further pressure on Iran by "shrinking Iran's oil export markets and isolating its Central Bank from the world financial system."[98] In addition, the European Union ban on the purchase of crude oil from Iran went into effect in July 2012. These actions contributed to a 12 percent decline in Iranian oil production and a decrease in the number of states willing to buy Iranian oil.[99]

The sanctions regime is an attempt by some in the international community to cajole Tehran into cooperating in a more transparent fashion. It has also had an effect on domestic politics. Some politicians, including Rafsanjani, have called for a more pragmatic and less confrontational approach to nuclear negotiations.[100] However, Tehran has not yet bowed to this pressure by reducing its production of uranium.

Although many in the international community have voiced concerns about a nuclear Iran, many within the country support the nuclear program: "84 percent said that it was very important for Iran to have a full-fuel cycle nuclear program."[101] A poll taken in 2009 suggested that the majority of Iranians want the government to develop nuclear power. A total of 55 percent said they supported only the development of nuclear power, whereas 38 percent said they supported the development of nuclear power and atomic bombs.[102] This is consistent with Ahmadinejad's efforts to turn the right of nuclear energy into a source of national pride. Many Iranians question the double standards that exist in global politics. Some countries (India, Pakistan, and Israel) possess nuclear weapons but are not threatened with sanctions, whereas other nuclear powers (the United States, the United Kingdom, and France) debate sanctions at the United Nations Security Council. As Seyed Hossein Mousavian, a former adviser to Ali Larjani, noted, "It is simply not acceptable for P5+1 countries, which controls 98 per cent of the world's stockpile of nuclear weapons, to deprive others from the pursuit of peaceful nuclear energy and fuel cycle."[103] It is easy to understand why Iranians believe they are trapped in an unfair system.

Contradiction between Religious Rhetoric and Realpolitik

Policymakers around the world must also be aware of circumstances where the religious rhetoric directed toward domestic audiences directly refutes the realism that often guides Tehran's actions in international relations. There have been a few occasions where the realism that influenced foreign policy was contrary to the religious rhetoric often used in the domestic environment. In these instances political elites in Tehran must engage in a careful balancing act to ensure their legitimacy.

Iran's arms deal with the United States and Israel is the best example of an incongruity between realism and religious oratory. Many hard-line conservatives in Iran demanded to know who had betrayed the principles of the Revolution by cooperating not only with the "Great Satan" but also with Israel. Supreme Leader Khomeini put an end to this embarrassing policy and criticized members of Parliament who wanted someone to answer for this policy by saying "you should not create schism. This is contrary to Islam."[104]

The arms deal between the United States and Iran proves Tehran's willingness to put realism and survival of the state above the religious ideology of the Revolution. It also demonstrates the difficulties that arise when policies directly contradict religious rhetoric and require a direct intervention by the supreme leader.

Implications for Makers of Foreign Policy

Given the realism at the heart of many foreign policy decisions in Tehran, national leaders around the world have guidance when dealing with the Islamic Republic. Policymakers should develop policies toward Iran with an understanding of Iranian national interest, and the realism pursued by Tehran. Actions that threaten the regime or the survival of the state will produce a hostile reaction from Iran. Policies that contribute to shared interests and common goals will likely result in greater cooperation from Tehran. As Kayhan Barzegar, an analyst at the Centre for Scientific Research and Middle East Strategic Studies (a think tank with ties to the supreme leader) noted: "If Iran faces threats, it adopts a confrontational strategy designed to safeguard its fundamental interests. That was the case in Iraq when the US harbored aggressive aims towards us. . . . But once our security interests are met, Iran's foreign policy sheds its more ideological trappings and reverts to a pragmatic form of realpolitik."[105]

One conclusion to draw from the realism of Iran's foreign policy is that the George W. Bush administration's aggressive policies and harsh rhetoric toward Iran were a mistake. Nick Burns, a former State Department adviser in the Bush administration, came to this conclusion: "We had advocated regime change. We had a very threatening posture toward Iran for a number of years. It didn't produce any movement whatsoever."[106] Thus this aggressive approach increased tensions between the two countries without producing any security gains.

Although the change in American presidents offered an opportunity to improve relations between the two countries, this was a very limited opportunity. Although President Obama assumed the office without the baggage of President George W. Bush (descriptions of the Axis of Evil) he was not operating with a blank slate. A poll conducted in 2009 suggested that most Iranians (72 percent) did not have much confidence in President Obama.[107] Furthermore, Obama must deal with a long legacy of failed policies. In January 2009, President Ahmadinejad greeted the new American president with a demand for an apology for "crimes committed against Iran," including the 1953 coup and US support for Iraq in the 1980s.[108] Though Obama has gone further than his predecessor by offering Tehran a less hostile government in Washington, this alone did not result in improved relations.

President Obama inherited a complicated and hostile relationship dating back to the 1950s. To deal with the decades of distrust, Washington will need to construct policies that demonstrate respect and coincide with Tehran's national interests. American policies that encourage regime change should be avoided, given Iran's resentment of past foreign invasions and interference. Treating Tehran with respect would lessen the perceived threat from Washington and could induce greater cooperation on regional issues. The administration's efforts to include Iran at a conference on Afghanistan in March 2009 were a step in the direction of mutual respect. Iran's participation in a conference in Bonn in December 2011 also showed that Tehran understands that there are areas where they shared some interests with Washington.

Working with Tehran on Afghan issues would also further both countries' mutual interests. Although Tehran does not want tens of thousands of foreign troops near its borders, it does want a stable Afghanistan. A stable Afghanistan would produce fewer refugees. The Office of the UN High Commissioner for Human Rights estimated that there were more than 900,000 registered Afghan refugees in Iran.[109] Iran also desires a stable government that can control its production of opium. One Iranian official, Esmaeel Ahmadi-Moghadam, Iran's police chief, suggested that some 3,000 tons of opium entered Iran from Afghanistan in one year alone.[110] Because Iran has an estimated 2 million drug addicts, it does not want to see lawlessness or an increase in production from poppy fields in Afghanistan.[111] A strong, stable government in Kabul that can control Afghanistan is something that both Tehran and Washington would be keen to see. Thus the United States should make a concerted effort to work with Tehran on Afghan issues.

Washington's and Tehran's security interests also coincide in Iraq. At the end of 2011, the United States withdrew its military forces from Iraq. Instability in Iraq would create problems for Washington, especially if Baghdad were engulfed in chaos, bloodshed, or political infighting among Sunnis, Shiites, and Kurds. Likewise, Iran wants a stable and secure Iraq, preferably one run by its Shiite allies. The development of increased violence or a civil war in Iraq would create major problems for both Tehran and Washington. Although Tehran has been accused of providing weapons to different groups in Iraq (some who have killed Americans) in the past, with the withdrawal of American military forces, Iran does not want to see an outbreak of violence in the future. Thus it is in both countries' mutual interests to cooperate in Iraq. This would also have the additional benefit of improving relations between the United States and Iran, which could be the basis for cooperation on other issues.

There are additional reasons to believe that cooperation might stimulate additional benefits. Easing relations with Washington might help to encourage better relations with the rest of the world. Although many Iranians would prefer not to be isolated from the global community, some in Europe would also prefer to see improved relations with Iran, especially if Tehran were more open about its nuclear program. Europe has been vulnerable to gas disruptions from Russia. In December 2008 and January 2009, some European states suffered from Russia's contract dispute with Ukraine. Thus investment in Iran's energy production could provide Europe with an alternate source of gas. Further development of the gas sector would also be in Tehran's economic interests. Thus the possibility exists for improved relations between Tehran and Washington and other foreign capitals. Although it will take time to develop the trust needed to improve relations significantly, even the Supreme Leader Khamenei suggested that it would be possible to improve relations with Washington in the future.

Conclusion

When examining Iranian foreign policy during the last few decades, scholars have seen Tehran pursue realism in its foreign policy. Although we have heard much religious rhetoric emanating from Friday prayers, by and large, Iranian leaders, with the exception of the early years of the Revolution, have been guided by realpolitik. Knowing that realism, and not a radical Islamic ideology, influences Iranian foreign policy should reassure makers of foreign policy.

Tehran has demonstrated a willingness to deal with its sworn enemies (the United States and Israel in the 1980s) to ensure its survival. Thus religious rhetoric about the "Great Satan" or the Zionist regime took a backseat to the national interests of the state. Even Tehran's pursuit of nuclear energy, and possibly nuclear weapons, can be viewed in terms of the state's national interests. Some in Iran believe that nuclear weapons would ensure the survival of the regime because the United States would not invade a nuclear-armed Iran as it invaded Iraq and Afghanistan. Although the wars in Afghanistan and Iraq have removed some threats (Saddam Hussein and the Baath Party), Iran is still in an unstable region. Tehran's lack of dependable allies contributes to its insecurity. Iran's first priority is self-preservation, which may be enhanced with nuclear capabilities.

Backing for Islamic groups such as Hamas and Hezbollah, though consistent with the religious ideology of the Revolution, is also compatible with Tehran's national interests. Iran's continued support—both materially and rhetorically—for Hezbollah has given Iran legitimacy within the Middle East. That Iran's affiliated group was able to survive Israel's military campaign in the summer of 2006 and maintain its influence in Lebanon contributed to the credibility and status of Hezbollah in the Middle East, and by extension those of its backer, Iran.

Ultimately, if makers of foreign policy want to see more cooperation and less confrontational policies from Tehran, they should collaborate on shared interests. Threatening Tehran has not produced any significant policy goals. However, working with Tehran on regional issues may open the door to finding accommodation on more difficult issues such as transparency on the nuclear program. This chapter has argued that foreign leaders need to understand that Iran is a state that is motivated by traditional national interests more than by religious ideology, despite its rhetoric. Understanding the motivation for Iranian foreign policy may be the first step toward a more cooperative relationship with the rest of the world. It will at least produce fewer misunderstandings in international relations.

Notes

1. This chapter builds on my earlier work "Islamic Realpolitik: Two-Level Iranian Foreign Policy," *International Journal on World Peace* 26, no. 4 (December 2009): 7–35.

2. Ray Takeyh, *Hidden Iran* (New York: Times Books, 2006), 2; Ali Ansari, *Confronting Iran* (New York: Basic Books, 2006); Ken Pollack, *The Persian Puzzle* (New York: Random House, 2004).

3. Wm Scott Harrop, "Muhammad Khatami: A Dialogue beyond Paradox," in *The Iranian Revolution at 30* (Washington, DC: Middle East Institute, 2009). Available at www .mideasti.org.

4. Akbar Ganji, the journalist and dissident called him "the latter-day sultan," given how extensive his powers are in domestic and foreign policy. Akbar Ganji, "The Latter-Day Sultan: Power and Politics in Iran," *Foreign Affairs* 87, no. 6 (November–December 2008): 45–66.

5. Article 52: "The foreign policy of the Islamic Republic of Iran is based upon the rejection of all forms of domination, both the exertion of it and submission to it, the preservation of the independence of the country in all respects and its territorial integrity, the defense of the rights of Muslims, nonalignment with respect to the hegemonist superpowers, and the maintenance of mutually peaceful relations with all nonbelligerent states."

6. The Supreme National Security Council is a body of high-ranking officials that are responsible for foreign policy, military, and intelligence operations.

7. Sandra Mackey, *The Iranians: Persia, Islam and the Soul of a Nation* (New York: Plume, 1998), 344.

8. International Crisis Group, *US–Iranian Engagement: The View from Tehran*, Middle East Briefing 28 (Tehran/Brussels: International Crisis Group, 2009), 2.

9. Conservatives and Reformists differ more on domestic social policy.

10. Various realists emphasize some theoretical concepts more than others. But most acknowledge that because the international system is anarchic states must be concerned with the security and survival of the state. To ensure the survival of the state, leaders must enhance their military and economic capabilities. Thus power, although sometimes difficult to measure, is an important aspect of realism. For a discussion of realism, see Jack Donnelly, *Realism in International Relations* (Cambridge: Cambridge University Press, 2000).

11. Flynt Leverett, *Dealing with Tehran: Assessing US Diplomatic Options towards Iran* (New York: Century Foundation, 2006), available at www.tcf.org. The author served on the National Security Council. See also Ted Galen Carpenter, "Toward a Grand Bargain with Iran," *Mediterranean Quarterly* 18, no. 1 (Winter 2007): 12–27.

12. This was not the first time this had occurred. An initial overtaking of the embassy occurred in February. Some of the hostages—African Americans and women—were released prior to Reagan's inauguration. The remaining hostages were ultimately released after Ronald Reagan had taken the oath of office. Some Iranians ironically believed that they would have better relations with Reagan, a Republican, than with the Democrat Carter. Some have argued that Khomeini and the revolutionaries struck a secret deal with the Reagan administration to have the hostages released after Reagan was inaugurated. See especially Abol Hassan Bani Sadr, *My Turn to Speak: Iran, the Revolution and Secret Deals with the United States* (Arlington, VA: Brassey's, 1991), chap. 3.

13. Ansari, *Confronting Iran*, 89.

14. That President Carter had allowed the shah entry into the United States on October 22, 1979, for medical treatment only made Iranian hostility worse.

15. Mark Bowden, *Guests of the Ayatollahs* (New York: Grove Press, 2006), 12.

16. Ibid., 140.

17. Mackey, *Iranians*, xix.

18. Khomeini, *Islam and Revolution: Writings and Declarations of Imam Khomeini*, translated and annotated by Hamid Algar (Berkeley, CA: Mizan Press, 1981), 306. Many accounts suggest that Khomeini was not informed of the students' plans prior to the event. He endorsed their actions after the fact. Bowden, *Guests*, 13–14, 94.

19. He said, "America is the number one enemy of the deprived and oppressed people in the world. There is no crime America will not commit in order to maintain its political, economic, cultural and military domination of those parts of the world where it predominates. Were we to compromise with America and the other superpowers, we would not suffer from these misfortunes. But our nation is no longer ready to submit to humiliation and abjection; it prefers a bloody death to a life of shame. We are ready to be killed and we have made a covenant with God to follow the path of our leader, the Lord of the Martyrs." Khomeini, *Islam and Revolution*, 305.

20. Takeyh, *Hidden Iran*, 24. Bani-Sadr echoes these views when he says that "the purpose of taking the hostages was to unify the power structure." Bani-Sadr, *My Turn*, 49. See also Bowden, *Guests*, 94.

21. Robin Wright, *In the Name of God* (New York: Simon & Schuster, 1989), 88. See also Gary Sick, *All Fall Down* (New York: Penguin Books, 1986), xxiv.

22. Wright, *In the Name of God*, 87.

23. Wright suggests that Iraq had "a five to one advantage in tanks, a nine to one edge in heavy artillery, and a six to one advantage in warplanes." Wright, *In the Name of God*, 25, 28.

24. Mohammed Ayoob, "Challenging Hegemony: Political Islam and the North-South Divide," *International Studies Review* 9, no. 4 (2007): 629–43, at 632.

25. Wright, *In the Name of God*, 175.

26. Sick, *All Fall Down*, xx. See also Mackey, *Iranians*, 322.

27. Tehran aided in obtaining Anderson's release. Congress had legislated against support to the Contras; Mackey, *Iranians*, 326–27.

28. Kasra Naji, *Ahmadinejad: The Secret History of Iran's Radical Leader* (Berkeley: University of California Press, 2008), 142.

29. Ansari, *Confronting Iran*, 119.

30. Quoted by Mehdi Moslem, *Factional Politics in Post-Khomeini Iran* (Syracuse, NY: Syracuse University Press, 2002), 225.

31. Unfortunately for him, this was rejected because of various political pressure by groups such as the American Israeli Public Affairs Committee. Ansari, *Confronting Iran*, 142.

32. Pollack, *Persian Puzzle*, 287.

33. Takeyh, *Hidden Iran*, 121.

34. Ansari, *Confronting Iran*, 155.

35. Barbara Rieffer-Flanagan, "Improving Democracy in Religious Nation-States: Norms of Moderation and Cooperation in Ireland and Iran," *Muslim World Journal of Human Rights* 4, no. 2 (2007): 17.

36. Bahram Rajaee, "Deciphering Iran: The Political Evolution of the Islamic Republic and US Foreign Policy after Sept. 11," *Comparative Studies of South Asia, Africa and the Middle East* 24, no. 1 (2004): 165.

37. International Crisis Group, *US–Iranian Engagement*, 3.

38. Iran also pledged over $500 million in aid to Afghanistan starting in 2002. Thus we see that in Afghanistan, American and Iranian national interests overlapped. Rajaee, 166.

39. Interview with the *New York Times*, September 26, 2008. In addition, some neoconservatives do not want the reformists to get credit for improving relations with the United States for the domestic impact it may have.

40. Shahriar Sabet-Saeidi, "Iranian-European Relations: A Strategic Partnership," in *Iran's Foreign Policy: From Khatami to Ahmadinejad*, edited by Anoushiravan Ehteshami and Mahjoob Zweiri (Reading, UK: Ithaca Press, 2008), 58.

41. Rafsanjani and other leading political figures were implicated in the assassinations at the Mykonos restaurant in Berlin. See Roya Hakakian, *Assassins of the Turquoise Palace* (New York: Grove Press, 2011).

42. Ansari, *Confronting Iran*, 167.

43. Sabet-Saeidi, "Iranian-European Relations," 57.

44. Quoted by Robin Wright, *The Last Great Revolution: Turmoil and Transformation in Iran* (New York: Alfred A. Knopf, 2000), 66.

45. Moslem, *Factional Politics*, 15.

46. Khomeini called the House of Saud "a bunch of pleasure-seeking mercenaries." Quoted by Mackey, *Iranians*, 312.

47. Takeyh, *Hidden Iran*, 69.

48. David Sanger and Andrew Kramer, "U.S. Lauds Russia on Barring Arms for Iran," *New York Times*, September 22, 2010, www.nytimes.com/2010/09/23/world/europe/23prexy.html. . . .

49. One of the cables leaked by WikiLeaks suggested that Iran had obtained missiles from North Korea with a range of 2,000 miles. That would give Iran the ability to hit Moscow. William Broad, James Glanz, and David Sanger, "Iran Fortifies Its Arsenal with the Aid of North Korea," *New York Times*, November 28, 2010, www.nytimes.com/2010/11/29/world/middleeast/29missiles.htm.

50. Andrei Shleifer and Daniel Treisman, "Why Moscow Says No: A Question of Russian Interests, Not Psychology," *Foreign Affairs* 90, no. 1 (January–February 2011): 122–38, at 135.

51. David Sanger, James Glanz, and Jo Becker, "Around the World, Distress over Iran," *New York Times*, November 28, 2010, www.nytimes.com/2010/11/29/world/middle east/29iran/html.

52. Friday Prayers at Tehran University, February 4 2011, www.leader.ir/langs/EN/print.php?sec=content&id=7774. He repeated these claims at a talk on April 3, 2011.

53. Rashid Khalidi, "Reflections on the Revolution in Tunisia and Egypt," *Foreign Policy*, February 24, 2011, http://mideast.foreignpolicy.com/posts/2011/02/24/reflections_on_the_revolutions_in_tunisia_and_egypt.

54. Shahram Chubin, "Iran and the Arab Spring: Ascendancy Frustrated," *GRC Gulf Papers*, September 2012, 34.

55. Jeffrey Feltman, "Acting Assistant Secretary, Bureau of Near Eastern Affairs, Testimony before the Subcommittee on Near Eastern and South Central Asian Affairs of the Senate Committee on Foreign Relations," June 8, 2010, Washington, DC.

56. Alexander Wilner and Anthony Cordesman suggest that Iran's financial and military support for Hezbollah is about $100 million a year. Alexander Wilner and Anthony Cordesman, "US and Iranian Strategic Competition: The Gulf Military Balance," Center for Strategic and International Studies, November 2, 2011, 67. Thanassis Cambanis, *A Privilege to Die* (New York: Free Press, 2010), 221. While Cambanis suggests that Hezbollah has some independence and does not take orders from Tehran, he acknowledges the benefits to Iran: "At any rate, without Hezbollah Iran would lose much of its ability to project power, pose an active threat to Israel and perhaps most important, influence Arab politics," p. 225.

57. Ze'ev Schiff, "Israel's War with Iran," *Foreign Affairs* 85, no. 6 (November–December 2006): 23–31.

58. In January 2011, the speaker of the Majlis, Ali Larjani, stated Iran's continuing support for Hamas and Hezbollah: "It is Iran's policy to fight against the global arrogance and support the oppressed, so we say openly that we back Hezbollah and Hamas." *Tehran Times*, "Iran Will Stand by Hezbollah and Hamas," January 5, 2011, www.tehrantimes.com/NCMS/2007.asp?code=233569.

59. In May 2007, SCIRI changed its name to the Supreme Islamic Iraqi Council.

60. According to some leaked cables, Iran has also sent over $100 million to political groups in Iraq with some $70 million going to ISCI. The cable also showed Tehran's pragmatism by their willingness to fund Kurdish and Sunni groups as well. Michael Gordon, "Meddling Neighbors Undercut Iraq," *New York Times*, December 5, 2010, www.nytimes.com/2010/12/06/world/middleeast/06wikileaks-ir. . . .

61. Erica Downs and Suzanne Maloney, "Getting China to Sanction Iran," *Foreign Affairs* (March–April 2011): 20.

62. International Crisis Group, *The Iran Nuclear Issue: The View from Beijing*, Asia Briefing 100 (Beijing/Brussels: International Crisis Group, 2010), 5.

63. Takeyh argues that in Tehran's approach to Israel it is not upholding realism: "During the last two decades Iran has gradually displaced ideological imperatives with national interest calculations as a guide to its international policy, but this trajectory has not affected its approach to Israel, which still reflects the lingering influence of its revolutionary Islamic heritage," p. 190.

64. Supreme Leader Khamenei stated his opposition to Israel and its people in September 2008 saying, "They (Israelis) are partners to occupying the land and possessions of Palestinian people and are the instruments of the Zionist authorities." Nazila Fathi, "Iran's Chief Cleric Says Country Is Not a Friend to Israelis," *New York Times*, September 20, 2008, www.nytimes.com./2008/09/20/world/middleeast/20iran.html.

65. "No Plan to Escort Gaza Bound Ships," *Tehran Times*, June 15, 2010, www.tehran times.com/NCMS/2007.asp?code=221355.

66. Michael Slackman, "Iran Gives Hamas Enthusiastic Support, but Discreetly, Just in Case," *New York Times*, January 13, 2009, www.nytimes.com/2009/01/13/world/ middleeast/13iran.html.

67. It is worth mentioning that some have questioned the translation of his phrase. Naji argues that a more accurate translation would be: "This Jerusalem-occupying regime must vanish from the pages of time." Kasra Naji, *Ahmadinejad: The Secret History of Iran's Radical Leader* (Berkeley: University of California Press, 2008), 140. Neither translation would likely reassure Israel. However, the latter is far less of a direct threat. Of course, he is not alone in expressing hostility toward Israel. Khomeini also referred to Israel as "that cancerous growth in the Middle East" in a message on September 24, 1979. Khomeini, *Islam and Revolution*, 276.

68. Naji, *Ahmadinejad*, 114.

69. "Islamic Law Prohibits Production of Nuclear Arms: Leader," *Tehran Times*, January 13, 2008. www.tehrantimes.com/index_view.asp?code=161066. He reiterated these views in June of 2008: "You know the Iranian nation is in principle and on religious grounds against the nuclear weapon. Nuclear weapons only incur high costs and have no use to us." Nazila Fathi, "Chief Cleric Says Iran Does Not Seek Nuclear Arms," *New York Times*, June 4, 2008, www.nytimes.com/2008/06/04/world/middleeast/04iran.html. He issued a fatwa in 2005 prohibiting the development of nuclear weapons. Michael Slackman, "Some See Iran as Ready to Strike a Deal," *New York Times*, October 15, 2009.

70. Alan Cowell, "Tehran's Mayor Speaks of Making Iran Less Isolated," *New York Times*, January 27, 2008, www.nytimes.com./2008/01/27/world/middleeast/27tehran.html. The former foreign minister, Manouchehr Mottaki, echoed his opposition to nuclear weapons: "Our position regarding nuclear weapons is very clear. We fundamentally believe that nuclear weapons—not only for small states, but for big states, big powers—is not a resolution to the problems they have, and cannot bring about security for anyone of them." Interview with Fareed Zakaria, July 6, 2008, CNN. See also "Iran Leader Denies Nuclear Claims," BBC, February 20, 2010, www.newsvote.bbc.co.uk/2/hi/middle_east/85233. . . . Khamenei said, "The West's accusations are baseless because our religious beliefs bar us from using such weapons."

71. Naji, *Ahmadinejad*, 127; Therese Delpech, *Iran and the Bomb: The Abdication of International Responsibility*, translated by Ros Schwartz (New York: Columbia University Press, 2006), 30.

72. Mark Lander, "Iran Policy More in Sync with Clinton's Views," *New York Times*, February 17, 2010. www.nytimes.com/2010/02/17/world/middleeast/17diplo.html? . . .

The secretary of defense echoed these remarks: "We have to face the reality that if Iran continues and develops nuclear weapons, it almost certainly will provoke nuclear proliferation in the Middle East. And that's a huge danger." Alan Cowell and Thom Shanker, "Iran's Nuclear Move Prompts New Calls for Sanctions," *New York Times*, February 9, 2010, www .nytimes.com/2010/02/09/world/middleeast/09iran.html? . . .

73. Eric Edelman, Andrew Krepinevich, and Evan Braden Montgomery, "The Dangers of a Nuclear Iran: the Limits of Containment," *Foreign Affairs* 90, no. 1 (January–February 2011): 66–81, at 67.

74. Some have questioned whether an Israeli attack would even be successful. Kenneth Pollack, Daniel Byman, Martin Indyk, Suzanne Maloney, Michael O'Hanlon, and Bruce Riedel, *Which Path to Persia? Options for a New American Strategy towards Iran* (Washington, DC: Brookings Institution Press, 2009), 131. Isabel Kershner, "Israeli Strike on Iran Would Be 'Stupid,' Ex-Spy Chief Says," *New York Times*, May 8, 2011, www.nytimes .com/2011/05/09/world/middleeast/09israel.html. . . .

75. Wilner and Cordesman, "US and Iranian Strategic Competition," 17. They note that "strikes against some 400 targets would be necessary to dismantle the program" (p. 104).

76. William Yong and Alan Cowell, "Bomb Kills Iranian Nuclear Scientist," *New York Times*, November 29, 2010, www. nytimes.com/2010/11/30/world/middleeast/30tehran .html. . . . ; William Yong, "Iran Says It Arrested Computer Worm Suspects," *New York Times*, October 2, 2010, www.nytimes.com/2010/10/03/world/middleeast/03iran.html? . . . See also David Sanger, "America's Deadly Dynamics with Iran," *New York Times*, November 6, 2011.

77. William Broad and David Sanger, "Iran Reports a Major Setback at a Nuclear Plant," *New York Times*, February 25, 2011, www.nytimes.com/2011/02/26/world/ middleeast/26nuke.html? . . .

78. There are a variety of estimates on how close Iran is to nuclear breakout capacity. In June 2010, US Central Intelligence Agency director Leon Panetta suggested Iran could build a nuclear bomb within two years. Other experts suggest that Iran is three to five years away from developing a nuclear weapon. Joseph Cirincione and Elice Connor, "How Iran Can Build a Bomb," *Foreign Policy*, July 1, 2010. At times Israeli leaders have believed that Iran is much closer to crossing the nuclear threshold than the Americans do. David Sanger and William Broad, "Allies' Clock Tick Differently on Iran," *New York Times*, March 15, 2009, www.nytimes.com/2009/03/15/weekinreview/15SANGER.html.

79. Ansari, *Confronting Iran*, 202.

80. Elaine Sciolino, "Atomic Monitor Signals Concern over Iran's Work," *New York Times*, May 27, 2008, www.nytimes.com/2008/05/27/world/middleeast/27.iran.html. International Atomic Energy Agency (IAEA), "Implementation of the NPT Safeguards Agreement and Relevant Provisions of Security Council Resolutions 1737 (2006), 1747 (2007) and 1803 (2008) in the Islamic Republic of Iran," May 26, 2008, available at www.iaea.org.

81. BBC, "UN Nuclear Agency Criticizes Iran," September 15, 2008, http://news.bbc .co.uk/go/pr/fr/-/2/hi/middle_east/7616744.stm. An IAEA report in November 2007 also complained that "the Agency's knowledge about Iran's current nuclear programme is diminishing" due to the lack of complete cooperation on the part of Tehran. IAEA, "Implementation of the NPT Safeguards Agreement and Relevant Provisions of Security Council Resolutions 1737 (2006) and 1747 (2007) in the Islamic Republic of Iran," November 15, 2007.

82. IAEA, "Implementation of the NPT Safeguards Agreement and Relevant Provisions of Security Council Resolutions in the Islamic Republic of Iran," November 18, 2011, GOV/2011/65.

83. In 2002 an Iranian opposition group—the National Council of Resistance of Iran—informed the world that it had evidence of Iran's nuclear program. Ansari, *Confronting Iran*, 198.

84. David Sanger, "Iran Agrees to Draft of Deal on Exporting Nuclear Fuel," *New York Times*, October 22, 2009, www.nytimes.com./2009/10/22/world/middleeast/22nuke.html? . . .

85. The deal was apparently rejected by the military and Supreme Leader Khamenei. David Sanger, "Obama Set to Offer Stricter Nuclear Deal to Iran," *New York Times*, October 27, 2010, www.nytimes.com/2010/10/28/world/middleeast/28iran.html? . . .

86. US State Department, "Background Briefing on Nuclear Nonproliferation Efforts with Regard to Iran and the Brazil/Turkey Agreement," Washington, DC, May 28, 2010.

87. *Tehran Times*, November 4, 2007.

88. Sue Pleming, "New US Audit Questions Efficacy of Iran Sanctions," Reuters, January 16, 2008, available at www.reuters.com. An analysis by the *New York Times* suggested that the United States was not enforcing the sanctions regime and hence limiting the effects of the sanctions. See Jo Becker and Ron Nixon, "US Enriches Companies Defying Its Policy on Iran," *New York Times*, March 6, 2010, www.nytimes.com/2010/03/07/world/middleeast/07sanctions.html?emc=eta1&pagew. . . .

89. Robert Einhorn, "Implementation of Iran Sanctions, House Committee on Oversight and Government Reform," Washington, DC, July 29, 2010.

90. UNSCR 1929: "—It bans transfers of major conventional weapons to Iran; —It bans all Iranian activities related to ballistic missiles that could deliver a nuclear weapon; —It establishes a framework for cargo inspections to detect and stop Iran's smuggling and acquisition of illicit items; —It prohibits Iran from investing abroad in sensitive nuclear activities, such as uranium mining; —It targets directly the role of the IRGC in Iran's proliferation efforts, etc. . . . "

91. William Burns, "Under Secretary for Political Affairs, Statement before the House Foreign Affairs Committee," Washington, DC, December 1, 2010.

92. Ibid.

93. Ibid. See also Philip Crowley, "Assistant Secretary, Daily Press Briefing," Washington, DC, December 1, 2010.

94. Ron Nixon, "Two Large Multinationals Pull Back from Iran," *New York Times*, March 10, 2010, www.nytimes.com/2010/03/11/world/middleeast/11iran.html? . . . Lukoil has said that it has lost more than $60 million due to US sanctions. See also "Anything to Declare?" *Economist*, July 3, 2010, 58. Office of the Spokesman of the State Department, "Companies Reducing Energy Related Business with Iran," Washington, DC, September 30, 2010. Total of France, Statoil of Norway, and Eni of Italy also "agreed to end their investment in Iran's energy sector." James B. Steinberg, "Deputy Secretary of State, Briefing on New Developments Pursuant to the Comprehensive Iran Sanctions, Accountability and Divestment of 2010," Washington, DC, September 30, 2010.

95. BBC, "US Warns Iran on Missile Threat," July 10, 2008, http://news.bbc.co.uk/go/pr/fr/-/2/hi/middle_east/7499198.stm.

96. Dmitri Trenin and Alexey Malashenko, *Iran: A View from Moscow* (Washington, DC: Carnegie Endowment for International Peace, 2010), 23.

97. One assessment suggested that "crude oil imports from Iran dropped by 35 percent during the first half of 2010," which "coincided with Washington's efforts to get Beijing to support UN sanctions." The authors suggest that while China has economic interests tied to Iran's energy capabilities, Beijing does not want a complete break with Washington. Erica Downs and Suzanne Maloney, "Getting China to Sanction Iran," *Foreign Affairs*, March–April 2011, 18–19.

98. Hillary Rodham Clinton, "Statement on Significant Reductions of Iranian Crude Oil Purchases," March 20, 2012, Washington, DC.

99. Thomas Erdbrink, "OPEC Sees Sanctions Taking Toll on Iran Oil Production," *New York Times*, May 17, 2012, www.nytimes.com/2012/05/18/world/middleeast/iran-oil -produc. . . .

100. Nazila Fathi, "Iran's Stocks Plunge after Vote for UN Review of Nuclear Program," *New York Times*, October 9, 2005. The *Tehran Times* has also echoed that this is in the country's national interest. In January 2009 Rafsanjani told the French ambassador, Poletti, that "using the language of threat, and unfriendly rhetoric will not help resolve the problems. Iran is truly ready to settle issues through negotiations without preconditions and within the framework of international law." "Rafsanjani Slams France's Stance on Iran's Nuclear Issue," *Tehran Times*, January 19, 2009.

101. Rieffer-Flanagan, "Improving Democracy," 25. See also www.WorldOpinionPoll .org.

102. "Iranians on Their Nuclear Program," September 22, 2009, poll taken by World-PublicOpinion.org. Only 31 percent said that they would prefer not to enrich uranium in return for the removal of sanctions.

103. Semira Nikou, interview with Seyed Hossein Mousavian, August 15, 2011, http:// iranprimer.usip.org/discussion/2011/aug/15/hossein-mousavian-iran-ready-negotiate-if.

104. Takeyh, *Hidden Iran*, 109.

105. International Crisis Group, *Iran Nuclear Issue*, 9.

106. BBC, "Iran in 'Backroom Offers' to West," February 20, 2009, http://news.bbc .co.uk/go/pr/fr/-2/hi/Europe/7901101.stm.

107. Alvin Richman, "Post-Election Crackdown in Iran Has Had Limited Impact on the Minority Expressing Strong Opposition to the Regime," available at WorldPublicOpinion,org.

108. BBC, "Iranian Leader Demands US Apology," January 28, 2009, http://news .bbc.co.uk/go/pr/fr/-/2/hi/middle_east/7855444.stm. Former secretary of state Albright had offered an apology toward the end of the Clinton administration. This apology was rejected as meaningless by the Supreme Leader Khamenei.

109. US State Department, "Report on Human Rights," February 25, 2009.

110. "Iran Ready to Train Afghan Police," *Tehran Times*, April 14, 2009.

111. International Crisis Group, *Iran Nuclear Issue*, 10.

CHAPTER 7

Economic Policies in the Midst of Ideological Infighting

Iran faces numerous economic challenges as it navigates its way through a globalized world. The unemployment rate is about 15 percent.[1] Every year an additional 1.6 million people are added to the ranks of the unemployed, most of whom are university graduates.[2] Many young Iranians graduate from college with no job prospects. And many have gone abroad in search of work, which contributes to the brain drain in Iran. The International Monetary Fund stated that Iran has the highest rate of educated citizens emigrating in the world.[3] Those individuals who are lucky enough to have a job will still have to contend with inflation. Corruption has been a consistent problem since the Revolution. Many of these economic troubles were inherited from the Pahlavi regime. However, government policies, mismanagement, ideological divisions among policymakers, and international sanctions have also exacerbated the economic problems of the Islamic Republic of Iran.

This chapter examines the evolution of economic policies developed during the last few decades and the economic challenges that Iran faces in the future. Some of the economic difficulties in Iran stem from the ideological differences of the revolutionaries. Some revolutionaries, including many clerics who owned land, held conservative views about property rights and supported a market-based economy. However, there were also numerous individuals who were part of the Islamic left and had been influenced by Marxist thought. They wanted to implement Islamic ideas about social justice and the suffering of the poor through government policies of land redistribution and the nationalization of various industries. The fundamental differences between these two groups led to political disagreements and, at times, incoherent policies. The factional infighting over what constituted an Islamic economy created significant problems that continue to plague Iran today. To explain these factional debates I describe the role that Islamic principles and interpretations have played in determining economic policy since the Revolution.

Beyond looking at traditional economic measures such as gross domestic product (GDP) and the rate of inflation, this chapter also analyzes how government policies affect the economic well-being of Iranians. To do so, I discuss whether the government is addressing the basic needs of its people (access to food, health care, etc.) and the extent of poverty and inequality in society. By looking at a range of economic issues, one can see that some of these economic problems are a long-term threat to the stability of the regime. Iran is far from a free-market, capitalist system. The inability of the Iranian government to develop long-term economic plans that produce economic growth and provide for the basic needs of the people has been a consistent problem during the last few decades, and it exacerbates the regime's lack of legitimacy. In addition, this chapter analyzes the role of economic threats to the regime in the form of international sanctions and how Tehran has adopted a pragmatic policy to deal with international sanctions. Finally, I examine several improvements in basic needs that are not considered threatening to the regime and are consistent with Khomeini's message of social justice.

Energy Resources

Iran's economy has long been dependent on its natural energy resources, especially oil. More than 60 percent of the government's revenues come from oil alone.[4] In 2011, Iran was the second-largest producer of crude oil and has extensive proven oil reserves, and this gives it the ability to influence global markets.[5] In addition, it has largely untapped natural gas resources. Iran's vast gas reserves are second only to Russia's; however, sanctions have precluded Iran from reaching its potential in this sector. Iran needs foreign technology (often from American companies) to develop liquefied natural gas that could then be exported. International sanctions have limited foreign investment in this energy sector.[6]

Although Iran possesses significant oil reserves, it lacks the ability to refine all its oil and hence it must import gasoline. In January 2008, Mohammad Javad Assemipur, the head of production at the National Iranian Oil Company, stated that Iran's crude oil output would rise to 4.2 million barrels per day by mid-March.[7] But this goal was not realized because Iran only produced 3.7 million barrels per day in 2010.[8] In 2011, this figure was down to 3.5

million barrels.[9] This is still far below prerevolutionary levels.[10] Iran's oil capacity has not reached the prerevolutionary levels of 6 million barrels per day
due to a number of factors. First, many foreign companies were forced to
leave Iran in 1979. When they left, their technological know-how went with
them. Thus Iran's ability to maintain its aging oil wells has suffered since the
Revolution.[11] Furthermore, sanctions have hampered efforts to attract foreign
investment, which is needed to increase Iran's oil production. One estimate
suggested that Iran needs approximately $1 billion per year in foreign invest-
ment to maintain its current production levels.[12] International sanctions via
the United Nations, European Union, United States, and a number of countries in the international community, plus an unfriendly business environment, have contributed to low levels of investment in the oil sector.[13] Iran's
aging oil infrastructure will likely lead to a decline in oil revenue. Analysts pre-
dict a decline in oil production: "Production capacity is likely to fall because
of geological constraints, the lack of domestic technical capacity, financial
constraints and international sanctions."[14] If Tehran is unable to improve its
oil infrastructure, this will have an adverse effect on Iran's long-term economic
growth and stability.

Natural resources such as oil have proven to be a blessing and a curse both
for Iran and for many actors in global politics. Many countries, including
growing economies such as China and India, are looking for stable sources of
energy. Iran's oil and natural gas offer energy-dependent countries around the
world a means to fuel their economic growth. China has entered into numerous energy contracts with Tehran as it searches for oil to satisfy the growing
economic needs of its middle class. India is also seeking partners with energy
resources to address its energy needs. The Delhi Declaration in 2003 demonstrates India's willingness to work with Tehran to see its energy needs ful-
filled.[15] However, Iran's oil, and the wealth that it derives from it, also presents
a problem for diplomats who would like to use economic incentives to curtail
Iran's more radical behaviors, especially the potential development of nuclear
weapons and support for violent groups in the Middle East. In 2008, Iran
earned more than $70 billion in revenues from the 2.5 million barrels that it
exported.[16] The higher the price of oil, the less likely it will be that Tehran can
be induced or persuaded to change its actions. When the price of oil is about
$100 a barrel, Iran sees its wealth increase. At various times during the past
few years, the price of oil has risen above $120 a barrel, and in 2008, the price
of oil was more than $140 a barrel. Thus when the European Union–3 (i.e.,
France, the United Kingdom, and Germany) tried to convince Iran to halt

the uranium enrichment program with financial incentives such as increased trade, its proposals fell on deaf ears.

But oil wealth has also proven to be a curse for Iran itself. The curse of oil tends to result in the neglect of economic development and investment in other areas of the state's economy. Because oil revenue has recently provided Iran with much income, there has been less of an incentive to develop other industries. Some observers have also suggested that reliance on oil production tends to inhibit the development of democracy because most of the major oil-producing states (e.g., Saudi Arabia, Kuwait, and Iran) are far from democratic.[17] Furthermore, because much of Iran's economy is dependent on oil, it is vulnerable to market forces. If oil prices drop precipitously (as they did in January 1999, when they sank to $20 a barrel), Iran's economy and budget will be adversely affected.[18]

Problems Inherited from the Shah

As noted in chapter 2, Iran faced many economic problems in the 1960s and 1970s, despite revenues generated from oil production. Although Iran saw sustained economic growth from 1964 to 1979, most Iranians did not benefit from it.[19] Many struggled to find jobs. Prosperity generated from the oil industry did not benefit many Iranians because the oil sector did not produce a significant number of jobs. Less than 1 percent of the population was employed in the oil sector.[20] The inability of many Iranians to find a job that provided a sustainable wage contributed to a variety of problems, including the fact that for many Iranians their basic needs went unmet.

Many in urban areas could not find affordable housing. Iranians living in Tehran often spent half their income on housing.[21] Those living outside major cities faced a different set of problems. Those Iranians living in rural areas often lacked access to electricity, adequate sources of nourishment, and health care.[22] Further, there was the continuing problem of inflation throughout much of the 1970s. According to the government, inflation was more than 25 percent toward the end of the 1970s.[23] However, the International Monetary Fund suggested that inflation was even higher than this.[24] The inflationary problems in Iran adversely affected the middle and lower classes.

These economic problems were more troubling given the significant oil revenues that the country benefited from in the 1960s and 1970s. In the last years of the Pahlavi regime, Iran was enjoying billions of dollars of revenue from oil exports.[25] The monarchy was more concerned with the economic growth of the country as a whole and an enhanced military than income distribution.[26] The shah used much of this oil revenue to build up Iran's military. He spent billions of dollars in the 1970s on military equipment, including F-16 fighter-bomber aircraft.[27] Instead of spending billions on military expenditures, he could have invested the country's oil revenues in his people. Iranians might have been less inclined to push the shah from his throne if their basic needs for food, housing, and jobs had been met.

Many Iranians resented the failed economic policies of their monarch. American diplomats serving in Iran noted their Iranian contacts complained about this: "There is also a general, deep seated concern voiced for the economic plight of the nation's poor masses. This generalization is usually accompanied by the contention that, given the country's vast income from oil and the extensive aid which has been received from foreign countries, the wealth of the nation would be greater and far more equitably divided were it not for what the clerics view as endemic corruption in the highest levels of the government."[28]

The shah's efforts to transform Iran into a modern industrial power were ineffective.[29] The White Revolution and especially the government's efforts at land reform were also largely a failure. Ultimately, the shah's efforts at economic reform and modernization failed to bring much-needed relief to his people. His mismanagement of the economy despite the country's oil wealth contributed to his downfall. This also meant that Khomeini and his cadre inherited many economic problems in the aftermath of the Revolution.

Economic Problems in the Aftermath of the Revolution

The Revolution of 1979 disrupted the economy almost as much as the political system. The theocratic government would dominate many aspects of the economy after 1979. In its first decade the Islamic Republic experienced a general economic decline, which can be explained by a number of factors including the war with its neighbor, inefficient economic policies, and a drop in oil prices. These problems were compounded by the ideological differences among the revolutionaries in their approach to the economy. The economy saw a general decline after the Revolution, which affected most Iranians but had a large impact on the poor.[30]

Initial Problems
Iran experienced a large flight of capital.[31] Investment in the new theocracy came with enhanced risk. Private investors could not be certain that their

investments would be honored under the new political leaders in Iran. Many factories, agricultural lands, and companies were confiscated in the aftermath of the Revolution.[32] Coupled with the fact that the new government national-ized many factories, banks, and other businesses, investors were understand-ably hesitant to invest.[33] In addition, the first few years of the 1980s saw many skilled workers emigrate due to the political changes. This brain drain had a negative effect on the economy. The country also saw an increase in inflation, while GDP declined. [34]

Ideological Differences among the Revolutionaries

Those groups that made up the Revolution had competing ideas about the di-rection of the economy. Some of the revolutionaries were influenced by Marx-ism and wanted to transform the economic system drastically. Others were conservatives who wanted to uphold property rights. Thus there were major philosophical differences over what an Islamic economy entailed:[35] "The Is-lamic Left supported a kind of Islamic socialism, with state control over the economy. But private property was entrenched in Islamic Law, many clerics owned land, and the Islamic conservatives, allied with bazaar merchants, fa-vored a mostly private economy and disliked government controls to help the poor. The Islamic Left had Majles majorities and the support of Prime Minis-ter Mousavi in the 1980s, but the conservatives in the Guardian Council often vetoed their measures."[36]

Although Khomeini spoke often about social justice, he was less clear about which economic principles would dominate his new political system. Some scholars have suggested that Khomeini "was a staunch defender of prop-erty rights and the role of the private sector."[37] However, the early years of the theocracy would see the government nationalize some industries. Islamic tenets are compatible with aspects of a free market economy as well as notions of social justice. Islam allows for trade and the private ownership of property, and it encourages freedom of enterprise.[38] Shia Islam does not provide a spe-cific guide to an Islamic economy: "The writings of Shi'ite scholars on Islamic economics (as compared with those of the Sunnis) are even more ambiguous as to the exact form or nature of an Islamic economy. This . . . allows Shi'ite Muslim fundamentalists considerable flexibility in interpreting Islamic eco-nomic rules and principles."[39]

Many clerics owned large tracts of land and hence supported a capitalist economy. Those merchants in the bazaar were also in favor of limited govern-ment interference and a hands-off economic approach. Rafsanjani, a wealthy landowner, pushed for a free market economy both while in Parliament and as president. These conservatives were opposed by the Islamic left, which wanted the government to take an active role in helping the poor in society. Those on the Islamic left, such as Mousavi, argued that the government should play an assertive role in directing the economy. The Islamic left won some early economic policy debates as some major Iranian industries were nationalized in the early 1980s. Rafsanjani's liberal economic approach would gradually play a large role in Iran's economy. However, during the 1980s these two factions clashed over economic policy in various political institutions with harmful consequences. These contrasting philosophies prevented Tehran from adopting a coherent approach to the economy and contributed to some of Iran's economic problems.

War with Iraq in the 1980s

Iran's war with Iraq, which dominated many aspects of politics throughout the 1980s, had a significant impact on Iran's economy in the 1980s and in the decade that followed. The war began in September 1980, when Iraq's president, Saddam Hussein, decided to attack the newly created Islamic Republic. Hussein thought that after a brief military engagement Iraq would emerge victorious and would benefit from the material spoils of war (additional land and oil wealth). The Iraqi leadership did not believe that Iran and its inexperienced clerical leaders would put up much of a fight. Hussein would learn over the course of eight bloody years just how determined the new religious leaders could be. In the end, the United Nations negotiated a cease-fire between the two sides. Neither side emerged victorious, and hundreds of thousands of Iranians and Iraqis lost their lives in the process. The war had a lasting impact on the Iranian economy.

The war cost Iran significantly in blood and treasure. One scholar described the extent of the economic hardship: "The costs were enormous: Productivity plummeted. Urban poverty doubled. Real per capita income dropped by 45 percent since the Revolution. And price controls and strict rationing of basic consumer goods failed to prevent rampant inflation."[40]

One estimate suggested that the war resulted in more than $590 billion in damages.[41] There were more than 300,000 casualties, and at least six cities, primarily in the western part of the country, were leveled.[42] Even cities further from the major battles suffered significant damage. Tehran, for example, was frequently hit by missiles. Damage done to the capital required reconstruction after the war. Iranians suffered during the war not only with rationing but also with unemployment. For example, almost 30 percent of the labor force was out of work in 1986.[43] Iran had to rebuild and address the damage caused by the war, including the bombing of cities and the destruction of Khorramshahr, Iran's main port.[44] Various businesses and industries needed to be reconstructed, including the Abadan refinery and the Kharg loading facilities.[45]

Reducing Inequality

One of Ayatollah Khomeini's prominent criticisms was that the shah had mismanaged the economy and was indifferent to the suffering of the masses. These criticisms were coupled with promises that an Islamic political system would be a more just system and would address the prevailing inequality in Iranian society. This was also consistent with those on the Islamic left who had been influenced by Marx and Shariati. Khomeini had incorporated aspects of Marxist ideology into his revolutionary discourse. He wanted to combine Islam and justice for the poor, as one scholar notes: "Khomeini's populist agenda was to empower the state with the mission to revitalize 'the authentic' Islam that would create a self-sufficient, independent society that would answer the woes of the devout and disinherited masses. Wealth and oil earnings were abundant, argued Khomeini, but were not distributed evenly under the shah's regime, and it was the revolutionary's duty to take an active role in abolishing inequality by redirecting expenditures."[46]

Many Iranians, especially the poor, supported Khomeini and the revolutionaries because they believed that their material well-being would be improved under the new regime. His successors have continued to stress the importance of helping the poor. Ayatollah Khamenei stated, "We should present a successful economic model to the world and prove the efficiency of our country in economic development by eradicating poverty and deprivation and establishing justice."[47] However, inequality in Iran has remained largely unchanged during the last three decades.[48] In 1996, after fifteen years in power, the government still had not dealt with the issue of poverty. The Iranian Chamber of Commerce acknowledged that about 40 percent of the population lived below the poverty line.[49] The *Tehran Times* reported that there were 12 million Iranians living below the poverty line in 2007.[50] Numerous sources both in Iran and in the West suggest that some "9 million Iranians live in absolute poverty."[51] The Department of Statistics in Iran concluded that 10 million citizens lived below the absolute poverty line.[52] Thus Khomeini's promise of social justice has been largely unfulfilled.

Subsidies

Because Khomeini criticized the monarchy for its neglect of the oppressed (*mostaz'a fin*), improving the lives of the downtrodden became one of the goals of the Revolution. One way these efforts were institutionalized was the policy of government subsidies. Initially, the government subsidized a number of products, including gas, milk, rice, sugar, and wheat, and also utilities, such as water and power, to help Iranians deal with the difficulties associated with the war in Iraq.[53] Tehran maintained these subsidies after the end of the war in 1988 in order to avoid provoking a frustrated and disillusioned population that had suffered greatly during eight painful years of war. Thus Iranians benefited from low prices, including cheap gasoline—roughly 38 cents per gallon in 2009.[54]

Government subsidies became an entrenched part of the system, a third rail, that was impossible for politicians to deal with despite the significant economic problems associated with these policies. Subsidies have been a drain on the economy costing more than $85 billion a year.[55] Some scholars have suggested that subsidies ate up to 25 to 30 percent of GDP.[56] In addition to the negative economic effects of the subsidies, gas subsidies contribute to increased gas consumption, pollution, and environmental problems.[57]

President Rafsanjani attempted to reform the subsidies program but faced a significant backlash from the population, including riots in a number of cities. President Khatami's efforts to deal with the subsidies problem were thwarted by conservatives in Parliament because of factional infighting.[58] It was only under President Ahmadinejad that Tehran passed a subsidy reform bill in 2010. The bill eliminated $20 billion in subsidies on gasoline and food products. This changed the price of gasoline from 38 cents a gallon to more than $2.50 a gallon. To offset the hardships for the poor, the government offered a onetime payment of $77 per person.[59] The bill also requires parliamentary oversight of the subsidies reform program, for the Majles had expressed significant concerns about Ahmadinejad's ability to implement the plan without corruption.[60]

The subsidies reform bill demonstrates that Iranian leaders can act in a pragmatic manner, irrespective of Islamic tenets. Subsidies were a long-term economic threat to financial viability and a financial strain on the economy. Dealing with this economic threat despite the potential anger from the population demonstrates that Iranian leaders can take a pragmatic approach to address a problem. The International Monetary Fund offered an initial positive assessment of the subsidy reform program. In June 2011 it praised the government:

The mission commended the authorities for the early success in the implementation of their ambitious subsidy reform program. The increases in prices of energy products, public transport, wheat, and bread adopted on December 19, 2010, are estimated to have removed close to US$60 billion (about 15 percent of GDP) in annual implicit subsidies to products. At the same time, the redistribution of the revenues arising from the price increases to households as cash transfers has been effective in reducing inequalities, improving living standards, and supporting domestic demand in the economy. The energy price increases are already leading to a decline in excessive domestic energy consumption and related energy waste. While the subsidy reform is expected to result in a transitory slowdown in economic growth and temporary increase in the inflation rate, it should considerably improve Iran's medium term outlook by rationalizing domestic energy use, increasing export revenues, strengthening overall competitiveness, and bringing economic activity in Iran closer to its full potential.[61]

Although subsidy reform was needed for long-term economic stability, there are still fears that the program will substantially increase inflation. Inflation in 2008 was 30 percent. Ahmad Tarakoli, a conservative in Parliament, warned that inflation could rise to 60 percent, especially for basic goods.[62] Although Iran's long-term economic prospects may be better since it has ended the subsidies program, inflation continues to be a problem. The Central Bank's governor, Mahmoud Bahmani, put the rate of inflation at close to 20 percent in November 2011. This was up from the figure for July of 15.4 percent.[63] By the middle of 2012 the rate of inflation had doubled. Some economists have suggested that the inflation rate was close to 50 percent in the fall of 2012.[64]

The Activities of Quasi-Government Agencies

Iran has a few organizations with ties to the government that engage in significant economic activities. The first are the *bonyads*, or charitable foundations. Charitable foundations that existed during the Pahlavi reign and were controlled by the monarchy were transferred to the revolutionaries when the king went into exile. Some of these foundations received millions of dollars in assets when they were taken over.[65]

Although the *bonyads* are technically independent from the government, they are deeply intertwined with clerics who have ties to the supreme leader.

Individuals selected to lead the foundations are often chosen because of their loyalty to Khamenei. There are numerous *bonyads* in Iran with millions of dollars worth of assets, including the Foundation for the Oppressed (Bonyad-e Mosta'zafin) and the Martyrs' Foundation (Bonyad-e Shadid). These *bonyads* provide assistance to the families of those killed during the war with Iraq, and they operate without parliamentary oversight and enjoy favorable economic policies: "The state channels resources to *bonyads* through a set of financial and legal means, including budgetary payments, interest subsidies, below-market exchange rates, special credits from state banks, tax exemption, immunity from legal restrictions, and monopoly status in various sectors. By some estimates, the total share of *bonyads* amounts to at least 20 percent of GDP."[66]

To give one example of the financial reach of an Islamic charitable foundation, the Foundation for the Oppressed is estimated to have more than $10 billion in assets, employs 200,000 people, and has investments both foreign and domestic in energy, agriculture, transportation, mining, and construction industries, to name a few.[67]

Another powerful economic actor is the Islamic Revolutionary Guards Corps (IRGC). As noted in chapter 3, the IRGC was created to protect the new political system from a counterrevolution. During the last few decades the IRGC has morphed into a powerful economic institution with investments throughout the country. The IRGC has a variety of investments in construction projects, manufacturing, real estate, and telecommunications.[68] This creates problems for the Iranian economy, because the IRGC has often purchased companies in no-competition bids. One consequence of these no-competition bids is that the bazaar has been pushed aside.[69] This puts other businesses at a competitive disadvantage. One estimate suggested that the IRGC controlled a third of Iran's economy.[70] The IRGC's military power has allowed it to expand its economic power. For example, in May 2004 the IRGC shut down the new Imam Khomeini International Airport after a Turkish consortium won the right to run the airport's operations. The IRGC claimed that allowing the Turks to run airport operations "was a threat to Iran's security and dignity."[71]

These quasi-governmental agencies hamper the economy because they hinder competition that could help the economy grow, as was noted by one Iranian scholar: "About 60 percent of the economy is still controlled and planned by the state, and another 10–20 percent by five large foundations that are also tied to the supreme leader. They have preferential access to credit, foreign exchange, and licenses and contracts, which makes it difficult for others to compete."[72]

The rise of the *bonyads* and the IRGC has had the effect of marginalizing the bazaar.[73] Merchants in the bazaar have a long history in Iran. They have been active in politics and were supportive of the Revolution in 1979. They have long had ties to clerics and conservatives in government. However, since the Revolution government policies—including regulations, licensing requirements, and the economic activities of charitable foundations—have reduced the economic strength and independence of the bazaar.[74] The *bazaaris* have faced additional problems since the Revolution, including the impact of sanctions. Many merchants have complained of trouble obtaining credit. They have had trouble opening foreign bank accounts and foreign banks have denied them access to credit.[75]

Despite the economic problems facing the bazaar and their weaker position in society, the *bazaaris* have, from time to time, voiced their discontent. In 2008 and 2010 the *bazaaris* in major cities went on strike to oppose the government's plan for increased taxes. These strikes were largely successful. Specifically, in 2008 the Ahmadinejad administration's attempt at a 3 percent value-added tax to increase government revenues was set aside due to bazaar strikes.[76]

Sanctions

The Islamic Republic of Iran has been dealing with sanctions since the Revolution. In the early 1980s the Carter administration enacted sanctions against Iran due to the hostage crisis. More recently, the international community has placed economic sanctions on Iran due to the lack of transparency concerning Tehran's nuclear program. The purpose of the sanctions is to discourage Iran from developing nuclear weapons and to encourage it to engage in more cooperative behavior with the international community.

The sanctions regime against Iran has been gradually increasing in intensity. Washington has led the way by placing sanctions on a number of entities in Iran, including Bank Mellat and the IRGC, due to their support for the nuclear program.[77] The Obama administration has continued to strengthen the sanctions regime against Iran since 2009. These more stringent sanctions can be seen in UN Security Council Resolution 1929 (passed in June 2010) and the Comprehensive Iran Sanctions Accountability and Divestment Act (passed in July 2010).[78] The Obama administration has described these efforts as "the strongest and most comprehensive set of sanctions that the Islamic Republic of Iran has ever faced."[79] In 2012 the Obama administration initiated further sanctions on Iran's Central Bank. By using a section of the USA Patriot Act, the Treasury Department prohibited financial institutions from dealing with Iran's Central Bank. Because the Central Bank is the institution through which most financial transactions, including oil sales, are made, this has the effect of significantly limiting Iran's access to international financial institutions and oil revenues.[80] In addition, the European Union has imposed strict sanctions:

> Iran continues to refuse to comply with its international obligations and to fully co-operate with the IAEA to address the concerns on its nuclear programme, and instead continues to violate those obligations. In this context and in accordance with the Council conclusions of 1 December 2011, the Council has agreed additional restrictive measures in the energy sector, including a phased embargo of Iranian crude oil imports to the EU, in the financial sector, including against the Central Bank of Iran, in the transport sector as well as further export restrictions, notably on gold and on sensitive dual-use goods and technology, as well as additional designations of persons and entities, including several controlled by the Islamic Revolutionary Guards Corps.[81]

American sanctions, coupled with the European Union's decision to ban oil imports from Iran after July 2012, have put increasing pressure on Iran.[82] The general push has been to dissuade foreign companies from doing business in Iran. For businesses that invest in Iran, especially in the energy sector, there is the potential for monetary fines and sanctions from the United States.

Various US officials have said that the sanctions are hurting the regime. In testimony before Congress, Robert Einhorn, special adviser for nonproliferation and arms control, explained that "at least $50–60 billion in oil and gas development deals have either been put on hold or have been discontinued in the last few years—due in part to our conversations with companies about the threat of ISA [Iran Sanctions Act] sanctions."[83] William Burns, the undersecretary for political affairs at the State Department, stated that a number of multinational corporations have already pulled out of Iran or limited their economic transactions with Iran, including Daimler, Toyota, Deutsche Bank, HSBC, Royal Dutch Shell, Reliance, and Lukoil.[84] Lukoil admitted that the reason it suspended development on the Anraran oil field was American sanctions: "We opened the largest field in Iran, but we can't work there because the US State Department has banned third countries from investing more than $20 million."[85] This hurts Iran's energy development, which could have increased Iran's gas exports and the economic profit that comes with it. The undersecretary for terrorism and financial intelligence, David Cohen, noted that Iran's crude exports were down more than 50 percent. Iran exported 2 million barrels of crude oil a day in 2011, but by 2012 its daily exports had plummeted to 1 million barrels.[86] Various scholars have noted the impact of sanctions on Iran. Steve Marsh suggests the various ways in which sanctions have been painful for Tehran: "American-led pressure can and does restrict Tehran's opportunities to develop its energy capacity quickly. Some leading western companies are either pulling out of or soft-pedalling involvement in the Iranian energy sector, and the risky political climate coupled with the global capital squeeze makes major banks even more reluctant to finance the development of Iran's untapped natural resources."[87]

Akbar Torbat has suggested that sanctions have cost Iran about 1.1 percent of GDP annually. This suggests that although the sanctions have not changed Tehran's behavior, they are having an impact.[88] Other scholars have suggested that US sanctions may have slowed foreign investment in Iran, even if they have not cut it off completely.[89]

Many in Iran, including Ahmadinejad, have also dismissed the sanctions regime as ineffective and irrelevant. Because Tehran has been dealing with sanctions for more than thirty years, many in the Islamic Republic believe that they can weather the latest phase of the economic sanctions storm. Iran has engaged in a number of efforts to mitigate the effects of the sanctions regime. Iran has tried to find non-Western markets for its exports, and it has also tried to lessen its reliance on US dollars. And as has been noted by one scholar, Tehran has had some success in these efforts: "Iran is using its energy resources to diversify its foreign reserves away from dollars in an obvious effort to ameliorate the impact of US-led economic sanctions. One way in which it is doing this is by insisting on selling its oil in non-dollar currencies. Thus, for example, China's state-run Zhuhai Zhenrong Corporation, the biggest single buyer of Iranian crude worldwide, pays for its oil in euros rather than in dollars."[90]

Tehran's efforts to export to a diverse group of states have also been successful, and thus have lessened its dependence on the West. Iran is exporting more of its oil and nonoil products to Asia: "In 2005–6 Asian economies accounted for 56.4 percent of Iran's oil exports, whilst the share of Western Europe was only 25.8 percent. In the same year United Arab Emirates (17.9 percent), Iraq (10.5 percent), India (6.9 percent) and Japan (5.0 percent) were the most important destinations for Iran's non-oil exports, with Asia accounting for

72.8 percent of Iran's non-oil exports as compared to 22.1 percent for Europe."[91] By 2009, Iran's largest trading partners were China, Japan, United Arab Emirates, and India.[92]

Iran's ability to find additional markets for its exports, especially oil, allows Tehran to soften some of the economic sanctions its faces. However, in rare moments of candor, Iranian officials have admitted the bite of sanctions. Ahmad Qalebani, the deputy oil minister, admitted that Iran's oil production was down from the previous year "due to lack of investment in oil field development."[93] Although the international community tried to cajole Tehran into cooperating on its nuclear program, thus far Tehran has been able to withstand this pressure. Given that the Islamic Republic of Iran has been under a sanctions regime for most of its existence, it is not clear that sanctions have changed Tehran's behavior. Iran continues to support Hamas and Hezbollah, and it has not backed away from its uranium enrichment program. Hence there is no definitive evidence that the sanctions regime has been effective in its stated goals.

Efforts at Reform

Given the various economic problems that Iran has faced, it is not surprising that some efforts have been undertaken to reform economic policies. These efforts at reform have stalled due to factional infighting and ineffectual policies.

Rafsanjani's Efforts at Reform

As 1989 drew to a close, Iran embarked on a new economic path. This was possible due to the fact that Ayatollah Khomeini died in 1989 and opened some space for some new economic policies. In addition, the war with Iraq was over, and this provided an opening to rebuild the country. President Rafsanjani led many of these economic reforms, which had modest results.

President Rafsanjani attempted numerous economic reforms after the war to try to jump-start the stalled economy. He privatized a number of government-owned industries, and he tried to reduce some of the market controls that had been implemented in the aftermath of the Revolution.[94] He created free trade zones, including one on Kish Island in the Persian Gulf. These efforts to develop a market economy also included reducing government subsidies.[95] This liberal economic approach was motivated by Rafsanjani's attempt to get a loan from the International Monetary Fund, which often places conditions on loans that entail free trade, reducing government spending, and freeing the economy from government interference.

Rafsanjani understood the economic difficulties that Iran faced and tried to improve its relations with the West, including the United States, to try to attract foreign investment. Foreign investment could help the economy grow, so the administration reduced some of the hurdles to foreign investment. The Rafsanjani administration offered $1 billion contract to the American oil company Conoco.[96] These efforts at rapprochement and economic cooperation were rejected by President Clinton. Instead, the Clinton administration hit Iran with a comprehensive sanctions package in 1995.[97] In 1996 the US Congress passed the Iran-Libya Sanctions Act in 1996, which put sanctions on companies that invested more than $40 million in Iran's (or Libya's) energy industry.[98]

Although Rafsanjani was able to encourage some Iranian professionals living abroad who had fled after the Revolution to return to Iran and contribute to improving the economy, his efforts at economic reform were far from successful. Although increased oil prices brought in more revenues, it could not keep up with the increase in Iran's foreign debt. For example, foreign debt more than tripled between 1991 and 1993.[99] When oil prices declined again in 1993, this contributed to a balance-of-payments crisis.[100]

Rafsanjani's attempts to create a market economy, encourage foreign investment, and promote privatization never came to complete fruition due to political and ideological infighting. The result was that many of these efforts were abandoned and the economic problems of the country persisted.[101]

Khatami's Efforts

President Rafsanjani bequeathed a stuttering economy to his successor, Mohammad Khatami. Inflation and unemployment rates were high and oil prices were low for much of his presidency. President Khatami and the reformists spent much of their energy on improving aspects of the political system, including enhancing press freedoms and the rule of law. Although there was not a complete neglect of the economy, the economy was not the primary focus for Khatami. His administration's failure to fully address the economic problems of the country would contribute to the weakness of the reformists. However, it is worth noting that some of his efforts were hampered by domestic political infighting and opposition from conservatives: "Those in government and foundations who control businesses discourage competition. Merchants who support the status quo and oppose change are still favored by the conservative clerics who control major governmental and judicial institutions. Nonetheless, the Khatami government took some steps to improve the economy. Khatami backed a five-year plan for 2000–5, much of which is devoted to promoting the rule of law, non-oil exports, privatization, and de-regulation. But relatively little has come of it, as most of these reforms would weaken the ruling clerics or their allied *bazaaris*."[102]

To deal with an economy dependent on and vulnerable to market fluctuations in the price of oil, Khatami created the Oil Stabilization Fund in 2000. The purpose of creating a stabilization fund was to save some money for a rainy day. By putting some excess oil revenues into a fund, the government can mitigate the economic pain of a future decrease in the price of oil. Thus the government is not completely vulnerable to market prices and in particular a steep decline in the price of oil.

Ahmadinejad's Changes

President Ahmadinejad shifted Iran's economic policies upon becoming president. He replaced Rafsanjani and Khatami's liberal economic philosophy with a more populist approach. The fourfold increase in oil prices since 2002 has allowed Ahmadinejad to spend freely.[103] While campaigning for the presidency, Ahmadinejad promised the poor that he would bring the country's "oil money to people's tables." In addition to government subsidies, Ahmadinejad also made numerous trips to rural areas and gave people cash handouts.[104] These policies have not lowered the unemployment rate, nor have they had a significant impact on inflation. His subsidy reform program can also be seen in a populist framework. The subsidy reform would still allow government support for the poor. It would eliminate subsides for the wealthy. Thus Ahmadinejad can continue to offer financial help to his base of supporters (the poor) while hurting those who are often critical of his policies.

Additional populist programs under Ahmadinejad's administration include low-interest loans. Low-interest loans have been given by the government for agricultural and tourism projects. Ahmadinejad also established the Imam Reza Compassion Fund to help young people with interest-free loans for marriage.[105] To fund these populist programs he has tapped into the Oil Stabilization Fund.[106] During his first two years in office Ahmadinejad took out $78.3 billion from the Oil Stabilization Fund.[107] But as noted above, this fund was designed to protect against a significant downturn in oil prices, not for cash handouts. Depleting the fund will only leave Iran vulnerable to a drop in oil prices.

Additional economic problems have occurred due to the nuclear standoff with the United Nations. Over the course of a two-week period in October 2005, Iran's stock market dropped almost 30 percent.[108] Some investors were moving their investments to safer financial markets in places such as Dubai. The fear was that the confrontation with the UN Security Council over Iran's nuclear ambitions was going to result in sanctions and a further economic backlash. Although the supreme leader controls foreign policy, Ahmadinejad's remarks in this area have not been well received. He questioned the Holocaust and suggested that Israel "be wiped off the map." Neither of these remarks was welcomed by the international community. Given these foreign policy difficulties, some have openly criticized the president. Furthermore, some members of Parliament have suggested that the president refrain from engaging in this heated rhetoric, which makes international relations more difficult and does nothing to improve the economy. They have argued that the stock market woes are a direct reaction to the country's confrontational policies over the nuclear issue and a response to President Ahmadinejad's aggressive speech at the UN in September 2005. Rafsanjani and Nabiollah Ibrahimi have called on the government to adopt a more pragmatic and less confrontational approach to nuclear negotiations.[109]

Iranians have been critical of Ahmadinejad's time in office due to his inability to improve the country's economic situation. There is still widespread corruption in Iran. To tackle this problem, the president would need to confront some members of the conservative establishment. The sharp decline in the value of Iran's currency, the rial, in the last months of 2011 and again in the middle of 2012 caused additional fears about the weakness of the economy.[110] In addition, Ahmadinejad has not been able to improve the financial well-being of the poorest Iranians. And inflation continues to be a problem. At the end of 2007, the president gave an interview on national television to explain why the country was experiencing high inflation. He gave a litany of reasons, including the fall of the dollar (causing the price of imported goods to rise), an injection of liquidity into the country's economy, and the media's overblown reporting on imports and exports.[111] In fact, the president seemed to blame everyone from the Majles, to his political opponents, to the global economy for the economic problems that Iran is facing. What he refused to do is acknowledge any responsibility for the crisis. Even onetime conservative supporters such as Mohammad Reza Katouzian called on the president to criticize others less and do more to fix the economy.

In addition, there are signs that the supreme leader is concerned about the president's rhetoric and inability to deal with Iran's economic problems. There have been reports from Tehran that the supreme leader is dissatisfied with the economic health of the country and Ahmadinejad's inability to address the country's economic woes—high inflation, the lack of heat and electricity at times, rising prices for food and rent.[112]

Economic Improvement

Although Iran has many economic problems (corruption, oil dependence, etc.), it has made some economic progress, especially in rural areas. Rural Iranians have seen some aspects of their lives improve since the Revolution, including access to water, health care, and education. These rights, which are necessary to survive and prosper in society, are not viewed as threatening by many in the regime. In fact, providing these basic rights to Iranians is consistent with the rhetoric used by Khomeini in the 1970s. He argued that the shah had ignored the needs of the poor. Thus improving the lives of the poor was one of the central goals of the Revolution.

In the thirty years since Khomeini was the voice of the oppressed, Iran has improved the lives of rural Iranians. Efforts to help the poor in rural areas can be seen in the Reconstruction Jihad, which initially sent volunteers to rural areas to assist farmers with the harvest in 1979. However, it evolved to take on a large economic role in rural areas by building roads, schools, and health clinics.[113] The Reconstruction Jihad's projects also involved bringing water and electricity to rural areas.[114] Furthermore, access to electricity and piped water in rural areas has increased substantially since the Revolution.[115] Access to electricity was below 20 percent in 1977, but by 2004 it was more than 95 percent. Similar improvements can be seen with access to water.[116] These government efforts have helped to secure the loyalty of the poor in rural areas of the country.

The Islamic Republic has also made a dramatic commitment to improving the health services it provides to its citizens. Between 1991 and 2006 Iran developed numerous social service complexes in both urban and rural areas. These complexes doubled in urban areas (from 414 to 980) and saw significant increases in rural areas as well (from 1,121 to 1,495). The purpose of these institutions is to provide Iranians with such resources as health care services, orphanages, and day care centers.[117] The number of doctors per capita doubled during the first twenty years of the theocracy.[118] The increase in access to medical services in Iran has resulted in a decrease in child mortality rates.[119] The *2011 UN Human Development Report* estimated that Iran's child mortality rate was 31 per 1,000 live births.[120] Furthermore, various charities that receive government funding also provide direct assistance to more than 2 million Iranians.[121] The results are laudable. The World Bank reports that health care has improved significantly during the last two decades and "now generally exceeds regional averages."[122] Furthermore, life expectancy is up to seventy-three years.[123]

Improving Women's Lives

Additional government funding has helped women improve their economic standing in society. Female literacy rates have improved since the days of the monarchy, and married women have gained greater access to birth control. In the late 1980s the government developed the National Birth Control Policy, which "provided free contraceptives (to married couples) through the primary health care system."[124] This policy was developed to help with family planning and encourage women to have fewer children. These policies were generally praised by international organizations such as the World Health Organization. The fertility rate in Iran dropped from 6.6 births in 1977 to 1.9 births in 2006.[125] Such policies have helped women not only to have fewer children but also to find better-paying jobs.

Educational Progress

Women have also benefited from the government's efforts on education. They have enjoyed greater access and opportunities via the education policies implemented since the Islamic Revolution. For some conservative Iranians, the segregation of education by gender and the classes offered at mosques facilitated the ability of girls to get an education.[126] The improvement in literacy rates has been remarkable. Between 1976 and 1996, women's literacy doubled (in 1976, 36 percent of Iranian women were considered literate; by 1996 the figure had risen to 72 percent). Overall adult literacy has improved more than 25 percent since the Revolution.[127] By 2006, the literacy rate for girls ten years and older was 80 percent.[128] According to the United Nations, adult literacy had risen to 85 percent by 2011.[129] Beyond achieving basic literacy— the ability to read and write a simple sentence—women were also attending universities in much greater numbers.[130] The human rights lawyer and Nobel Prize winner Shirin Ebadi noted that close to 65 percent of the students in universities were women.[131]

Women have used their increasing educational opportunities to enhance their work opportunities. Although many women lost their jobs as lawyers and judges in the immediate aftermath of the Revolution, the members of the younger generation of educated women have not remained in a domestic role. More women have entered the workforce in the last thirty years, and many are working in the service sector. In 1976, women made up 38.2 percent of the manufacturing force; 39.5 percent in education, health care, and social services; and 18.3 percent in social, personal, and financial services. By 2006, women in manufacturing had declined to 18.7 percent; in education, health care, and social services, they had increased to 48.6 percent; and in social, personal, and financial services, they were up to 28.2 percent.[132] Thus the increase in women working outside the home has not been limited to cheap jobs in manufacturing or the textile industry. Rather, many were using their education to secure higher-paying jobs.[133]

Conclusion

Many observers have voiced skepticism about Tehran's ability to get its economic house in order. With so many economic difficulties and so many vested interests, it is not surprising that the Iranian scholar Nikki Keddie sounded a pessimistic note: "The rise in unemployed, educated youth, and continued population growth as young people have babies have created an explosive economic situation. Strict limits on foreign investment, a weak legal framework, the majority economic role of corrupt governmental institutions and foundations, and the dearth of productive investment by the bazaar bourgeoisie create obstacles to economic reform and development. Iran remains overwhelmingly dependent on fluctuating oil income."[134]

Although Iran has experienced some economic growth during the last few years—GDP averaged more than 2.5 percent annual growth between 2009 and 2011—it has largely been based on oil revenues.[135] If oil prices were to decline significantly, Iran's economic growth would experience a significant setback. Hence, long-term growth based primarily on oil revenues is not a solid foundation for the future.

Iran's inability to develop policies that contribute to its long-term economic growth is a major threat to the regime's stability. Economic problems such as continuing inequality and poverty contribute to a population that is not satisfied. When those suffering under unfavorable economic circumstances also see the country receiving increasing oil revenues, this decreases the legitimacy of the regime. When coupled with Khomeini's claims of social justice in Islam, the theocracy's overall inability to improve the lives of the vast majority of its citizens adds to a crisis of legitimacy. Ineffective economic policies and the shah's failure to improve the economic well-being of much of the population contributed to his fall from power.

For Tehran to alter its economic course and reduce its reliance on oil production (and its potential vulnerability to market fluctuations), it will need to rethink some of its policies. It must further diversify its exports and develop more competitive industries. To do so, it must reduce the power of the quasi-governmental actors such as the IRGC and the *bonyads*. Doing so would allow for a more competitive economy. Addressing international concerns about its nuclear program, including greater transparency with regard to its enrichment activities, could lessen the sanctions regime. This might allow for greater investment in a variety of industries, which could put Iran on the path to increased growth and economic stability. But if Tehran chooses not to confront these economic problems, its dimming long-term economic prospects could potentially threaten the regime's political power, just as they did that of the shah in 1979.

Notes

1. "Iran's Bold Economic Reform: Economic Jihad," *Economist*, June 23, 2011, 59.

2. Ladane Nasseri, "Iran's Unemployed Rise by 1.6 Million Each Year, Sharagh Reports," Bloomberg, May 9, 2011.

3. Shayerah Ilias, "Iran's Economic Conditions: US Policy Issues," Congressional Research Service, April 22, 2010, 6.

4. Elliot Hen-Tov, "Understanding Iran's New Authoritarianism," *Washington Quarterly* 30, no. 1 (Winter 2006–7): 163–79, at 172; Fareed Mohamedi, "The Oil and Gas Industry," in *The Iran Primer*, edited by Robin Wright (Washington, DC: US Institute of Peace Press, 2010), 100–103, at 100.

5. Thomas Erdbrink, "OPEC Sees Sanctions Taking Toll on Iran Oil Production," *New York Times*, May 17, 2012, www.nytimes.com/2012/05/18/world/middleeast/iran-oil-produc. . . . See also US Central Intelligence Agency, *CIA World Factbook*, www.cia.gov/library/publications/the-world-factbook/geos/ir.html.

6. Ilias, "Iran's Economic Conditions," 13.

7. "Iran Oil Output to Reach 4.2 Mbpd by March '08," *Tehran Times*, January 2, 2008, www.tehrantimes.com/index_View.asp?code=160464.

8. Mohamedi, "Oil and Gas Industry," 101.

9. Rick Goldstone, "Iran Admits Western Sanctions Are Inflicting Damage," *New York Times*, December 20, 2011, www.nytimes.com/2011/12/20/world/middleeast/iran-admits-we. . . .

10. A total of 4 million barrels a day would be about 30 percent less than production levels in 1979. Between 1975 and 1978 Iran was producing more than 5 million barrels of oil a day. Cyrus Bina, "Global Oil and the Oil Politics of the Islamic Republic," in *Modern Capitalism and Islamic Ideology in Iran*, edited by Cyrus Bina and Hamid Zangeneh (New York: St. Martin's Press, 1992), 121–58, at 127. See also Hen-Tov, "Understanding Iran's New Authoritarianism," 170.

11. Nikki Keddie, *Modern Iran: Roots and Results of Revolution* (New Haven, CT: Yale University Press, 2003), 265.

12. Ilan Berman, "Toward an Economic Strategy against Iran," *Comparative Strategy* 27 (2008): 20–26, at 21.

13. Ilias, "Iran's Economic Conditions," 4.

14. Mohamedi, "Oil and Gas Industry," 101.

15. Steve Marsh, "Thirty Years On: Iran's "Silent Revolution," *Iranian Studies* 42, no. 2 (April 2009): 213–29, at 225. See also C. Christine Fair, "Indo-Iranian Ties: Thicker Than Oil," *Middle East Review of International Affairs* 11, no. 1 (March 2007), www.meria.idc .ac.il/journal/2007/issue1/jv11no1a9.html.

16. Ilias, "Iran's Economic Conditions," 21.

17. See, e.g., Michael Ross, "Blood Barrels," *Foreign Affairs* 87, no. 3 (May–June 2008): 2–8.

18. Hadi Salehi Esfahani and M. Hashem Pesaran, "The Iranian Economy in the Twentieth Century: A Global Perspective," *Iranian Studies* 42, no. 2 (April 2009): 177–211, at 185.

19. M. H. Pesaran discusses fifteen years of economic growth from 1963–64 to 1977–78. Pesaran cites the growth in GDP at 9 percent a year and the rise in per capita income from $176 to $2,160. M. H. Pesaran, "The System of Dependent Capitalism in Pre- and Post-Revolutionary Iran," *International Journal of Middle East Studies* 14, no. 4 (November 1982): 501–22.

20. Fred Halliday, "Iran: The Economic Contradiction," *MERIP Reports*, no. 69 (July–August 1978): 9–18, at 11.

21. Kenneth Pollack, *The Persian Puzzle: The Conflict between Iran and America* (New York: Random House, 2004), 110–12.

22. Sandra Mackey, *The Iranians: Persia, Islam and the Soul of a Nation* (New York: Plume, 1998), 220; Pollack, *Persian Puzzle*, 113.

23. "The economy overheated and started experiencing high and rising inflation in the mid-1970s." Esfahani and Pesaran, "Iranian Economy," 190–91.

24. Ali Ansari, *Modern Iran since 1921: The Pahlavis and After* (London: Pearson Education, 2003), 151–52; Pollack, *Persian Puzzle*, 83, 111; Halliday, "Iran," 16.

25. Patrick Clawson, "Iran's Economy: Between Crisis and Collapse," *MERIP Reports*, no. 98 (July–August 1981): 11–15.

26. Esfahani and Pesaran, "Iranian Economy," 189.

27. Ervand Abrahamian, *A History of Modern Iran* (Cambridge, Cambridge University Press, 2008), 125.

28. "Confidential Letter from Francis H. Thomas, American Consul, Isfahan, to William Helseith, Consular Coordinator, American Embassy in Tehran," August 6, 1965, RG 59 General Records of the Bureau of Near Eastern and South Asian Affairs, US Department of State, 1964–66, box 12, ARC.

29. Arang Keshavarzian, *Bazaar and State in Iran* (Cambridge: Cambridge University Press, 2007), 4.

30. Keddie, *Modern Iran*, 256.

31. Ibid., 256.

32. Ibid., 246.

33. Ibid., 256.

34. Esfahani and Pesaran, "Iranian Economy," 192.

35. Suzanne Maloney, "The Revolutionary Economy," in *Iran Primer*, ed. Wright, 95–99.

36. Keddie, *Modern Iran*, 256.

37. Maloney, "Revolutionary Economy," 95.

38. Hamid Hosseini, "From *Homo Economicus* to *Homo Islamicus:* The Universality of Economic Science Reconsidered," in *Modern Capitalism and Islamic Ideology in Iran*, edited by Cyrus Bina and Hamid Zangeneh (New York: St. Martin's Press, 1992), 103–17, at 111–12. However, Islam does not allow usury.

39. Pesaran, "System of Dependent Capitalism," 512.

40. Maloney, "Revolutionary Economy," 96.

41. Hooshang Amirahmadi, "Economic Costs of the War and Reconstruction in Iran," in *Modern Capitalism*, ed. Bina and Zangeneh, 257–81, at 261.

42. Ibid., 260.

43. Behzad Yaghmaian, "Recent Developments in the Political Economy of Iran: The Triangle Crisis," in *Modern Capitalism*, ed. Bina and Zangeneh, 159–88, at 173.

44. Keddie, *Modern Iran*, 264; Yaghmaian, 176.

45. Keddie, *Modern Iran*, 264.

46. Keshavarzian, *Bazaar and State*, 151.

47. "Poverty Casts Its Dark Shadow over the Masses," *Tehran Times*, April 29, 2007.

48. Eshahani and Pesaran note that "the overall inequality measured by the Gini coefficient has remained unchanged." They also suggest that some of the inequality in Iranian society had started to decline before 1979. Esfahani and Pesaran, "Iranian Economy," 195.

49. Robin Wright, *The Last Great Revolution: Turmoil and Transformation in Iran* (New York: Alfred A. Knopf, 2000), 24.

50. "Poverty Casts Its Dark Shadow."

51. Semira Nikou, "The Subsidies Conundrum," in *Iranian Primer*, ed. Wright, 106.

52. "Ten Million Iranians under Absolute Poverty Line," Payvand Iran News, May 29, 2010, www.payvand.com/news/10may/1316.html.

53. Nikou, "Subsidies Conundrum," 104–7.

54. Ibid., 105.

55. "Iran Parliament Moves Ahead with Fuel Subsidies Cuts," Associated Press, October 12, 2009.

56. Nikou, "Subsidies Conundrum," 104.

57. Ibid., 105. See also "Iran's Bold Economic Reform: Economic Jihad," *Economist*, June 23, 2011, 59.

58. Maloney, "Revolutionary Economy," 97.

59. William Yong, "Iran Lets Gas Prices Soar, but Drivers Seem Unfazed," *New York Times*, December 20, 2010, www.nytimes.com/2010/12/21/world/middleeast/21iran.html?e. . . .

60. Nikou, "Subsidies Conundrum," 105.

61. International Monetary Fund, "Statement by IMF Article IV Mission to the Islamic Republic of Iran," Press Release 11/228, June 13, 2011, www.imf.org/external.np/sec/pr/2-11/pr11228.htm.

62. Robert Worth, "Iran's Plan to Phase Out Subsidies Brings Frenzied Debate," *New York Times*, December 2, 2009, www.nytimes.com/2009/12/02/world/middleeast/02iran.html?ref=wor. . . . The IMF suggested in June 2011 that inflation was 12.4 percent in 2010–11. International Monetary Fund, "Statement by IMF Article IV Mission to the Islamic Republic of Iran," Press Release 11/228, June 13, 2011. www.imf.org/external.np/sec/pr/2-11/pr11228.htm.

63. Najmeh Bozorgmehr, "Food Inflation Threatens Stability in Iran," *Financial Times*, November 8, 2011, www.ft.com/cms/s/0/b8bc5c40-09fc-11e1-85ca-00144feabc0.html; "Inflation Hits 15.4 Percent in Iran," *Tehran Times*, July 21, 2011, www.tehrantimes.com/NCms/2007.asp?code=244461.

64. Jay Newton-Small, "One Nation under Sanctions," *Time*, September 24, 2012, 39.

65. Keddie, *Modern Iran*, 246.

66. Hen-Tov, "Understanding Iran's New Authoritarianism," 174.

67. Ilias, "Iran's Economic Conditions," 8; Keshavarzian, *Bazaar and State*, 167. Arjomand suggests that bonyads controls some 40 percent of the economy. Said Amir Arjomand, *After Khomeini: Iran under His Successors* (Oxford: Oxford University Press, 2009), 61.

68. Fredric Wehrey, Jerrold Green, Brian Nichiporuk, Ali Reza Nader, Lydia Hansell, Rosool Nafisi, and S. R. Bohandy, *The Rise of the Pasdaran: Assessing the Domestic Roles of Iran's Islamic Revolutionary Guards Corps* (Santa Monica, CA: RAND Corporation, 2009), xv.

69. Arjomand, *After Khomeini*, 61.

70. Mark Gregory, "Expanding Business Empire of Iran's Revolutionary Guards," BBC, July 26, 2010, www.bbc.co.uk/news/world-middle-east-10743580? . . . See also Ali Reza Nader, "The Revolutionary Guards," in *Iran Primer*, ed. Wright, 59.

71. Arjomand, *After Khomeini*, 60.

72. Keddie, *Modern Iran*, 273.

73. Arjomand, *After Khomeini*, 122.

74. Ibid.

75. Ilias, "Iran's Economic Conditions," 12.

76. Arjomand, *After Khomeini*, 123.

77. "Iran Bank Says US Sanctions, Accusations Wrong," *Tehran Times*, November 14, 2009, www.tehrantimes.com/index_View.asp?code=156400.

78. UNSCR 1929: —It bans transfers of major conventional weapons to Iran; —It bans all Iranian activities related to ballistic missiles that could deliver a nuclear weapon; —It establishes a framework for cargo inspections to detect and stop Iran's smuggling and acquisition of illicit items; —It prohibits Iran from investing abroad in sensitive nuclear activities, such as uranium mining; —It targets directly the role of the IRGC in Iran's proliferation efforts, etc. . . .

79. William Burns, "Under Secretary for Political Affairs, Statement before the House Foreign Affairs Committee," Washington, DC, December 1, 2010.

80. David Cohen, "Under Secretary for Terrorism and Financial Intelligence, US Policy on Iran, Testimony before the Senate Committee on Foreign Relations," December 1, 2011, Washington, DC; Mark Lander and Clifford Krauss, "Gulf Nations Aid US Push to Choke Off Iran Oil Sales," *New York Times*, January 12, 2012, www.nytimes.com/2012/01/13/world/asia/asia-buyers-of-iran-c. . . .

81. Council of the European Union, "Council Conclusions on Iran," January 23, 2012, http://eeas.europa.eu/index_en.htm.

82. US State Department, Office of the Spokesperson, "United States Welcomes Additional European Union Sanctions on Iran," January 23, 2012.

83. Robert Einhorn, "Implementation of Iran Sanctions, House Committee on Oversight and Government Reform," Washington, DC, July 29, 2010.

84. Ron Nixon, "Two Large Multinationals Pull Back from Iran," *New York Times*, March 10, 2010, www.nytimes.com/2010/03/11/world/middleeast/11iran.html? . . . Lukoil

has said that it has lost over $60 million due to US sanctions. See also "Anything to Declare?" *Economist,* July 3, 2010, 58; Office of the Spokesman of the State Department, "Companies Reducing Energy Related Business with Iran," Washington, DC, September 30, 2010. Total of France, Statoil of Norway, and Eni of Italy also "agreed to end their investment in Iran's energy sector." James B. Steinberg, "Deputy Secretary of State, Briefing on New Developments Pursuant to the Comprehensive Iran Sanctions, Accountability and Divestment of 2010," Washington, DC, September 30, 2010.

85. Berman, "Toward an Economic Strategy," 23.

86. David Cohen, "The Law and Policy of Iran Sanctions," remarks at New York University School of Law, September 12, 2012.

87. Marsh, "Thirty Years On," 229.

88. Esfahani and Pesaran, "Iranian Economy," 210. See Akbar Torbat, "Impacts of the US Trade and Financial Sanctions on Iran," *World Economy* 28, no. 3 (2005): 407–34.

89. Esfahani and Pesaran, "Iranian Economy," 209. It is worth noting that their article was published in 2009, before some of the more crippling sanctions were imposed under the Obama administration.

90. Marsh, "Thirty Years On," 223.

91. Esfahani and Pesaran, "Iranian Economy," 209.

92. Ilias, "Iran's Economic Conditions," 23.

93. Rick Goldstone, "Iran Admits Western Sanctions Are Inflicting Damage," *New York Times,* December 20, 2011, www.nytimes.com/2011/12/20/world/middleeast/iran-admits-we. . . .

94. Esfahani and Pesaran, "Iranian Economy," 193.

95. Keddie, *Modern Iran,* 264.

96. Unfortunately for him, this was rejected because of various political pressure by groups such as the American Israeli Public Affairs Committee. Ansari, *Confronting Iran,* 142.

97. President Clinton went further in March 1995 when he issued Executive Order 12957, which included "comprehensive sanctions" to "deal with the unusual and extraordinary threat to the national security, foreign policy, and economy of the United States constituted by the actions and policies of the Government of Iran."

98. Pollack, *Persian Puzzle,* 287.

99. This rose from a total of $9 billion in 1991 to $34 billion in 1993. Keddie, *Modern Iran,* 267.

100. Esfahani and Pesaran, "Iranian Economy," 194.

101. Keddie, *Modern Iran,* 264.

102. Ibid., 273.

103. Ilias, "Iran's Economic Conditions," 21.

104. Ibid., 6.

105. Ibid., 7.

106. Ibid.

107. Kasra Naji, *Ahmadinejad: The Secret History of Iran's Radical Leader* (Berkeley: University of California Press, 2008), 233.

108. Nazila Fathi, "Iran's Stocks Plunge after Vote for UN Review of Nuclear Program," *New York Times,* October 9, 2005.

109. Ibid. The *Tehran Times* has also echoed that this is in the country's national interest.

110. The rial declined 50 percent in approximately two months. Rick Gladstone, "As Further Sanctions Loom, Plunge in Currency's Value Unsettles Iran," *New York Times*, December 20, 2011, www.nytimes.com/2011/12/21/world/middleeast/currency-plung. . . .

111. "President Elaborates on High Price Rises," *Tehran Times*, December 18, 2007, www.tehrantimes.com/NCms/2007.asp?code=159428.

112. Nazila Fathi, "A President's Defender Keeps His Distance," *New York Times*, January 8, 2008, www.nytimes.com/2008/01/08/world/middleeast/08iran.html; Michael Slackman, "A Frail Economy Raises Pressure on Iran's Rulers," *New York Times*, February 3, 2008, www.nytimes.com/2008/02/03/world/asia/03iht-03iran.9691705.html.

113. Keddie, *Modern Iran*, 286.

114. Ibid.

115. Hen-Tov, "Understanding Iran's New Authoritarianism," 173.

116. Electricity: 16.2 percent (1977) to 98.3 percent (2004); piped water: 11.7 percent (1977) to 89.0 percent (2004). Statistical Center of Iran, 1984–2005 Household Income and Expenditure Surveys.

117. Iran Statistical Yearbook 1385 (2006-7), www.sci.org.ir.

118. Hen-Tov, "Understanding Iran's New Authoritarianism," 173.

119. In 1960 there were 281 deaths per 1,000 births versus 42 deaths per 1,000 births in 2001. World Bank, *World Development Indicators 2003* (Washington, DC: World Bank, 2003).

120. United Nations, *2011 Human Development Report* (New York: United Nations, 2011), www.undp.org.ir/doccenter/reports/HDR_2011_EN_Complete.pdf.

121. Djavad Salehi-Isfahani, "Oil Wealth and Economic Growth in Iran," in *Contemporary Iran: Economy, Society, Politics*, edited by Ali Gheissari (Oxford: Oxford University Press, 2009), 15–16.

122. World Bank, "Iran: Country Brief," June 2009.

123. United Nations, *2011 Human Development Report*.

124. Pardis Mahdavi, "Who Will Catch Me If I Fall? Health and the Infrastructure of Risk for Urban Young Iranians," in Ali Gheissari edition, at page 165.

125. Farzaneh Roudi, "Iran Is Reversing Its Population Policy," *Viewpoint* 7 (Woodrow Wilson International Center for Scholars), August 2012, www.wilsoncenter.org/sites/default/files/iran_is_reversing_its_population_policy.pdf.

126. Roksana Bahramitash and Hadi Salehi Esfahani, "Nimble Fingers No Longer! Women's Employment in Iran," in *Contemporary Iran*, ed. Gheissari, 92.

127. "Adult literacy rates have increased from 50 percent to 78 percent in 2002." Hen-Tov, "Understanding Iran's New Authoritarianism," 173.

128. Statistical Center of Iran, www.sci.org. The World Bank has also noted the improvement. The overall literacy rate in 2008 was 85 percent; Data.worldbank.org/country/iran-islamic-republic.

129. United Nations, *2011 Human Development Report*.

130. Jane Howard, *Inside Iran: Women's Lives* (Washington, DC: Mage, 2002), 85, 79.

131. Rebecca Barlow and Shahram Akbarzadeh, "Prospects for Feminism in the Islamic Republic of Iran," *Human Rights Quarterly* 30 (2008): 21–40, at 24.

132. Statistical Center of Iran.

133. As Bahramitash and Saleshi Esfahani note, this is contrary to the female work-force in other parts of the global south: "The trend has been the opposite: Women have increasingly left nimble-finger jobs in the carpet industry to go to school so as to take on clerical, technical and professional positions." Bahramitash and Saleshi Esfahani, "Nimble Fingers," 79.

134. Keddie, *Modern Iran*, 274.

135. Esfahani and Pesaran, "Iranian Economy," 195. See also US Central Intelligence Agency, *CIA World Factbook*.

PART III

The Future

CHAPTER 8

Conclusion
Emancipating Iranian Politics

> Revolution gives ordinary people the false belief that they can remake
> not just themselves, their country, and the whole wide world but
> human nature itself. That such grand designs always fail, that human
> nature is immutable, that everyone's idea of perfection is different—
> these truths are all for a time forgotten.
> —Mark Bowden, *Guests of the Ayatollahs*

Iran's political and social landscape changed dramatically in the twentieth century. The religious movement that developed late in the 1970s in Iran was a
direct response to the alienation felt by Iranians at the shah's Westernization
programs and his relationship to the West.[1] Beginning with Reza Shah in
1925, and continuing in 1941 under Mohammad Reza Pahlavi, the monarchy initiated secular reforms in Iranian society in education, banking, and the
judicial system.[2] These were viewed by many in Iran as an attack on the indigenous culture and Islam. Mohammad Reza Pahlavi was also viewed as beholden
to the West, especially after the United States restored him to the throne in
1953 via the US Central Intelligence Agency's Operation Ajax.[3]

Shia Islam, which is the faith of more than 90 percent of the population,
became the vehicle for the mobilization of discontented Iranians.[4] The clergy
maintained control over the mosques and religious schools, and this allowed
them to sustain their influence at the grassroots level.[5] The discourse of the
religious movement led by Ayatollah Khomeini emphasized the importance of
religious identity and social justice, and of the removal of foreign influences.[6]

Claims of unjust treatment, Western imperialism, and foreign domination under the shah found a receptive audience.

Furthermore, by working from an Islamic base the movement was able to promote a simple message that the population could understand and to which it could relate. The "dualistic idea of a cosmic clash of good versus evil, light and darkness, order and chaos, truth and falsehood" has been prevalent in Iranian society for centuries.[7] Khomeini chose to frame his message in this Manichean worldview.

The ability to mobilize the public around a religious message was an advantage that Khomeini had over the communists and liberal groups in Iran, which were also dissatisfied with the shah. Khomeini drew on a preestablished base—a grassroots religious network—to overthrow the shah.[8]

In March 1979 a referendum changed Iran's government from a monarchy to an Islamic Republic. Out of roughly 39 million citizens, more than 20 million Iranians went to the polls to vote and roughly 98 percent of them voted for the creation of an Islamic Republic.[9] At the end of that year, 16 million people ratified the new Constitution by popular referendum.[10]

The political system, as codified in the Constitution, is a combination of semidemocratic and undemocratic institutions. This represents the inherent contradiction within the system. An overwhelming degree of power rests with the supreme leader and the Guardian Council, a body of senior clerics. Neither institution is elected by the population. The Guardian Council has veto power over members of the Parliament and over legislation developed in the Majles.[11] This unaccountable part of government has vetoed legislation passed in Parliament concerning women's rights, family law, the prevention of torture, and electoral reform.[12] Another unelected political body in Iran is the judiciary, which has closed newspapers and jailed publishers, and has also imprisoned members of political groups for insulting religious values.[13] Thus Iran has the veneer of a democratic system rather than a fully functioning democracy.

Having examined the creation and history of the Islamic Republic of Iran, we now turn to the future. Predicting the future is a difficult endeavor, especially in a country as complicated as Iran. However, it is worth examining a few possible political developments. As the Islamic Republic of Iran moves further into the twenty-first century, it will face many internal and external challenges and threats, and the pertinent question concerns how Iran and its theocratic authoritarian leadership will tackle them. Iran's leaders could adopt the Chinese approach (as practiced in the wake of Tiananmen Square) and implement a harsh crackdown to retain power. They certainly proved capable of this in 2009, when they quashed political protests. Or a gradual opening could occur, whereby power would be devolved from religious bodies to more democratically elected bodies, placing Iran on a path toward greater democratization.

Specifically, this concluding chapter focuses on those political, economic, and social conditions that will be conducive for the gradual transformation from an illiberal, religiously defined nation-state to a more moderate democratic one. The international community's ability to influence Iranian policy will be considered, including pressure to adhere to international norms concerning human rights and nuclear development. If Iran, with its religiously based political system, can develop into a more rights respective society and cooperate with the international community, then other countries would be less concerned about state-sponsored terrorism and threats from this Middle Eastern state. A more democratic system would also protect the basic rights of Iranian citizens and respect their basic dignity.

The Evolution of Iran: How Iran Has Changed

In many ways it is remarkable that the revolutionary Iranian government set up in 1979 survived into its fourth decade. Many revolutions have not lasted as long. During the last few decades, Iran has changed significantly in a number of areas. Its efforts to spread its Revolution throughout the Middle East have been scaled back. Beyond foreign policy, its domestic politics has also been transformed during the last few decades. The Iranian political system has changed not simply because some of the main revolutionary leaders (e.g., Khomeini) have left the scene, but also because the political factions have changed. New political infighting has occurred not just between the conservatives and the reformists but also within the conservative faction. As a result a variety of policies (e.g., family planning) have been pursued that deviate from the Islamic foundation of the political system. This can be explained by the tensions that exist between pragmatism and radicalism, and it demonstrates that a radical form of Islam did not determine all the policies in the Islamic Republic of Iran.

Political Changes

There have been numerous changes to the political players in Iran since the early years of the Revolution. In the early 1980s the two dominant factions competing for power and political influence were the Islamic left—those with a Marxist influence—and the more conservative right—with a focus on free markets. These two factions competed for seats in Parliament and for control over policy. As the 1980s drew to a close, the conservatives had come out on top. This was a result of political maneuvering as well as international developments (the demise of the Soviet Union and its Eastern European counterparts). In the 1990s Iranians saw the rise of the reformists. As the politics and policies of the Islamic Republic of Iran have changed, so have some of the individuals who were soldiers in the Revolution. Some prominent and devoted revolutionaries, who were at the forefront of the Revolution in 1979, have argued for change. And some of these individuals have become disillusioned with the Islamic Republic.

Individuals such as Ganji, Soroush, Mousavi, Montazeri, and Massoumeh Ebtekar all played vital roles in the Revolution and its aftermath. In the decades since, they have called for political change and moderation. Ebtekar was part of the group of students who took American hostages at the US embassy in Tehran. Soroush helped to revise the university curriculum and hence was part of the cultural revolution that took place in the early 1980s. Ganji served in the Revolutionary Guards. All three would support the reform movement in one form or another (as, variously, vice president, intellectual, and journalist). They sought to improve the political system, "not to abolish but to transform non-violently the system they themselves had helped establish. . . . They would attempt to change it from within."[14]

Despite their efforts, many within the reform movement have complained about the lack of concrete results. Efforts to produce greater individual rights and freedoms were blocked by the judiciary and also by the Guardian Council, which vetoed more than a hundred of Khatami's legislative initiatives between 1997 and 2004.[15] Many student protesters were imprisoned and tortured. Numerous newspapers were closed. The reform efforts failed to achieve their goals.

Although many have been critical of the reformists' failure to fundamentally transform the power structure in Iran, they did make a lasting contribution. And though it is true that many of Khatami's political efforts were stymied, his accomplishments not only in foreign policy but also in changing the political culture of Iran live on. People in Iran believe in his message of greater democratization. The protests that followed the presidential elections in June 2009 demanded a more democratic political system. This message will continue even after Khatami has stepped away from the political scene.

The months after the presidential election in 2009 saw Iran consumed by protests, demonstrations, arrests, trials, and much factional fighting. This battle was a power struggle for the political direction of the country. It demonstrated a willingness by those in power, especially the supreme leader, to do whatever was necessary to eliminate political rivals and threats to their power.

The first year of President Ahmadinejad's second term (2009–10) saw the hard-line conservatives in government initiate a harsh crackdown on the reformers associated with the Green Movement. Demonstrations were suppressed. Many protesters were physically attacked and arrested, and some were even killed. Many faced trials that lacked fairness and due process. Others were tortured and raped in prison. The government efforts to silence the Green Movement were largely successful. Its leaders, Mousavi and Karroubi, were placed under house arrest in February 2011. Since then, they have been largely unable to organize or further the goals of the movement.

The political feuding has gone beyond conservatives and reformists. The next subject at the center of the crossfire was President Ahmadinejad and his associates. He became the target of the supreme leader's fury when he challenged Khamenei on who would lead the Intelligence Ministry. Ahmadinejad fired the intelligence minister, Moslehi, and Khamenei ordered the president to reinstate him. Ahmadinejad was trying to enhance his powers via one of the most powerful ministries in the country, and the supreme leader quickly put Ahmadinejad back in his place. The president's assertive behavior was not appreciated and would not be tolerated. To signal Khamenei's disapproval, Mohammed Sharif Malekzadeh, the deputy foreign minister and a close ally of Ahmadinejad, was arrested in June 2011.[16] The next shot across the bow was directed at Ali Akbar Javanfeker, the director of the state's official news agency and Ahmadinejad's political associate, who was briefly arrested in November 2011.[17] Beyond threats to the president's friends and political advisers, a warning was also sent to Ahmadinejad. Ayatollah Khamenei indicated that Iran's political system could be improved if the office of the president were to be eliminated. Instead, Khamenei suggested an increase in the powers of Parliament.[18] Eliminating the office of the president would place even greater powers in the hands of the supreme leader.

Although these political changes are not imminent, they were intended to put Ahmadinejad on notice. The concern from the supreme leader's office was that Ahmadinejad and his allies wanted to displace the clergy and gradually shift power to the president and his associates. The supreme leader again demonstrated that he would tolerate no threats to his control over the political system. He would not tolerate a challenge from Khatami, Mousavi, or even conservatives such as Ahmadinejad. Khamenei indicated to the political elites that Ahmadinejad, regardless of his beliefs, was dispensable.[19] Ahmadinejad is a much weaker political figure as a result of his confrontation with the supreme leader.

The Evolution of the Elections

Elections have been an important element of Iran's political system for the last thirty years. Beginning with a referendum to change the political system to an Islamic republic, Iran has held repeated elections for a number of political offices. Although there are other political institutions that are not subject to voting (the supreme leader), democratic elements are a fundamental aspect of this political system. And though some elections have been criticized for irregularities, most notably the 2009 presidential election, Iran has also carried out free and fair elections. Some of these produced surprising results, such as the presidency of Khatami in 1997.

The international community has also seen more competition within political factions in Iran. Elections in the 1980s were often between those on the Islamic left and those on the conservative right. In the last few presidential and parliamentary elections, observers have seen more competition both within and among conservatives.[20] This competition within the conservative ranks will continue in future parliamentary elections and presidential elections.

Changes in Human Rights

Although there have been many human rights violations in Iran during the last three decades, the international community has also seen some limited progress on this issue. Although a number of rights have been violated, including an array of civil and political rights, one should understand that the motivation for these human rights violations is perceived threats to the regime. Limitations on political rights, including freedom of expression, occur to limit political opposition to the regime and especially the hard-line conservatives in power. It is also important to note that Iran has experienced some improvements in human rights since the Revolution, namely, in some socioeconomic rights including education and health care. Improving education, especially for girls, and efforts to improve access to health care services are not perceived as a threat to the regime and are consistent with the Islamic themes that Khomeini used before the Revolution.

Thus, one can see a road map to improving Iran's human rights record. The international community has already seen some limited steps in Iran's socialization toward protecting human rights. To see further progress, the international community and especially the United States must refrain from threats (i.e., of fomenting regime change). Although one should not expect the Islamic Republic to emerge overnight as a liberal democracy that protects a wide range of human rights, neither should one be utterly pessimistic about the chances for progress.

Changes in Foreign Policy

There has been a trend toward realism in Iranian foreign policy during the last few decades. Despite harsh religious rhetoric, the Islamic Republic of Iran has demonstrated that Islam and religious principles mostly take a backseat to realism, power politics, and the survival of the state. The inability of foreign policymakers to understand the realism at the heart of Iranian foreign policy has created mutual hostilities and confrontations that make improving relations with Tehran rather difficult.

Although religious rhetoric has often billowed from Friday sermons and speeches, pragmatic policies driven by a basic understanding of realism have generally determined foreign policy during the last thirty years. Thus the hostage crisis and the desire to spread the Islamic Revolution throughout the Middle East gradually gave way to more pragmatic policies. Despite harsh language, Tehran has avoided a direct military confrontation with Israel for more than thirty years. After the first decade of the Revolution, the international community witnessed Iran's willingness to trade arms with the United States through Israel. It also saw Iran's cooperation in the war in Afghanistan and efforts by Khatami and others to improve relations with Saudi Arabia and other Persian Gulf states.

Iran's development of nuclear energy and potentially nuclear weapons can also be seen as a way to ensure the survival of the regime in a way that is consistent with realism. This is not surprising given the wars and instability in the region. Likewise, Tehran's support for Hezbollah and Hamas, though consistent with the religious ideology of the Revolution, can also serve to strengthen Iran's national interests. The more Israel is forced to deal with hostilities on its borders, the less likely it will be to strike Iran. Thus many of Iran's foreign policies can be understood as a pragmatic response to secure its national interests.[21] This is more consistent with realism then with revolutionary Islam.

Economic Changes

Iran's economy has faced numerous challenges during the last few decades, including the destructive war with Iraq, inflation, international sanctions, unemployment, and corruption. Although some of these economic problems were inherited at the time of the Revolution, other economic difficulties stem from ideological differences among the revolutionaries. Many revolutionaries had been influenced by Marxism and thus argued that Islamic tenets demanded social justice for the poor. The Islamic left wanted the government to redistribute large estates and nationalize various industries. For the conservative-leaning revolutionaries who had large landholdings, they opposed large-scale government intervention into the economy. Conservatives argued that property rights and free trade had a long tradition in Islamic history. The factional infighting over what constituted an Islamic economy created significant problems that continue to plague Iran today.

Iran today continues to face a number of economic problems. A significant percentage of its people live below the poverty line.[22] Unemployment is extensive.[23] Oil revenues are not finding their way to the vast majority of Iranians. And charitable foundations run by clerics, such as the Imam Reza Foundation, have billions of dollars in assets.[24] To make matters worse, the ruling clerics enjoy luxury lifestyles that suggest they are out of touch with the normal struggles of everyday Iranians. These wealthy individuals have increased their prosperity at the cost of millions of unemployed Iranians. (Many Iranians support normal relations with the United States, if for no other reason than to improve their country's economic condition.)

Creating a vibrant economy is essential to Iran for a number of reasons. Economic growth and especially the creation of jobs are essential for the young people (under twenty-five years of age) who make up half the population. The youth of Iran are educated and frustrated. Many will obtain a university degree that does not translate into a well-paying job. Young people who are unemployed will put off getting married or will be forced to live with relatives, which will increase their sense of inadequacy and frustration. When this frustration is coupled with their access to the outside world via the Internet, their resentment will grow. This resentment is something that Iranian leaders must address, or it could lead to unrest.

The Future of Iran

Policymakers in Washington and around the world have to deal with Iran due to its geopolitical and economic importance. Although Iran is not a superpower, it aspires to be a regional power and one whose influence and role in the Middle East must be respected. Given these factors, policymakers need to understand Iranian politics. Though predicting political outcomes in Iran is a difficult task, one can spell out a few potential scenarios that policymakers might encounter in the future. One possible development in Iran would be a movement toward greater democratization, which would result in a more liberal democratic polity. Alternatively, the international community might witness greater repression by the clerical regime. This section examines both possibilities and assesses the likelihood of democratic change in Iran.

Toward a More Liberal Democracy

Many in the international community would welcome a more liberal and democratic Iran. This would mean less support for groups that have used violence against civilians, such as Hamas and Hezbollah. It could also mean that the threat of a nuclear Iran would decline. When South Africa transformed its political system from an apartheid-led government to a more democratic one, the government gave up its former nuclear program. A more democratic Iran, with power concentrated in the hands of popularly elected bodies such as the Majles, would also be more likely to improve its human rights record. Given these progressive policy changes, what are the chances for significant political change in Iran? And what would be required to accomplish these changes?

It is not impossible for a religiously inspired nation-state such as Iran to undertake fundamental political change. The international community has witnessed other states with a strong religious tradition make a transition to a more secular and democratic polity. This change occurs for a number of reasons. First, some religiously inspired nation-states have experienced a decline in the intensity of religion in their society. Many national movements experience a lull in ardent support over time.[25]

A second reason why religious influence declines in a society concerns corruption. Corruption can lead to the decline of religious influence, especially when the corruption stems from religious leaders. Religion can be used by leaders to mobilize a population, not only because its symbols and beliefs are familiar to the people but also because the moral component of many religious traditions gives religious leaders the *presumption* of integrity and character. When religious leaders are found to have violated basic moral precepts, their support declines. The more the clergy preach about equality, morality, solidarity with the poor, and spiritual and sexual purity, and then act contrary to those values, the less support they will find in the population. When religious figures assume positions of power or have a significant influence on a society, this can result in inappropriate behaviors and a susceptibility to corruption. When religious figures are accused of corruption or political abuse, this results in a loss of legitimacy. And this loss of legitimacy can also lead individuals to lose faith in their religion. Thus citizens may desire a more secular polity. In a similar fashion, as clerics in Iran have amassed wealth, many Iranians have come to resent the clerics in power. The continuing economic problems facing the country—including unemployment, inflation, and a depreciating currency—all exacerbate a loss of legitimacy for the ruling elites. Because Iran has billions in oil revenues, many question why these revenues are not helping more Iranians. The more the ruling elites talk about justice and authorize torture, the less legitimacy they have.

In addition, international influence should not be ignored. International norms can change the behavior of a state, even one that is based on religious principles. The role of international norms has received more attention from scholars in the last decade. Scholars have argued that states are socialized over time through domestic and international pressure to internalize and implement policies that respect international norms.[26] This international socialization can promote policy change in states. International norms concerning human rights, international cooperation, and peaceful coexistence also affect religious nation-states.

Finally, religiously defined states that adopt more secular and democratic policies often do so after a significant threat has been removed. A looming political threat, whether of an international or domestic variation, will often hinder significant change in a religious nation-state because its leaders will use the threat to scare their citizens. Hence, removing perceived threats is more likely to produce political moderation over time.

What steps are necessary for gradual change and greater democratization in Iran? The first step typically requires that the people are disillusioned with their regime. The 2009 presidential election and its violent aftermath demonstrated the frustration and resentment that many Iranians have for the theocracy. This is a result of the corruption and the illegitimacy of the June 2009 elections, not to mention the country's growing social and economic problems.

The ruling elite have failed to address numerous social and economic problems. Although Khomeini and his revolutionary cadre promised a more just society, many Iranians have failed to see significant improvement in their lives on a variety of issues. Numerous problems exist in Iran that need to be addressed: "Homeless children wandering the streets, widespread drug addiction, flagrant and flourishing prostitution are only a few of the most visible symptoms of the bankruptcy of what claims to be a religious state. Everything that the regime forbids is available provided one is prepared to pay the price . . . or has the right connections. Prohibition has generated a lucrative parallel market; corruption thrives at all levels of society: What the Iranians call 'mullah connections' are enough to sidestep laws and regulations. The regime's great families have developed their own networks of favoritism; the *aqazadeh*—the daddy's boys of the establishment—move effortlessly into key positions in the business world."[27] Some have noted that Iranians are disillusioned with religion along with the government. Omid Memarian suggested as much: "We're beginning to understand where religion has led us. We can judge the impact it's had on political life, on society. Religion has meant the institutionalization of corruption. What a joke! It's not surprising that today religion has left the hearts and lives of young people. Our youth has become secularist in its outlook, in its way of life, in its hopes. And this is happening in a time of crisis, when the Islamic Republic is in danger."[28]

Even some high-level clerics have voiced their discontent with the political system. Ayatollah Jalaluddin Taheri—the Friday prayers leader of Isfahan—resigned due to the repressive policies of the clerics. He charged "Iran's clerical leaders with directing and encouraging a bunch of club wielders and of marrying the ill-tempered, ugly hag of violence to religion." Further, he claimed, "the centers of power were unchecked and unbridled; . . . neither reproached by the executors of justice nor reproved by the law."[29] These criticisms stem from the oppressive governing system. Thus one of the greatest hindrances to the long-term survival of the theocracy is the illegitimacy within the political system.

Beyond the internal criticism, a variety of changes in international relations could affect the future of Iran. The changes taking place in Iraq are especially relevant. Arguably, the Islamic Revolution was strengthened most by the invasion from Iraq in 1980. This threat led to a rally-around-the-flag effect and increased domestic support for the new political system more than anything Khomeini could have initiated. The threat from the nonbeliever Saddam Hussein has passed since the American invasion in 2003. Furthermore, because Shia political parties and leaders have exerted much political influence in Iraq since the fall of Saddam Hussein, the threat from an attack by Iraq has decreased substantially.

Although the threat from Iraq has been removed, the perceived threat from the United States still remains. Iran's incorporation into the so-called

Axis of Evil during President Bush's 2002 State of the Union Address was not well received in Tehran. The wars and regime change in Iran's neighbors—Afghanistan and Iraq—have also given some of the ruling clerics pause.[30] Though relations with the United States have been difficult since 1979, these military endeavors and the Axis of Evil speech did not improve relations.[31]

Improving American–Iranian relations, though difficult, should be a priority for both countries. The United States could provide Iran with security guarantees so that Tehran would feel less threatened. [32] Many Iranians have voiced their support for improved relations with the United States.[33] Compromise with Iran will be difficult so long as there are internal tensions between neoconservatives and pragmatic conservatives in the Iranian regime. Ultimately, Washington's best approach may be to manage Iran's decline. Iran has numerous economic problems, including corruption, inflation, and a lack of competition due to the IRGC and the *bonyads*. Furthermore, Iran has a frustrated young population. Coupled with demands for greater freedom, Iran has numerous internal problems with which to deal. Iran's regime has shown signs of significant political divisions not only between reformists and conservatives but also between conservatives. The political infighting between Supreme Leader Khamenei and President Ahmadinejad is evidence of this. Thus an Iran marked by internal divisions is not in a position to make a grand bargain with the United States.

Washington would be wise to develop a policy of strategic patience or containment vis-à-vis Tehran. If the United States and other countries in the international community accept that Iran has a number of self-generated problems (corruption, inflation, a lack of legitimacy) that have the potential to weaken the regime in the long term, then they should patiently wait for these self-inflicted wounds to lead to the internal decay of the system. Containing Iran and waiting for the theocracy's internal problems to weaken it from within may not be a politically correct policy, especially among hawkish politicians who talk of an attack on Iran. And though President Obama specifically ruled out a policy of containment, it still may be the best long-term policy stance for dealing with Iran. Iran's political leaders do not inspire many of their citizens, and the political system has inherent contradictions built into it that prevent it from dealing with a range of problems. Because the United States and the West have a superior military capability when compared with Iran, Washington and its allies can contain Iran in the short term and wait for the regime to tear away at its foundations.

The United States may have to wait for a generational change to occur in Iran. A new supreme leader may have a different global perspective and may be more open to international cooperation. Although patiently waiting for Tehran to change may not appear to be very satisfying, it may be Washington's best option. Thus, instead of threatening Iran, the United States should try to manage the internal decay within the Iranian system.

Another Revolution?

Many have speculated on Iran's future and its movement toward democracy. The presidential elections in June 2009 and the subsequent demonstrations that summer led some commentators to assert that we were witnessing another revolution in Iran. Although we have seen an Arab Awakening, so far this has not happened in Iran. First, many reformers such as Khatami do not want to use violence against the regime to achieve their goals. Others, such as Said Hajjarian, who was the strategist behind the reformers, have said they do not want another revolution.[34] It is not clear that most Iranians have any desire for a violent overthrow of the government. They, unlike some of their counterparts in the Middle East (e.g., Syrians), have not taken to the streets repeatedly in the face of violence. They want peaceful political change. Many reformists in the Green Movement want to make the political system more democratic. They do not want to bring down the system. Nor are they arguing for a secular democracy. Khatami explained: "I do not mean 'liberal democracy.' Democracy means the government is chosen by the people and they have the power to change it if they are unhappy, but Islam is one of the foundations of our culture and it will influence our democracy."[35]

Further development of civil society can advance the goal of democracy. When a country has a vibrant civil society that is tolerated by the individuals in charge, change is possible. In Poland the international community witnessed an active grassroots movement in Solidarity. When coupled with compromises by communists, change occurred in Poland. The Polish communists (due in part to Gorbachev's unwillingness to send in the military to crush the protesters) did not engage in a large-scale massacre of Solidarity supporters. Similarly, the African National Congress was able to assume power when the apartheid-led government decided to compromise instead of initiating more bloodshed in the 1990s. This was also evident in Iran in the late 1970s. The shah elected not to slaughter his people when faced with a strong civil society movement based on Shia Islam.

Iran's civil society has shown moments of vibrancy. Women are more active and educated than in the past, and they are demanding their rights. They have also started numerous organizations dedicated to improving women's condition in Iranian society. And they have developed newspapers and magazines to address the inequality in their society.

We have seen the growth of Islamic feminism within Iran, especially "among highly educated, middle-class Muslim women who are unwilling to break away from their religious orientation."[36] Iran's Islamic feminists—who include female lawyers, politicians, academics, and writers—have argued for improvements in women's lives and in changes in Iranian laws. Some have been deeply influenced by Western and global feminism. Some Islamic feminists have challenged interpretations of Islamic texts that are "orthodox, literalist, or misogynist."[37] By focusing on verses in the Qur'an that support gender equality, Islamic feminists have argued for access to higher education and the repeal of discriminatory laws. And their efforts have resulted in some limited successes. As Valentine Moghadam notes, "As a result of pressure from Islamic feminists, parliament and government bodies passed legislation to support working mothers, to allow unmarried women to study abroad, and to permit war widows to retain custody of their children and to receive financial compensation. The 1992 amendments to the divorce laws enabled the court to place a monetary value on women's housework."[38] Thus we see grassroots efforts among women applying political pressure to the Iranian political system and using the discourse of Islam to try to accomplish their goals.

Beyond these efforts by female activists, Iran needs to develop a well-organized opposition. The Green Movement may have had significant support in the summer of 2009, but it has since demonstrated its weakness. First, its nominal leadership has been sidelined. Karroubi and Mousavi were placed under house arrest in 2011. The weakness or absence of a charismatic leader (like Khomeini in 1979) makes pursuing democratic change even harder. In addition, many of their supporters were thrown in prison. The movement also lacks a clear and distinct vision for the future. What specifically does the opposition stand for? Democracy and freedom are noble goals, but this has not united all Iranians across the political spectrum. Many supporters of the Green Movement who took to the streets in the summer of 2009 were students or from the middle class. The Green Movement and reformists cannot rely only on the middle class for change to occur. They must mobilize the support of the lower classes (Khomeini's downtrodden). This is especially true in the rural areas where Ahmadinejad has been popular. Any political change will require a grassroots movement that has broad support from rural areas as well as ethnic minorities. So far, the Green Movement has lacked an overarching strategy to reform the political system.

Every society needs a moral vision of how society should be organized. For the Iranian people, the Revolution of 1979 had provided that vision, based on Shia Islam. The problem today is that the moral vision of the Revolution has lost its legitimacy. For meaningful change to occur, Iran needs not only for the ruling elites to relinquish some of their power but also the development of a new moral vision. One of the weaknesses of the Green Movement is its lack of a clear moral strategy that is distinguished from the revolutionary vision. Because the Green Movement did not break completely with Islam, it has not provided a new, compelling vision.

Thus, though a number of factors exist to promote change (frustration with the ruling clerics, corruption, a desire for change, a reduction in threats and elements of civil society), it appears unlikely that the international community will see a significant political change in Iran in the short term. Without a significant change in leadership, especially in the supreme leader, Iran will not make progress toward greater democratization. Khamenei's strategy of divide and rule among political factions has served him well. He has also demonstrated his willingness to kill his citizens to maintain power. The clerical regime has also demonstrated its willingness to crush aspects of civil society that it perceives to be a threat. And there are additional problems within Iranian civil society: "There can be little doubt about the vibrancy of Iran's NGOs [nongovernmental organizations], but the pathway to success may be rocky. The movement is restricted to the upper and middle classes; mobilizing 'the masses' has proven to be more difficult than anticipated. NGOs lack the necessary tools and capacity for communicating with the least-favored strata of the population; radio, television, and much of the press are tightly controlled by the regime. NGOs have no access to them."[39]

When Khamenei leaves the political scene, whoever replaces him will have an opportunity to initiate change. If his successor is more Gorbachev and less Stalin, Iran could moderate its policy.

Toward More Repression

The June 2009 presidential elections showed just how far hard-line conservatives were willing to go to hold on to power. The 2009 elections offered a choice between four candidates and a series of free-wheeling debates. It ended with jail sentences, torture, and in some cases, death. A few hours after the polls closed, the Interior Ministry announced a resounding victory by Ahma-dinejad. His thirty-point victory over Mousavi led many in the Green Move-ment to cry voter fraud. The fact that some 40 million votes were counted so quickly also gave credence to the belief that this had not been a free and fair election. Thus it was not surprising when millions of Iranians who felt their vote had been stolen took to the streets to protest.

The protests and the regime's response indicated that many in the ruling elite were willing to spill their citizens' blood. In the weeks that followed, nu-merous protesters were killed. Neda's tragic shooting and the fact that she bled to death on the street became a symbol of the regime's brutality. The govern-ment alleged that the video of her death that circulated worldwide was a fake, and it even went so far as to prevent her mother from visiting her grave. This brutal response was promoted by the supreme leader, who on June 19, 2009, issued a warning to the protesters. He told the protesters that if they did not stay off the street, there would be violence.

Beyond the killings that took place on the streets of Tehran, numerous protesters and some opposition figures were arrested. Some told of the torture to which they were subjected in prison. Show trials were also conducted. The theocratic, authoritarian regime sought to terrorize the opposition through these acts of repression and violence.

Furthermore, those in power appear more than willing to unleash violence against any perceived threats to the regime. Although the shah was reluctant to engage in the bloodbath of his people, Khamenei and members of the IRGC are less constrained. The willingness of the regime's leaders to use force against the protesters indicates they are unwilling and unlikely to give up or share power in the next few years. One can thus expect more repression in Iran. Therefore, the leaders' willingness to resort to a harsh crackdown sug-gests similarities with the communists in Beijing. The Chinese Communist Party was willing to send the tanks into Tiananmen Square to prevent greater democratization in that country. Because Khamenei and others in power in Iran appear to be willing to do the same, change may be a long time coming.

The Arab Awakening

The Arab Awakening, which saw protests across much of the Middle East in 2011 and toppled dictators in Egypt and Tunisia, was of course followed with great interest by various political actors in Iran. Mousavi and Karroubi sought government permission to hold a rally in honor of the demonstra-tors in Tunisia and Egypt, who pushed autocratic leaders out of power. The government denied them permission for the rally. (This is another example of how the government silenced the Green Movement.) Mousavi and Karroubi attempted to use the Arab Awakening as a base for greater democratization in Iran. But they were unable to use the momentum and inspiration of the Arab Awakening to further their cause.

Ayatollah Khamenei also tried to claim ownership of the Arab Awakening. In April 2011 the supreme leader claimed that the popular uprisings throughout the Middle East had been inspired by the Iranian Revolution of 1979: "The blessed movements were a fruit of the perseverance and bravery of the Iranian nation."[40] His claim that the Revolution of 1979 inspired the Arab Awakening is far-fetched, considering that Arabs across the Middle East demanded freedom and democracy, neither of which Iranians fully enjoy. The Arab Awakening is a warning to the regime. Repression cannot always guarantee power.[41]

Aspects of the Arab Awakening are quite unsettling to the clerical leaders in Tehran. Although Iran may be happy that pro-Western leaders such as former Egyptian president Mubarak and former Tunisian president Ben Ali are no longer in office, they are deeply concerned about the revolts in Syria. The Assad regime in Damascus is one of the few consistent allies that Tehran has known in the Middle East. At the time of writing, protests and violence continue despite more than 60,000 deaths in Syria. The fall of Bashar al-Assad would harm Tehran's strategic interests. Iran has often used Syria as a means to transit supplies to Hezbollah in Lebanon. If the Assad regime falls due to continued protests, this could lead to a regime that is led by Sunnis. And a Sunni-led Syria may look to Saudi Arabia for support. This would further enhance Saudi Arabia's influence in the Middle East at the expense of Tehran.

Masses of people demonstrating in the streets make Iranian leaders very nervous. They fear a velvet revolution or a soft revolution—undermining the regime from within via foreign ideas, influence, and culture. Maziar Bahari, a journalist for *Newsweek* who was imprisoned for more than a hundred days, explains the government's mindset:

> Soon after my arrest, in addition to accusing me of working for various spy agencies, Mr. Rosewater [interrogator] had insisted that I'd masterminded the coverage of the election by the agents of the Western media in Iran. This played to a familiar fear. Ayatollah Khamenei liked to warn Iranians about a "cultural NATO" as threatening as the military one—a network of journalists, activists, scholars and lawyers who supposedly

sought to undermine the Islamic Republic from within. Anyone on the streets of Tehran in June [2009] would have known how spontaneous— even leaderless—the postelection protests had been. But Khamenei and the Guards clearly believed, or at least wanted Iranians to believe that they had been orchestrated by foreigners. They called the plot a "velvet revolution" or a "soft overthrow."[42]

Senior members of the IRGC, including Major General Mohammad Ali Jafari, have warned about a color revolution in Iran. In the days leading up to the June 2009 presidential election, IRGC Brigadier General Yadollah Javani warned Mousavi and the reformists that the Green Movement "will [be] suffocate[d] before it is even born."[43] Their fears of a color revolution will unfortunately result in more repression.

Threats and Retaliation

The beginning of 2012 saw verbal sparring between Iran and some of its long-time enemies. In response to additional US sanctions, Iranian vice president Mohammad-Reza Rahimi threatened to close the Strait of Hormuz, the vital waterway through which one-fifth of the oil consumed globally passes.[44] President Obama replied to this threat by sending a letter to the supreme leader indicating that the United States would not tolerate any attempts by Iran to close the strait.[45] But there are doubts that Iran would close the strait. If Tehran did decide to mine the strait's waters, it would inflict heavy economic damage on its economy because much of its oil passes through the strait. Tehran is unlikely to make this type of self-inflicted economic wound unless it is attacked.

Unfortunately, discussions about a possible attack on Iran by Israel increased at the start of 2012. Israeli leaders, including Prime Minister Netanyahu, view Iran's nuclear program as an existential threat. There has been much speculation that Israel will launch a military attack on nuclear sites in Iran in an attempt to set back the nuclear program. Although Washington has publicly discouraged Tel Aviv from doing this, the United States has no guarantees that Israel will not engage in a series of military strikes. Tehran has warned that any military actions on the part of the United States or Israel will be met with "an iron fist." Ayatollah Khamenei stated that "the Iranian nation will not invade any country or nation, but it will respond to any invasion or threat with full force."[46] At the time of writing, Iran has not caved in to threats from Israel or the international community regarding its nuclear program. These continuing threats do not bode well for diplomacy or for the moderation of the political system in Iran.

Iran in the Twenty-First Century

Iran faces numerous challenges as it navigates its way through a globalized world. If Iranian leaders feel less threatened and can see some economic benefits from cooperation with the West and additional European and American incentives, we may see a gradual change of the Iranian polity. This, coupled with a growing young population that does not want a stringent form of Islam to control their lives and is frustrated with the corruption within the religious leadership, could lead to a more moderate democratic polity. This is not to suggest that Iran will change overnight. There is still no credible, unified opposition movement to lead the cause. But economic incentives combined with a decrease in perceived threats and the loss of legitimacy of religious figures can lead to the gradual reform of the political system. Some, such as Akbar Ganji, have already called for this reform.

International norms have played and will continue to play a role in the transformation of the Iranian political system. The more Iranian leaders talk about specific international norms such as democracy or cooperation with the international community, the more they affirm the existence of the norm.[47] And the more difficult it becomes for them to criticize other states for violating a norm, when they are also violating the norm in question. Some have already noted the value of international cooperation and moderation.

Even Ahmadinejad has used language concerning the norms of human rights. In a message to the American people, he stated: "Both (nations) greatly value and readily embrace the promotion of human ideals such as compassion, empathy, respect for the rights of human beings, security, justice and equity." He went on to criticize the Bush administration because "civil liberties in the United States are being increasingly curtailed . . . judicial due process and fundamental rights are being trampled upon." So even he has used the language of human rights.

International norms, a decrease in threats, corruption, and the loss of the regime's legitimacy can all lead to changes in aspects of Iranian policy. Some religiously defined nation-states, including Ireland and Great Britain, have evolved from illiberal political systems to democracies that protect human rights. In addition, Iran's ties to Hezbollah and other organizations that employ violence against civilians might be weakened if the leadership of the country were viewed as less Islamic. Some human rights violations against women and religious minorities could be avoided if Islamic tenets were reinterpreted. A decrease in religious influence might also allow for an opening to promote the greater democratization of the political system. Iranians have indicated that they believe that living in a country that elects representatives is very important.[48] A more democratic government, in keeping with changes in leadership positions, may disavow its nuclear ambitions, as South Africa did after apartheid ended, and improve its record on human rights. Thus a moderation of Iranian politics could have potential benefits for Iranians with regard to human rights, as well as for the international community, in greater cooperation.

Although almost all religiously oriented national movements, especially in their early years of development, have engaged in illiberal policies, not all have continued to do so. For example, Ireland, Poland, and Great Britain—all countries with a strongly religious national legacy—are today liberal democracies that respect human rights. This is reflected by their consistent "free" status in Freedom House surveys. Under the right conditions, Iran could follow in their footsteps. At this point the international community can only hope that change will come sooner rather than later. I am not optimistic that Iran will change for the better in the next few years. I hope I am wrong.

Notes

1. John Esposito and John Voll, *Islam and Democracy* (Oxford: Oxford University Press, 1996), 58; Sandra Mackey, *The Iranians: Persia, Islam and the Soul of a Nation* (New York: Penguin Books, 1986).

2. See Eliz Sanasarian, *Religious Minorities in Iran* (Cambridge: Cambridge University Press, 2000), 15; Ali Akbar Mahdi, "Iranian Women: Between Islamicization and Globalization," in *Iran Encountering Globalization: Problems and Prospects*, edited by Ali Mohammadi (New York: RoutledgeCurzon, 2003), 50.

3. Kenneth Pollack, *The Persian Puzzle: The Conflict between Iran and America* (New York: Random House, 2004), 65. See also Elton Daniel, *The History of Iran* (Westport, CT: Greenwood Press, 2001).

4. Robin Wright, *In the Name of God* (New York: Simon & Schuster, 1989), 42.

5. Mahmood Monshipouri, *Islamism, Secularism, and Human Rights in the Middle East* (Boulder, CO: Lynne Rienner, 1998), 173.

6. Mahdi, "Iranian Women," 47.

7. Bernard Lewis, "The Roots of Muslim Rage," *Atlantic Monthly* 266, no. 3 (September 1990): 47–60, at 25.

8. Fred Halliday, *Nation and Religion in the Middle East* (Boulder, CO: Lynne Rienner, 2000), 137.

9. See John Esposito, *The Oxford History of Islam* (Oxford: Oxford University Press, 1999), 675–90. See also Wright, *Name of God*, 65; and Pollack, *Persian Puzzle*, 145, 152.

10. Esposito and Voll, *Islam and Democracy*, 62.

11. Monshipouri, *Islamism, Secularism, and Human Rights*, 178, 186.

12. Human Rights Watch, *World Report 2003, Iran*, available at www.hrw.org; US State Department, "Country Reports on Human Rights Practices: 2003—Iran," www.state.gov/g/drl/rls/hrrpt/2003/27927.htm.

13. Bureau of Democracy, Human Rights, and Labor, US State Department, "International Religious Freedom Report," October 7, 2002.

14. Jean-Daniel Lafond and Fred Reed, *Conversations in Tehran* (Vancouver: Talon Books, 2006), 13.

15. Bernd Kaussler, "European Union Constructive Engagement with Iran (2000–2004): An Exercise in Conditional Human Rights Diplomacy," *Iranian Studies* 41, no. 3 (June 2008): 269–95, at 279.

16. J. David Goodman, "Iran Rift Deepens with Arrest of President's Ally," *New York Times*, June 23, 2011, www.nytimes.com/2011/06/24/world/middleeast/24iran.html.

17. Rick Gladstone and Artin Afkami, "Top Media Aide of Iran's President Reported Held in Raid," *New York Times*, November 21, 2011, www.nytimes.com/2011/11/22/world/middleeast/ali-akbar-javan. . . .

18. Robert Worth, "Iran's Power Struggle Goes beyond Personalities to Future of Presidency Itself," *New York Times*, October 26, 2011, www.nytimes.com/2011/10/27/world/middleeast/in-iran-rivalry. . . .

19. Karim Sadjadpouri, "The Rise and Fall of Iran's Ahmadinejad," *Washington Post*, July 13, 2011, www.washingtonpost.com/opinions/the-rise-and-fall-of-irans-a. . . .

20. Vali Nasr, "The Conservative Wave Rolls On," *Journal of Democracy* 16, no. 4 (October 2005): 9–22. It also demonstrates the divisions within conservative ranks.

21. This does not discount the fact that individuals in the Iranian regime occasionally engage in aggressive policies, such as the storming of the British embassy or the plot to assassinate the Saudi ambassador to the United States in 2011. A number of questions remain about who was involved in the assassination attempt, and who in Tehran had knowledge of it. Iranian leaders, including the supreme leader, denied any involvement in the assassination attempt. Members of the Qods force have been implicated in the plot.

22. Mahmood Monshipouri, "The Revival of Populism in Iranian Politics," *Turkish Weekly*, www.turkishweekly.net/comments.php?id=1436.

23. Hen-Tov has suggested 16 percent. Elliot Hen-Tov, "Understanding Iran's New Authoritarianism," *Washington Quarterly* 30, no. 1 (Winter 2006–7): 163–79.

24. Amir Taheri, "Winners and Losers Turn the Fate of Iran," *Gulf News*, June 29, 2005, www.gulfnews.com/opinion.NF.asp?articleID=170841.

25. Crane Brinton, *The Anatomy of Revolution* (New York: Random House, 1965). Of course, this is not always the case. If one looks at the evolution of Turkey, one sees that the reverse has occurred. Turkey has witnessed a growth in religious influence in the political system since its founding by Ataturk.

26. Thomas Risse, Stephen Ropp, and Kathrin Sikkink, *The Power of Human Rights: International Norms and Domestic Change* (Cambridge: Cambridge University Press, 1999), 5.

27. Lafond and Reed, *Conversations*, 157.

28. Ibid., 110.

29. Human Rights Watch, *World Report 2003*. Other clerics have also voiced their concerns about the hard-line conservatives who have strayed from the Revolution's goals. Nazila Fathi, "Political Fervor of Iranian Clerics Begins to Ebb," *New York Times,* January 17, 2003.

30. As Gawdat Bahgart has suggested, "Iranian strategists feel threatened by the growing non-conventional capacities of several of their neighbors and also by the deployment of American troops next to their borders in almost all directions." Quoted in "Nuclear Proliferation: The Islamic Republic of Iran," *International Studies Perspectives* 7, no. 2 (May 2006): 128.

31. American–Iranian relations had thawed slightly before the axis-of-evil speech. The United States had removed the Taliban in Afghanistan and Iran was cooperating at the Bonn Conference (December 2001) on the restructuring of Afghanistan with the Karzai government. However a month later the Iranians felt betrayed by the axis-of-evil speech.

32. The truth is that the United States has limited options because a military strike is difficult and economic sanctions could harm civilians and the global economy.

33. A World Public Opinion Poll in 2008 indicated that close to 70 percent of Iranians wanted direct talks with the United States; see www.worldpublicopinion.org. International Crisis Group, *US–Iranian Engagement: The View from Tehran*, Middle East Briefing 28 (Tehran/Brussels: International Crisis Group, 2009).

34. Lafond and Reed, *Conversations*, 202.

35. Hooman Majd, *The Ayatollah Begs to Differ: The Paradox of Modern Iran* (New York: Anchor Books, 2009), 219.

36. Nayereh Tohidi, "'Islamic Feminism': Perils and Promises," *MEWS Review* xvi, nos. 3–4 (Fall 2001–Winter 2002). See also Ziba Mir-Hosseini and Richard Tapper, *Islam and Democracy in Iran: Eshkevari and the Quest for Reform* (New York: I. B. Tauris, 2006), 25.

37. Valentine M. Moghadam, "Feminism and Islamic Fundamentalism: A Secularist Interpretation," *Journal of Women's History* 13, no. 1 (Spring 2001): 42–45.

38. Valentine M. Moghadam, "Islamic Feminism and Its Discontents: Towards a Resolution of the Debate," *Signs* 27, no. 4 (Summer, 2002): 1135–71.

39. Lafond and Reed, *Conversations*, 113.

40. Ayatollah Khamenei, "Regional Uprisings, Fruit of 1979 Revolution," April 3, 2011, www.leader.ir/langs/EN/print.php?sec=content&id=7938. . . .

41. Both Ben Ali and Hosni Mubarak led repressive regimes, and both have fallen from power.

42. Maziar Bahari, "118 Days, 12 Hours, 54 Minutes," *Newsweek*, November 30, 2009, www.newsweek.com/id/223862.

43. Muhammad Sahimi, "Iran's Election Drama More Elaborate Than You Think," Payvand Iran News, June 25, 2009, http://payvand.com/news/09/jun/1279.html.

44. David Sanger and Annie Lowrey, "Iran Threatens to Block Oil Shipments, as US Prepares Sanctions," *New York Times*, December 27, 2011, www.nytimes.com/2011/12/28/world/middleeast/iran-threatens. . . .

45. Elisabeth Bumiller, Eric Schmitt, and Thom Skanker, "US Sends Top Iranian Leader a Warning on Strait Threat," *New York Times*, January 12, 2012, www.nytimes.com/2012/01/13/world/middleeast/us-warns-top-i. . . . The warning against closing the Strait of Hormuz was confirmed by the *Tehran Times*; see "Details of Obama's Letter to Iran Released," *Tehran Times*, January 18, 2012, www.tehrantimes.com/politics/94692-details-of-obamas-letter-to. . . .

46. Tehran Times, "Iran Will Respond to Any Attack with 'Iron Fist,'" November 10, 2011, www.tehrantimes.com/index.php/politics/4415-iran-will-respond-to-a. . . .

47. Finnemore notes that by talking about a norm or a violation of a norm, the state "indicates the existence of a norm." Martha Finnemore, *National Interests in International Security* (Ithaca, NY: Cornell University Press, 1996), 23.

48. See www.WorldOpinionPoll.org. When respondents were asked whether living in a country that is governed by representatives elected by the people was important on a scale where 1 signified "not at all important" and 10 signified "absolutely important," the mean was 9.1.

BIBLIOGRAPHY

Abdo, Geneive. "Re-Thinking the Islamic Republic: A Conversation with Ayatollah Hossein Ali Montazeri." *Middle East Journal* 55 (Winter 2001): 9–24.

Abrahamian, Ervand. *A History of Modern Iran*. Cambridge: Cambridge University Press, 2008.

Afary, Janet. *Sexual Politics in Modern Iran*. Cambridge: Cambridge University Press, 2009.

Agence France-Press. "Rafsanjani Boosts Pressure on Iran Regime before Anniversary." May 29, 2010. http://news.yahoo.com/s/afp/20100529/ts_afp/iranpoliticsoppositionra . . .

Akhan, Shahrough. "The Thought and Role of Ayatollah Hossein ali Montazeri in the Politics of Post-1979 Iran." *Iranian Studies* 41 (December 2008): 645–66.

Al-e Ahmad, Jalal. *Plagued by the West*, translated by Paul Sprachman. New York: Caravan Books, 1982.

Alexander, Yonah, and Milton Hoenig. *The New Iranian Leadership*. Westport, CT: Praeger Security International, 2008.

American Embassy, Ashgabat. "Iran Post-Election." Classified Cable, June 15, 2009. Reference ID09ASHGABAT757.Cablegate.wikileaks.org/cable/2009/06/09ASHGABAT757.html.

Amirahmadi, Hooshang. "Economic Costs of the War and Reconstruction in Iran." In *Modern Capitalism and Islamic Ideology in Iran*, edited by Cyrus Bina and Hamid Zangeneh. New York: St. Martin's Press, 1992.

Amnesty International. "Iran Dire Human Rights Situation Persists 2 Years after Disputed Elections," June 9, 2011. AI Index: 13/057/2011. Available at www.amnesty.org.

———. "Iran's Presidential Election amid Unrest and Ongoing Human Rights Violations." June 5, 2009. Available at www.amnesty.org.

An-Na'im, Abdullahi Ahmed. "Shari'a and Islamic Family Law: Transition and Transformation," *Ahfad Journal* 23 (December 2006): 2–30.

———. *Toward An Islamic Revolution: Civil Liberties, Human Rights, and International Law*. Syracuse, NY: Syracuse University Press, 1990.

Ansari, Ali. *Confronting Iran*. New York: Basic Books, 2006.

———. *Modern Iran since 1921: The Pahlavis and After*. London: Pearson Education, 2003.

Arjomand, Said Amir. *After Khomeini: Iran under His Successors*. Oxford: Oxford University Press, 2009.

————. "Constitutional Implications of Current Political Debates in Iran." In *Contemporary Iran: Economy, Society, Politics,* edited by Ali Gheissari. Oxford: Oxford University Press, 2009.

————. *The Turban for the Crown: The Islamic Revolution in Iran.* New York: Oxford University Press, 1988.

Associated Press. "Ahmadinejad Wants Opposition Tried." August 28, 2009. www.nytimes .com/aponline/2009/08/28/world/AP-ML-Iran.html?emc. . . .

————."Iran Parliament Moves Ahead with Fuel Subsidies Cuts." October 12, 2009.

Axworthy, Michael. *A History of Iran: Empire of the Mind.* New York: Basic Books, 2008.

Ayoob, Mohammed. "Challenging Hegemony: Political Islam and the North-South Divide." *International Studies Review* 9 (2007): 629–43.

Azimi, Fakhreddin. "Unseating Mossadeq: The Configuration and Role of Domestic Forces." In *Mohammad Mossadeq and the 1953 Coup in Iran,* edited by Mark J. Gasiorowski and Malcolm Byrne. Syracuse, NY: Syracuse University Press, 2004.

Bahari, Maziar. "118 Days, 12 Hours, 54 Minutes." *Newsweek,* November 30, 2009. www .newsweek.com/id/223862.

Bahgart, Gawdat. "Nuclear Proliferation: The Islamic Republic of Iran." *International Studies Perspectives* 7 (May 2006).

Bahramitash, Roksana, and Hadi Salehi Esfahani. "Nimble Fingers No Longer! Women's Employment in Iran." In *Contemporary Iran: Economy, Society, Politics,* edited by Ali Gheissari. Oxford: Oxford University Press, 2009.

Bani Sadr, Abol Hassan. *My Turn to Speak: Iran, the Revolution and Secret Deals with the United States.* Arlington, VA: Brassey's, 1991.

Barlow, Rebecca, and Shahram Akbarzadeh. "Prospects for Feminism in the Islamic Republic of Iran." *Human Rights Quarterly* 30 (2008): 21–40.

BBC. "Arrests after Protest in Tehran." http://news.bbc.co.uk/go/pr/fr/-/2/hi/middle_ east/7907276.stm.

————. "Ayatollah Demands End to Protests." June 19, 2009. http://news.bbc.co.uk/go/ pr/fr/-/2/hi/middle_east/8108661.stm.

————. "Clashes Erupt at Iran Mass Rally." September 18, 2009. http://news.bbc.co.uk .go/pr/fr/-/2/hi/middle_east/8262273.stm.

————. "Crowds Join Ahmadinejad Victory Rally." June 14, 2009.

————. "Fresh Rally Takes Place in Tehran." June 17, 2009. http://news.bbc.co.uk/2/hi/ midd. . . .

————."Iran Arrests Opposition Figures." December 28, 2009. http://news.bbc.co.uk/go/ pr/fr/-/2/hi/middle_east/8432297.stm.

————."Iran Backs First Woman Minister." September 10, 2009. http://newsvote.bbc .co.uk/mpapps/pagetools/print/news.bbc.co.uk/2/hi/midd. . . .

————. "Iran in 'Backroom Offers' to West." February 20, 2009. http://news.bbc.co.uk/ go/pr/fr/-2/hi/Europe/7901101.stm.

————. "Iran to Hold Election Recount." June 16, 2009. http://news.bbc.co.uk/go/pr/ fr/-/2/hi/middle_east/8102400.stm.

————. "Iranian Leader Demands US Apology." January 28, 2009. http://news.bbc .co.uk/go/pr/fr/-/2/hi/middle_east/7855444.stm.

————. "Iranians Vote in General Election." March 14, 2008. http://news.bbc.co.uk/go/ pr/fr/-/2/hi/middle_east/7295732.stm.

———. "Iran's Mousavi Defies Crackdown." June 15, 2009. www.news.bbc.co.uk/go/pr/fr/-/2/hi/middle_east/8118783.stm.

———. "New Iranian Dress Code Crackdown," June 17,2008. http://news.bbc.co.uk/go/pr/fr/-/2/hi/middle_east/7457212.stm.

———. "Row of Iran's Women Ministers." August 22, 2009. http://news.bbc.co.uk/go/pr/fr/-/2/hi/middle_east/8215880.stm.

———. "US Admiral Urges Caution on Iran." July 2, 2008. http://news.bbc.co.uk/go/pr/fr/-/2/hi/middle_east/7486338.stm.

Becker, Jo, and Ron Nixon. "US Enriches Companies Defying Its Policy on Iran." *New York Times*, March 6, 2010.

Behrooz, Maziar. "The 1953 Coup in Iran and the Legacy of the Tudeh." In *Mohammad Mossadeq and the 1953 Coup in Iran*, edited by Mark J. Gasiorowski and Malcolm Byrne. Syracuse, NY: Syracuse University Press, 2004.

Berman, Ilan. "Toward an Economic Strategy against Iran." *Comparative Strategy* 27 (2008): 20–26.

Bina, Cyrus. "Global Oil and the Oil politics of the Islamic Republic." In *Modern Capitalism and Islamic Ideology in Iran*, edited by Cyrus Bina and Hamid Zangeneh. New York: St. Martin's Press, 1992.

Boroumand, Ladan. "Civil Society's Choice." *Journal of Democracy* 20 (October 2009): 16–20.

———."The Role of Ideology." *Journal of Democracy* 16 (October 2005): 52–63.

Bowden, Mark. *Guests of the Ayatollahs*. New York: Grove Press, 2006.

Bozorgmehr, Najmeh. "Food Inflation Threatens Stability in Iran." *Financial Times*, November 8, 2011. www.ft.com/cms/s/0/b8bc5c40-09fc-11e1-85ca-00144feabc0.html.

Brinton, Crane. *The Anatomy of Revolution*. New York: Random House, 1965.

Broad, William, James Glanz, and David Sanger. "Iran Fortifies Its Arsenal with the Aid of North Korea." *New York Times,* November 28, 2010. www.nytimes.com/2010/11/29/world/middleeast/29missiles.htm.

Broad, William, and David Sanger. "Iran Reports a Major Setback at a Nuclear Plant." *New York Times,* February 25, 2011. www.nytimes.com/2011/02/26/world/middleeast/26nuke.html.

Bumiller, Elisabeth, Eric Schmitt, and Thom Skanker. "US Sends Top Iranian Leader a Warning on Strait Threat." *New York Times*, January 12, 2012. www.nytimes.com/2012/01/13/world/middleeast/us-warns-top-i. . . .

Burns, William. "Under Secretary for Political Affairs, Statement before the House Foreign Affairs Committee." Washington, DC, December 1, 2010.

Cambanis, Thanassis. *A Privilege to Die*. New York: Free Press, 2010.

Carpenter, Ted Galen. "Toward a Grand Bargain with Iran." *Mediterranean Quarterly* 18 (Winter 2007): 12–27.

Chubin, Shahram. "Iran and the Arab Spring: Ascendancy Frustrated." *GRC Gulf Papers*, September 2012.

———. "The Iranian Nuclear Riddle after June 12." *Washington Quarterly* 33 (January 2010): 163–72.

Cirincione, Joseph, and Elice Connor. "How Iran Can Build a Bomb." *Foreign Policy*, July 2010.

Classified Cable from Dubai to Secretary of State, Subject: Iran Domestic Politics, January 13, 2010. Reference ID 10RPODUBAI15. http://cablegate.wikileaks.org/cable/2010/01/10RPODUBAI15.html.

Clawson, Patrick. "Iran's Economy: Between Crisis and Collapse." *MERIP Reports*, no. 98 (July–August 1981): 11–15.

Clinton, Hillary. "Statement on Significant Reductions of Iranian Crude Oil Purchases." Washington, DC, March 20, 2012.

Cohen, David. "The Law and Policy of Iran Sanctions." Remarks at New York University School of Law, September 12, 2012.

———. "Under Secretary for Terrorism and Financial Intelligence, US Policy on Iran, Testimony before the Senate Committee on Foreign Relations." Washington, DC, December 1, 2011.

Cook, J. M. *The Persian Empire*. New York: Schocken Books, 1983.

Cordesman, Anthony. "The Conventional Military." In *The Iran Primer*, edited by Robin Wright. Washington, DC: US Institute of Peace Press, 2010.

Cordesman, Anthony, and Martin Kleiber, *Iran's Military Forces and War Fighting Capabilities*. Westport, CT: Praeger Security International, 2007.

Cottam, Richard. *Nationalism in Iran*. Pittsburgh: University of Pittsburgh Press, 1979.

Council of the European Union. "Council Conclusions on Iran." January 23, 2012. http://eeas.europa.eu/index_en.htm

Cowell, Alan. "Iranian Parliament Questions Ahmadinejad." *New York Times*, March 14, 2012. www.nytimes.com/2012/03/15/world/middleeast/iran-ahmadine. . . .

———."Rafsanjani Loses Key Post in Iranian Religious Assembly." *New York Times*, March 8, 2011. www.nytimes.com/2011/03/09/world/middleeast/09iran.html. . . .

———. "Tehran's Mayor Speaks of Making Iran Less Isolated." *New York Times*, January 27, 2008.

Cowell, Alan, and Thom Shanker. "Iran's Nuclear Move Prompts New Calls for Sanctions." *New York Times*, February 9, 2010. www.nytimes.com/2010/02/09/world/middleeast/09iran.html. . . .

Crowley, Philip. "Assistant Secretary, Daily Press Briefing." Washington, DC, December 1, 2010.

Cumming Bruce, Nick. "Iran Defends Human Rights Record before UN Council." *New York Times,* February 16, 2010. www.nytimes.com/2010/02/16/world/middleeast/16geneva.html.

Daniel, Elton. *The History of Iran*. Westport, CT: Greenwood Press, 2001.

Davenport, Christian. "Multi-Dimensional Threat Perception and State Repression: An Inquiry into Why States Apply Negative Sanctions." *American Journal of Political Science* 38 (1995): 683–713.

Davies, Graeme. "Inside Out or Outside In: Domestic and International Factors Affecting Iranian Foreign Policy towards the United States 1990–2004." *Foreign Policy Analysis* 4 (2008): 209–25.

Delpech, Delpech. *Iran and the Bomb: The Abdication of International Responsibility*, translated by Ros Schwartz. New York: Columbia University Press, 2006.

Donnelly, Jack. *Realism in International Relations*. Cambridge: Cambridge University Press, 2000.

Downs, Erica, and Suzanne Maloney. "Getting China to Sanction Iran." *Foreign Affairs*, March–April 2011, 18–19.

Ebadi, Shirin. *Iran Awakening: A Memoir of Revolution and Hope*. New York: Random House, 2006.

Economist. "Anything to Declare?" July 3, 2010, 58.

————."Iran's Bold Economic Reform: Economic Jihad." June 23, 2011, 59.

Edelman, Eric, Andrew Krepinevich, and Evan Braden Montgomery. "The Dangers of a Nuclear Iran: The Limits of Containment." *Foreign Affairs* 90 (January–February 2011): 66–81.

Einhorn, Robert. "Implementation of Iran Sanctions." House Committee on Oversight and Government Reform. Washington, DC, July 29, 2010.

Elleman, Michael. "Iran's Ballistic Missile Program." In *The Iran Primer,* edited by Robin Wright. Washington, DC: US Institute of Peace Press, 2010.

Erdbrink, Thomas. "OPEC Sees Sanctions Taking Toll on Iran Oil Production." *New York Times,* May 17, 2012. www.nytimes.com/2012/05/18/world/middleeast/iran-oil -produc. . . .

Esfahani, Hadi Salehi, and M. Hashem Pesaran. "The Iranian Economy in the Twentieth Century: A Global Perspective." *Iranian Studies* 42 (April 2009): 177–211.

Esfandiari, Haleh. *My Prison, My Home: One Woman's Story of Captivity in Iran.* New York: HarperCollins, 2009.

Esposito, John, and John Voll. *Islam and Democracy.* Oxford: Oxford University Press, 1996.

Fair, C. Christine. "Indo-Iranian Ties: Thicker Than Oil." *Middle East Review of International Affairs* 11 (March 2007). www.meria.idc.ac.il/journal/2007/issue1/jv11no1a9.html.

Falk, Richard. *Achieving Human Rights.* New York: Routledge, 2008.

Fathi, Nazila. "Authorities in Iran Arrest 18 Students." *New York Times,* October 3, 2009. www.nytimes.com/2009/10/03/world/middleeast/03iran.html.

————. "Chief Cleric Says Iran Does Not Seek Nuclear Arms." *New York Times,* June 4, 2008.

————. "Conservatives Prevail in Iran Vote, but Opposition Scores, Too." *New York Times,* April 27, 2008.

————. "Dismissal Is Setback for Iran's Leader." *New York Times,* November 5, 2008. www.nytimes.com/2008/11/05/world/middleeast/05iran.html. . . .

————. "Election Seen as a Setback for Iran's President." *New York Times,* December 18, 2006.

————. "Former Iranian President Publicly Assails Ahmadinejad." *New York Times,* December 12, 2007. www.nytimes.com/2007/12/12/world/middleeast/12iran.html.

————. "Grandson of Ex-Leader Is Arrested in Tehran." *New York Times,* March 22, 2010. http://www.nytimes.com/2010/03/23/world/middleeast/23iran.html.

————. "Hundreds of Women Protest Sex Discrimination in Iran." *New York Times,* June 12, 2005. www.nytimes.com/2005/06/12/international/middleast/13womencnd.html ?ei=5094. . . .

————."Iran Celebrates Revolution and Muzzles Reformers." *New York Times,* February 12, 2008. www.nytimes.com/2008/02/12/world/middleeast/12tehran.html?ei= 5070&en=325a2.

————. "Iran Lifts Ban Barring Women from Attending Sporting Events." *New York Times,* May 1, 2006. www.nytimes.com/2006/05/01/world/middleeast/01iran.html.

————."Iran Opposition Leader's Aide Is Freed." *New York Times,* September 14, 2009. www.nytimes.com/2009/09/14/world/middleeast/14iran.html?_r=1&e. . . .

————. "Iranian Candidate Taps Student Woes." *New York Times,* May 31, 2009. www.ny times.com/2009/05/31/world/middleeast/31iran.html?_r=1&e. . . .

————. "Iranian Court Shuts Down 3 Pro-Reform Newspapers as Dissent Continues to Simmer." *New York Times,* October 7, 2009. www.nytimes.com/2009/10/07/world/middleeast/07iran.html.

————. "Iranian Scholars Denounce Conference That Denied Holocaust." *New York Times,* February 27, 2007.

————."Iranian Women Are Arrested after Protests outside of Court." *New York Times,* March 6, 2007. www.nytimes.com/2007/03/06/world/middleeast/06iran.html.

————. "Iran's Chief Cleric Says Country Is Not a Friend to Israelis." *New York Times,* September 20, 2008. www.nytimes.com./2008/09/20/world/middleeast/20iran.html.

————. "Iran's Leader Said to Refuse Delay in Vote." *New York Times,* February 4, 2004.

————. "Iran's Religious Conservatives Are Expected to Solidify Power at Polls." *New York Times,* March 6, 2008. www.nytimes.com/2008/03/06/world/middleeast/06iran.htm lref=world&pagewanted. . . .

————. "Iran's Stocks Plunge after Vote for UN Review of Nuclear Program." *New York Times,* October 9, 2005.

————. "Iran's Supreme Leader Issues New Warning." *New York Times,* September 12, 2009. www.nytimes.com/2009/09/12/world/middleeast/12iran.html?emc=et. . . .

————. "Many Try to Run for President in Iran, but Few Will Be Allowed." *New York Times,* May 11, 2009. www.nytimes.com/2009/05/11/world/middleeast/11iran.html ?ref=wor. . . .

————. "Political Fervor of Iranian Clerics Begins to Ebb." *New York Times,* January 17, 2003.

————. "A President's Defender Keeps His Distance." *New York Times,* January, 8, 2008. www.nytimes.com/2008/01/08/world/middleeast/08iran.html.

————. "Reformers Gain in Iran Vote Despite Being Barred." *New York Times,* March 16, 2008. www.nytimes.com/2008/03/16/world/middleeast/16iran.html?ei=5070&en=a 255aaa. . . .

————. "Reformist Details Evidence of Abuse in Iran's Prisons." *New York Times,* September 15, 2009. www.nytimes.com/2009/09/15/world/middleeast/15iran.html.

————. "Student Cry 'Death to the Dictator' as Iranian Leader Speaks." *New York Times,* December 12, 2006.

————. "Tehran Protesters Defy Ban and Clash with Police." *New York Times,* December 27, 2009. www.nytimes.com/2009/12/27/world/middleeast/27iran.html?_r=1&emc =eta1&pa. . . .

Fathi, Nazila, and Alan Cowell. "Iran's Ruling Cleric Warns of Bloodshed If Protests Persists." *New York Times,* June 20, 2009.

Fathi, Nazila, and Michael Slackman. "As Confrontation Deepens, Iran's Path Is Unclear." *New York Times,* June 19, 2009.

Feltman, Jeffrey. "Acting Assistant Secretary, Bureau of Near Eastern Affairs, Testimony before the Subcommittee on Near Eastern and South Central Asian Affairs of the Senate Committee on Foreign Relations." Washington, DC, June 8, 2010.

Firoozi, Ferydoon. "Income Distribution and Taxation Laws of Iran." *International Journal of Middle East Studies* 9 (January 1978): 73–87.

Flecter, Martin. "The Face of Abbas Kargar Javid: Man Accused of Killing Neda Soltan." *The Times,* August 20, 2009.

Forsythe, David. *Human Rights in International Relations,* 2nd ed. Cambridge: Cambridge University Press, 2006.

Fuller, Graham. *The Future of Political Islam.* New York: Palgrave McMillan, 2003.

Ganji, Akbar. "The Latter-Day Sultan: Power and Politics in Iran." *Foreign Affairs* 87 (November–December 2008): 45–66.

———. *The Road to Democracy in Iran.* Cambridge, MA: MIT Press, 2008.

Ganji, Manoucher. *Defying the Iranian Revolution.* Westport, CT: Praeger, 2002.

Gasiorowski, Mark. "The Coup d'État against Mossadeq." In *Mohammad Mossadeq and the 1953 Coup in Iran,* edited by Mark J. Gasiorowski and Malcolm Byrne. Syracuse, NY: Syracuse University Press, 2004.

Ghahramani, Zarah, with Robert Hillman. *My Life as a Traitor.* New York: Farrar, Straus & Giroux, 2008.

Gladstone, Rick. "As Further Sanctions Loom, Plunge in Currency's Value Unsettles Iran." *New York Times,* December 20, 2011. www.nytimes.com/2011/12/21/world/middleeast/currency-plung. . . .

———. "Iran Admits Western Sanctions Are Inflicting Damage." *New York Times,* December 20, 2011. www.nytimes.com/2011/12/20/world/middleeast/iran-admits-we. . . .

Gladstone, Rick, and Artin Afkami. "Top Media Aide of Iran's President Reported Held in Raid." *New York Times,* November 21, 2011. www.nytimes.com/2011/11/22/world/middleeast/ali-akbar-javan. . . .

Goodman, J. David. "Iran Rift Deepens with Arrest of President's Ally." *New York Times,* June 23, 2011. www.nytimes.com/2011/06/24/world/middleeast/24iran.html.

Gordon, Michael. "Meddling Neighbors Undercut Iraq." *New York Times,* December 5, 2010. www.nytimes.com/2010/12/06/world/middleeast/06wikileaks-ir. . . .

Gregory, Mark. "Expanding Business Empire of Iran's Revolutionary Guards." BBC, July 26, 2010. www.bbc.co.uk/news/world-middle-east-10743580? . . .

Halliday, Fred. "Iran: The Economic Contradiction." *MERIP Reports* 69 (July–August 1978): 9–18.

———. *Nation and Religion in the Middle East.* Boulder, CO: Lynne Rienner, 2000.

Hanizadeh, Hassan. "Women's Rights in Iran." *Tehran Times,* July 8, 2007.

Harrop, Wm. Scott. "Muhammad Khatami: A Dialogue beyond Paradox." In *The Iranian Revolution at 30.* Washington, DC: Middle East Institute, 2009. Available at www.mideasti.org.

Herodotus. *The Histories,* translated by Aubrey de Selincourt. New York: Penguin Books, 2003.

Hers, Martin. "Counselor of Embassy, Confidential Memorandum of Conversation, November 26, 1966." RG 59 General Records of the Department of State, Bureau of Near Eastern and South Asian Affairs, Box 18.

Hosseini, Hamid. "From *Homo Economicus* to *Homo Islamicus:* The Universality of Economic Science Reconsidered." In *Modern Capitalism and Islamic Ideology in Iran,* edited by Cyrus Bina and Hamid Zangeneh. New York: St. Martin's Press, 1992.

Hosseini, Ziba Mir, and Richard Tapper. *Islam and Democracy: Eshkevari and the Quest for Reform.* London: I. B. Tauris, 2006.

Howard, Jane. *Inside Iran: Women's Lives.* Washington, DC: Mage Publishers, 2002.

Human Rights Council. "Report of UN Secretary General on the Situation of Human Rights in Iran at the Human Rights Council in Geneva." March 28, 2011. Document A/HRC/16/75.

Human Rights Watch. "Iran: Discrimination and Violence against Sexual Minorities." December 15, 2010.

———. "Iran: Escalating Repression of University Students," December 7, 2010.

———. "Iran: Four Journalists Sentence to Prison, Floggings," February 10, 2009. www.hrw.org/en/news/2009/02/10/iran-four-journalists-sentenced-prison -floggings? . . .

———. "Iran: Release Students Detained for Peaceful Protests." February 24, 2009.

———. "Iran: Reverse Closure of Nobel Laureate's Rights Group." December 21, 2008.

———. "Iran: Women on Trial for Peaceful Demonstration. Activists Arrested for Protesting Discriminatory Laws." February 27, 2007.

———. *World Report 2003, Iran.* Available at www.hrw.org.

Huntington, Samuel. "The Clash of Civilizations." *Foreign Affairs,* Summer 1993, 22–49.

Ignatieff, Michael. *Human Rights as Politics and Idolatry.* Princeton, NJ: Princeton University Press, 2001.

International Atomic Energy Agency, "Implementation of the NPT Safeguards Agreement in the Islamic Republic of Iran." November 15, 2004. www.iaea.org/Publications/ Documents/Board/2004/gov2004-83_derestrict.pdf.

International Campaign for Human Rights. "UN Resolution Ramps up Cross-Regional International Pressure on Iran's Human Rights Crisis," November 21, 2010.

International Crisis Group. *The Iran Nuclear Issue: The View from Beijing.* Asia Briefing 100. Beijing/Brussels: International Crisis Group, 2010.

———. *US–Iranian Engagement: The View from Tehran.* Middle East Briefing 28. Tehran/ Brussels: International Crisis Group, 2009.

International Monetary Fund. "Statement by IMF Article IV Mission to the Islamic Republic of Iran." Press Release 11/228, June 13, 2011. www.imf.org/external.np/sec/ pr/2-11/pr11228.htm.

Iranian Constitution. www.servat.unibe.ch/icl/ir00000_.html.

Kaussler, Bernd. "European Union Constructive Engagement with Iran (2000–2004): An Exercise in Conditional Human Rights Diplomacy." *Iranian Studies* 41(June 2008): 269–95.

Keddie, Nikki. *Modern Iran: Roots and Results of Revolution.* New Haven, CT: Yale University Press, 2003.

Kershner, Isabel. "Israeli Strike on Iran Would Be 'Stupid,' Ex-Spy Chief Says." *New York Times,* May 8, 2011. www.nytimes.com/2011/05/09/world/middleeast/09israel.html. . . .

Keshavarzian, Arang. *Bazaar and State in Iran.* Cambridge: Cambridge University Press, 2007.

Khalidi, Rashid. "Reflections on the Revolution in Tunisia and Egypt." February 24, 2011.

Khamenei, Ayatollah. "Iran Found New Identity after the Revolution." February 8, 2008. www.leader.ir/langs/EN/index.php?pnews&id=3852.

———."Nation Must Develop Insight Prior to Ballot." January 23, 2008. www.leader.ir/ langs/EN/print.php?id=3816.

———. "Regional Uprisings, Fruit of 1979 Revolution." April 3, 2011. www.leader.ir/ langs/EN/print.php?sec=content&id=7938. . . .

Khomeini, Ayatollah. *Islam and Revolution: Writings and Declarations of Imam Khomeini,* translated and annotated by Hamid Algar. Berkeley, CA: Mizan Press, 1981.

Lafond, Jean-Daniel, and Fred A. Reed. *Conversations in Tehran.* Vancouver: Talon Books, 2006.

Lander, Mark. "Iran Policy More in Sync with Clinton's Views." *New York Times,* February 17, 2010. www.nytimes.com/2010/02/17/world/middleeast/17diplo.html. . . .

Lander, Mark, and Clifford Krauss. "Gulf Nations Aid US Push to Choke Off Iran Oil Sales." *New York Times,* January 12, 2012. www.nytimes.com/2012/01/13/world/asia/ asia-buyers-of-iran-c. . . .

Leverett, Flynt. *Dealing with Tehran: Assessing US Diplomatic Options towards Iran.* New York: Century Foundation, 2006. Available at www.tcf.org.

Lewis, Bernard. "The Roots of Muslim Rage." *Atlantic Monthly,* September 1990, 47–60.

Limbert, John. *Negotiating with the Islamic Republic of Iran.* Special Report 199. Washington, DC: US Institute of Peace, 2008.

MacFarquhar, Neil. "Clerics May Be Key to Outcome of Unrest." *New York Times,* June 18, 2009. www.nytimes.com/2009.06/18/world/middleast/18clerics.html?emc=. . . .

———."Power Struggle in Iran Enters the Mosque." *New York Times,* May 6, 2011. www .nytimes.com/2011/05/07/world/middleeast/07iran.html? . . .

Mackey, Sandra. *The Iranians: Persia, Islam and the Soul of a Nation.* New York: Plume, 1998.

Mahdavi, Pardis. "Who Will Catch Me If I Fall? Health and the Infrastructure of Risk for Urban Young Iranians." In *Contemporary Iran: Economy, Society, Politics,* edited by Ali Gheissari. Oxford: Oxford University Press, 2009.

Mahdi, Ali Akbar. "Iranian Women: Between Islamicization and Globalization." In *Iran Encountering Globalization: Problems and Prospects,* edited by Ali Mohammadi. New York: RoutledgeCurzon, 2003.

Majd, Hooman. *The Ayatollah Begs to Differ: The Paradox of Modern Iran.* New York: Anchor Books, 2009.

Maloney, Suzanne. "The Revolutionary Economy." In *The Iran Primer,* edited by Robin Wright. Washington, DC: US Institute of Peace Press, 2010.

Marsh, Steve. "Thirty Years On: Iran's "Silent Revolution." *Iranian Studies* 42 (April 2009): 213–29.

Martin, Vanessa. *Creating an Islamic State: Khomeini and the Making of a New Iran.* New York: I. B. Tauris, 2000.

Mayer, Ann Elizabeth. *Islam and Human Rights.* Boulder, CO: Westview Press, 2007.

Mearsheimer, John, and Stephen Walt. *The Israel Lobby and US Foreign Policy.* New York: Farrar, Straus & Giroux, 2007.

Meyer, Karl, and Shareen Blair Brysac. *Kingmakers: The Invention of the Modern Middle East.* New York: W. W. Norton, 2009.

Milbank, Dana. "Live from New York: Mahmoud Ahmadinejad's Unreality Show." *Washington Post,* September 25, 2007.

Millspaugh, Arthur. *Americans in Persia.* Washington, DC: Brookings Institution, 1946.

Moghadam, Valentine. "Feminism and Islamic Fundamentalism: A Secularist Interpretation." *Journal of Women's History* 13 (Spring 2001): 42–45.

———. "Islamic Feminism and Its Discontents: Towards a Resolution of the Debate." *Signs* 27 (Summer 2002): 1135–71.

Mohammadi, Ali. "The Sixth Majles Election and the Prospects for Democracy in Iran." In *Iran Encountering Globalization: Problems and Prospects,* edited by Ali Mohammadi. New York: RoutledgeCurzon, 2003.

Molavi, Afsin. *The Soul of Iran.* New York: W. W. Norton, 2002.

Monshipouri, Mahmood. *Islamism, Secularism, and Human Rights in the Middle East.* Boulder, CO: Lynne Rienner, 1998.

———. *Muslims in Global Politics: Identities, Interests, and Human Rights.* Philadelphia: University of Pennsylvania Press, 2009.

————. "The Revival of Populism in Iranian Politics." *Turkish Weekly.* www.turkishweekly .net/comments.php?id=1436.

Moslem, Mehdi. *Factional Politics in Post-Khomeini Iran.* Syracuse, NY: Syracuse University Press, 2002.

————. "The State and Factional Politics in the Islamic Republic of Iran." In *Twenty Years of Islamic Revolution: Political and Social Transition in Iran since 1979*, edited by Eric Hooglund. Syracuse, NY: Syracuse University Press, 2002.

Mousavi, Mir. "Mousavi Issues 13th Statement." http://english.mowjcamp.com/article/ id/38750.

Mozaffari, Mehdi. "Rushdie Affair." In *The Oxford Encyclopedia of the Modern Islamic World*, edited by John L. Esposito. New York: Oxford University Press, 1995.

Nader, Ali Reza. "The Revolutionary Guards." In *The Iran Primer*, edited by Robin Wright. Washington, DC: US Institute of Peace Press, 2010.

Nader, Ali Reza, David E Thaler, and S. R. Bohandy. *The Next Supreme Leader: Succession in the Islamic Republic of Iran.* Santa Monica, CA: RAND Corporation, 2011.

Nafisi, Azar. *Reading Lolita in Tehran.* New York: Random House, 2003.

Naji, Kasra. *Ahmadinejad: The Secret History of Iran's Radical Leader.* Berkeley: University of California Press, 2008.

Nasr, Vali. "The Conservative Wave Rolls On." *Journal of Democracy* 16 (October 2005): 9–22.

————. "Politics within the Late Pahlavi State: The Ministry of Economy and Industrial Policy, 1963–1969." *International Journal of Middle East Studies* 32 (2000): 97–122.

————. *The Shia Revival.* New York: W. W. Norton, 2007.

Nasseri, Ladane. "Iran's Unemployed Rise by 1.6 Million Each Year, Sharagh Reports." Bloomberg, May 9, 2011.

National Security Council. "Statement of Policy on the Present Situation in Iran." NSC136/1.

Nemat, Marina. *Prisoner of Tehran.* New York: Free Press, 2007.

Newton-Small, Jay. "One Nation under Sanctions," *Time*, September 24, 2012, 39.

New York Times. "An Interview with President Mahmoud Ahmadinejad." September 26, 2008. www.nytimes.com/2008/09/26/world/middleeast/26iran-transcript.html?ref= world&. . . .

————. "Iran Vetoes Candidates." February 7, 2008. www.nytimes.com/2008/02/07/world/ middleeast/07tehran.html?ref=world&pagewant. . . .

————. "Violence Grips Tehran Amid Crackdown." June 21, 2009. www.nytimes.com/ 2009/06/21/world/middleeast/21iran.html?emc=et. . . .

Nikou, Semira. "The Subsidies Conundrum." In *The Iran Primer*, edited by Robin Wright. Washington, DC: US Institute of Peace Press, 2010.

Nixon, Ron. "Two Large Multinationals Pull Back from Iran." *New York Times*, March 10, 2010.

Nomani, Mohammad Manzoor. *Khomeini, Iranian Revolution and the Shi'ite Faith.* London: Furqan, 1988.

Osanloo, Arzoo. *The Politics of Women's Rights in Iran.* Princeton, NJ: Princeton University Press, 2009.

Payvand News. "Iran: Hashemi Rafsanjani under Growing Pressure." January 15, 2012. www.payvand.com/news/12/jan/1153.html.

———. "Iran: Women's Rights Activists Get Suspended Lashing Sentences." April, 24, 2008.

———. "Ten Million Iranians under Absolute Poverty Line." May 29, 2010. www.pay vand.com/news/10may/1316.html. . . .

Pesaran, M. H. "The System of Dependent Capitalism in Pre- and Post Revolutionary Iran." *International Journal of Middle East Studies* 14 (November 1982): 501–22.

Peterson, Scott. "Iran's New Hard-Liner Maps Path." *Christian Science Monitor*, June 27, 2005. www.csmonitor.com/2005/0627/p01s04-wome.htm.

Plato. *Republic*, translated by C. D. C. Reeve, Indianapolis: Hackett, 2004.

Pleming, Sue. "New US Audit Questions Efficacy of Iran Sanctions." Reuters, January 16, 2008. Available at www.reuters.com.

Pollack, Kenneth. *The Persian Puzzle: The Conflict between Iran and America*. New York: Random House, 2004.

Pollack, Kenneth, Daniel Byman, Martin Indyk, Suzanne Maloney, Michael O'Hanlon, and Bruce Riedel. *Which Path to Persia? Options for a New American Strategy towards Iran*. Washington, DC: Brookings Institution Press, 2009.

Posner, Michael. "Human Rights and Democratic Reform in Iran, Testimony before the Senate Foreign Relations Committee." Washington, DC, May 11, 2011.

Pouladi, Fardad. "Iran Reinstates More Reformist Candidates for Election." Agence France-Presse, February 16, 2008. http://news.yahoo.com/s/afp/20080216/w/_mideast/afp/iranpolticsvote_080216141906. . . .

Radio Free Europe/Radio Liberty. "Many Religious Figures Critical of Iran Election Results." July 2, 2009. www.payand.com/news/09/jul/1017.html.

Rajaee, Bahram. "Deciphering Iran: The Political Evolution of the Islamic Republic and US Foreign Policy after Sept. 11." *Comparative Studies of South Asia, Africa and the Middle East* 24 (2004): 165.

Ramazani, Rouhollah. "Iran's White Revolution: A Study in Political Development." *International Journal of Middle Eastern Studies* 5 (1974): 124–39.

Reporters Without Borders. "Arrest of Journalists since Disputed June Election Now Top 100." www.rsf.org/spip.php?page=impression&id_article=34918.

Richman, Alvin. "Post-Election Crackdown in Iran Has Had Limited Impact on the Minority Expressing Strong Opposition to the Regime." Available at http://worldpublic opinion.org.

Rieffer-Flanagan, Barb. "Improving Democracy in Religious Nation-States: Norms of Moderation and Cooperation in Ireland and Iran." *Muslim World Journal of Human Rights* 4 (2007): 1–36.

———. "Islamic Realpolitik: Two-Level Iranian Foreign Policy." *International Journal on World Peace* 26 (December 2009): 7–35.

———. "Religion and Nationalism: Understanding the Consequences of a Complex Relationship." *Ethnicities* 3 (June 2003): 215–42.

Risse, Thomas, and Kathryn Sikkink. "The Socialization of International Human Rights Norms into Domestic Practices: Introduction." In *The Power of Human Rights: International Norms and Domestic Change*, edited by Thomas Risse, Stephen C. Ropp, and Kathryn Sikkink. Cambridge: Cambridge University Press, 1999.

Rorty, Richard. "Human Rights, Rationality, and Sentimentality." In *The Philosophy of Human Rights*, edited by Patrick Hayden. Saint Paul: Paragon House, 2001.

Rosenberg, Tina. "An Enlightened Needle Exchange in Iran." *New York Times*, November 29,2010.http://opinionator.blogs.nytimes.com/2010/11/29/an-enlightened-exchange -in-iran/.

Ross, Michael. "Blood Barrels." *Foreign Affairs* 87 (May–June 2008): 2–8.

Roudi, Farzaneh. "Iran Is Reversing Its Population Policy." *Viewpoint* 7 (Woodrow Wilson International Center for Scholars), August 2012. www.wilsoncenter.org/sites/default/ files/iran_is_reversing_its_population_policy.pdf.

Rubin, Barry. *Paved with Good Intentions*. New York: Penguin Books, 1981.

Sabet-Saeidi, Shahriar. "Iranian–European Relations: A Strategic Partnership." In *Iran's Foreign Policy: From Khatami to Ahmadinejad*, edited by Anoushiravan Ehteshami and Mahjoob Zweiri. Reading, UK: Ithaca Press, 2008.

Sadjadpour, Karim. "Reading Khamenei: The World View of Iran's Most Powerful Leader." Washington, DC: Carnegie Endowment for International Peace, 2008.

———. "The Rise and Fall of Iran's Ahmadinejad." *Washington Post*, July 13, 2011. www .washingtonpost.com/opinions/the-rise-and-fall-of-irans-a. . . .

———. "The Supreme Leader." In *The Iran Primer*, edited by Robin Wright. Washington, DC: US Institute of Peace Press, 2010.

Sadri, Mahmoud, and Ahmad Sadri. "Introduction." In *Reason, Freedom, and Democracy in Islam: Essential Writings of Abdolkarim Soroush*, edited by Mahmoud Sadri and Ahmad Sadri. New York: Oxford University Press, 2000.

Sahimi, Muhammad. "Iran's Election Drama More Elaborate Than You Think." *Payvand Iran News,* June 25, 2009. www.payvand.com/news/09/jun/1279.html.

Said, Edward. "The Clash of Ignorance." *The Nation*, October 22, 2001.

Salehi-Isfahani, Djavad. "Oil Wealth and Economic Growth in Iran." In *Contemporary Iran: Economy, Society, Politics*, edited by Ali Gheissari. Oxford: Oxford University Press, 2009.

Sanandaji, Kaveh-Cyrus. "The Eighth Majles Elections in the Islamic Republic of Iran: A Division in Conservative Ranks and the Politics of Moderation." *Iranian Studies* 42 (September 2009): 621–48.

Sanasarian, Eliz. *Religious Minorities in Iran*. Cambridge: Cambridge University Press, 2000.

Sanger, David. "Iran Agrees to Draft of Deal on Exporting Nuclear Fuel." *New York Times*, October 22, 2009. www.nytimes.com./2009/10/22/world/middleeast/22nuke. html? . . .

———. "Obama Set to Offer Stricter Nuclear Deal to Iran." *New York Times*, October 27, 2010. www.nytimes.com/2010/10/28/world/middleeast/28iran.html? . . .

———."US Rejected Aid for Israeli Raid on Iranian Nuclear Site." *New York Times*, January 11, 2009. www.nytimes.com/2009/01/11/washington/11iran.html.

Sanger, David, and William Broad. "Allies' Clocks Tick Differently on Iran." *New York Times*, March 15, 2009. www.nytimes.com/2009/03/15/weekinreview/15SANGER .html.

Sanger, David, James Glanz, and Jo Becker. "Around the World, Distress over Iran." *New York Times*, November 28, 2010. www.nytimes.com/2010/11/29/world/middle east/29iran/html.

Sanger, David, and Andrew Kramer. "US Lauds Russia on Barring Arms for Iran." *New York Times*, September 22, 2010.

Sanger, David, and Annie Lowrey. "Iran Threatens to Block Oil Shipments, as US Prepares Sanctions." *New York Times*, December 27, 2011. www.nytimes.com/2011/12/28/world/middleeast/iran-threatens. . . .

Schiff, Ze'ev. "Israel's War with Iran." *Foreign Affairs* 85 (November–December 2006): 23–31.

Sciolino, Elaine. "Atomic Monitor Signals Concern over Iran's Work." *New York Times*, May 27, 2008.

———."Iranian Critic Quotes Khomeini Principles." *New York Times*, July 19, 2009. www.nytimes.com/2009/07/19/world/middleeast/19assess.html?_r=1. . . .

Secor, Laura. "Whose Iran?" *New York Times*, January 28, 2007.www.nytimes.com/2007/01/28/magazine/28iran.t.html?ref=magazine&pagewanted. . . .

Shane, Scott, and Michael R. Gordon, "Dissident's Tale of Epic Escape from Iran's Vise." *New York Times*, July 13, 2008. www.nytimes.com/2008/07/13/world/middleeast/13dissident.html.

Shleifer, Andrei, and Daniel Treisman. "Why Moscow Says No: A Question of Russian Interests, Not Psychology." *Foreign Affairs* 90 (January–February 2011): 122–38.

Sick, Gary. *All Fall Down*. New York: Penguin Books, 1986.

Slackman, Michael. "A Frail Economy Raises Pressure on Iran's Rulers." *New York Times*, February 3, 2008. www.nytimes.com/2008/02/03/world/asia/03iht-03iran.9691705.html.

———. "Iran Gives Hamas Enthusiastic Support, but Discreetly, Just in Case," *New York Times*, January 13, 2009.

———. "Iran Moderate Says Hard Liners Rigged Election." *New York Times*, June 19, 2005.

———."Iran Opposition Calls for End to Crackdown." *New York Times*, July 8, 2009. www.nytimes.com/2009/07/08/world/middleast/08iran.html?hp=&page. . . .

———. "An Iranian Revolutionary, Dismayed but Unbowed." *New York Times*, February 16, 2008, www.nytimes.com/2008/02/16/world/asia/16yazdi.html.

———. "Iranian Site Reports a Protester's Death Sentence." *New York Times*, October 9, 2009. www.nytimes.com/2009/10/09/world/middleeast/09tehran.html.

———. "Iran's Death Penalty Is Seen as a Political Tactic." *New York Times*, November 23, 2009. www.nytimes.com/2009/11/23/world/middleeast/23iran.html.

———. "No Candidate Wins Majority in Iranian Presidential Election, Forcing a Second Round." *New York Times*, June 18, 2005. www.nytimes.com/2005/06/18/international/middleeast/18iran.html.

———. "Some See Iran as Ready to Strike a Deal." *New York Times*, October 15, 2009.

Slackman, Michael, and Sharon Otterman. "Clerical Council in Iran Rejects Plea to Annul the Vote." *New York Times*, June 24, 2009.

Statistical Center of Iran. Available at www.sci.org.

Steinberg, James. "Deputy Secretary of State, Briefing on New Developments Pursuant to the Comprehensive Iran Sanctions, Accountability and Divestment of 2010." Washington, DC, September 30, 2010.

Taheri, Amir. *The Spirit of Allah: Khomeini and the Islamic Revolution*. Bethesda, MD: Adler & Adler, 1985.

———. "Winners and Losers Turn the Fate of Iran." *Gulf News*, June 29, 2005. www.gulfnews.com/opinion.NF.asp?articleID=170841.

Takeyh, Ray. *Guardians of the Revolution*. Oxford: Oxford University Press, 2009.

——. *Hidden Iran*. New York: Times Books, 2006.

Tehran Times. "Ahmadinejad Submits International War Crimes Bill." February 23, 2009. www.tehrantimes.com/index_View.asp?code=189890.

——. "Details of Obama's Letter to Iran Released." January 18, 2012. www.tehrantimes .com/politics/94692-details-of-obamas-letter-to. . . .

——. "Inflation Hits 15.4% in Iran." July 21, 2011. www.tehrantimes.com/NCms/ 2007.asp?code=244461.

——. "Iran Bank Says US Sanctions, Accusations Wrong." November 14, 2009. www .tehrantimes.com/index_View.asp?code=156400.

——. "Iran Oil Output to Reach 4.2 Mbpd by March '08." January 2, 2008. www.tehran times.com/index_View.asp?code=160464.

——. "Iran Will Respond to Any Attack with 'Iron Fist.'" November 10, 2011. www .tehrantimes.com/index.php/politics/4415-iran-will-respond-to-a. . . .

——. "Iranians Vote for a New Parliament." March 15, 2008. www.tehrantimes.com/ NCms/2007.asp?code=165090.

——. "Islamic Republic Has Elevated Status of Women: Leader." May 23, 2011. www .tehrantimes.com/index_View.asp?code=241201.

——. "Leader Advises Presidential Candidates Not to Delight Enemies." May 25, 2009. www.tehrantimes.com/NCms/2007.asp?code=195367.

——. "Leader: No Conflict Between Women's Social and Family Roles." July 5, 2007.

——."Mahdavi Kani Replaces Rafsanjani as Assembly of Experts Chief." March 9, 2011. www.tehrantimes.com/NCms/2007.asp?code=237109.

——. "Majlis Allocates $20 Million to Reveal Rights Violations by US, UK." November 30, 2009.

——."Mousavi Vows to Defend Women's Rights." May 19, 2009. www.tehrantimes .com/NCms/2007.asp?code=194903.

——. "MPs Showed Their Mettle in Impeachment of Interior Minister: Larijani." *Tehran Times*, November 5, 2008. www.tehrantimes.com/Names/2007.asp?code=181662.

——. "No Plan to Escort Gaza-Bound Ships." June 15, 2010. www.tehrantimes.com/ NCMS/2007.asp?code=221355.

——. "Poverty Casts Its Dark Shadow over the Masses." April 29, 2007.

——. "Tehran to Host Conference Calling for Prosecution of Zionist War Criminals." April 14, 2009. www.tehrantimes.com/index_View.asp?code=192197.

——. "West's Criticism of Iran's Human Rights Record Is Politically Motivated: IPM Director." October 1, 2007.

——. "Zionist Regime Is the New Face of Fascism: Leader." June 2, 2010. www.tehran times.com/index_View.asp?code=220586.

——. www.tehrantimes.com/NCms/2007.asp?code=159428.

Tetreault, Mary Ann. "God, the State, and Mammon: Religious Revivalism and the Modern World." Paper prepared for International Studies Association, New Orleans, March 25, 2002.

Thomas, Francis. "American Consul, Isfahan, to William Helseith, Consular Coordinator, American Embassy in Tehran, August 6, 1965." RG 59 General Records of the Department of State, Bureau of Near Eastern and South Asian Affairs (1964–66), box 12, ARC.

Tohidi, Nayereh. "'Islamic Feminism': Perils and Promises." *MEWS Review* 16 (Fall 2001–Winter 2002).

Torbat, Akbar. "Impacts of the US Trade and Financial Sanctions on Iran." *The World Economy* 8 (2005): 407–34.

Trenin, Dmitri, and Alexey Malashenko. *Iran: A View from Moscow.* Washington, DC: Carnegie Endowment for International Peace, 2010.

UN General Assembly. "The Situation of Human Rights in the Islamic Republic of Iran." September 23, 2011. Document A/66/374.

US State Department. "Background Briefing on Nuclear Nonproliferation Efforts with Regard to Iran and the Brazil/Turkey Agreement." May 28, 2010, Washington, DC.

———. "Country Reports on Human Rights Practices: 2003—Iran." www.state.gov/g/drl/rls/hrrpt/2003/27927.htm.

US State Department, Bureau of Democracy, Human Rights, and Labor. "2010 Country Reports on Human Rights Practices," Washington, DC, April 8, 2011. www.state.gov/g/drl/rls/hrrpt/2010/nea/154461.htm.

———. "International Religious Freedom Report," October 7, 2002.

US State Department, Office of the Spokesman of the State Department. "Companies Reducing Energy-Related Business with Iran." Washington, DC, September 30, 2010.

———. "United States Welcomes Additional European Union Sanctions on Iran." January 23, 2012.

Wehrey, Fredric, Jerrold Green, Brian Nichiporuk, Ali Reza Nader, Lydia Hansell, Rosool Nafisi, and S. R. Bohandy. "The Rise of the Pasdaran: Assessing the Domestic Roles of Iran's Islamic Revolutionary Guards Corps." Santa Monica, CA: RAND Corporation, 2009.

Wilner, Alexander, and Anthony Cordesman. "US and Iranian Strategic Competition: The Gulf Military Balance." Center for Strategic and International Studies, November 2, 2011.

World Bank. "Iran: Country Brief." June 2009. Available at www.data.worldbank.org/country/iran-islamic-republic.

Worth, Robert. "Accused Spies Offer Apologies at Iran Trial." *New York Times*, August 9, 2009. www.nytimes.com/2009/08/09/world/middleeast/09iran.html.

———. "Candidate Declares Iran May Face 'Disintegration'," *New York Times*, July 13, 2009. www.nytimes.com/2009/07/13/world/middleeast/13iran.html?ref=wor. . . .

———. "Iran Arrests Dissidents, Sites Report." *New York Times*, December 29, 2009. www.nytimes.com/2009/12/29/world/middleeast/29iran.html?emc=eta1&pagewant.

———. "Iran Invokes the West to Motivate Voters." *New York Times*, February 29, 2012. www.nytimes.com/2012/03/01/world/middleeast/iran-invokes-w. . . .

———. "Iran's Government Declares Huge Turnout in First National Vote since '09 Protests." *New York Times*, March 2, 2012. www.nytimes.com/2012/03/03/world/middleeast/iran-elections-pa. . . .

———. "Iran's Plan to Phase Out Subsidies Brings Frenzied Debate." *New York Times*, December 2, 2009. www.nytimes.com/2009/12/02/world/middleeast/02iran.html?ref=wor. . . .

———. "Iran's Power Struggle Goes beyond Personalities to Future of Presidency Itself." *New York Times*, October 26, 2011. www.nytimes.com/2011/10/27/world/middleeast/in-iran-rivalry. . . .

———. "Reports of Prison Abuse and Deaths Anger Iranians." *New York Times*, July 30, 2009. www.nytimes.com/2009/07/30/world/middleeast/30iran.html?ref=wor. . . .

———. "Tehran Losing Iranians' Trust, Ex-Leader Says." *New York Times*, July 18, 2009, www.nytimes.com/2009/07/18/world/middleeast/18iran.html.

Worth, Robert, and Nazila Fathi. "Iran Broadcasts Confessions by 2 Opposition Figures on Trial." *New York Times*, August 3, 2009. www.nytimes.com/2009/08/03/world/middle east/03iran.html?emc=eta. . . .

———. "Iran Gathering Is Broken Up." *New York Times*, July 31, 2009. www.nytimes.com/ 2009/07/31/world/middleeast/31iran.html.

Wright, Robin. *In the Name of God.* New York: Simon & Schuster, 1989.

———. *The Last Great Revolution: Turmoil and Transformation in Iran.* New York: Alfred A. Knopf, 2000.

Yaghmaian, Behzad. "Recent Developments in the Political Economy of Iran: The Triangle Crisis." In *Modern Capitalism and Islamic Ideology in Iran*, edited by Cyrus Bina and Hamid Zangeneh. New York: St. Martin's Press, 1992.

Yong, William. "Iranian Lawmakers Complain about Ahmadinejad." *New York Times*, November 23, 2010. www.nytimes.com/2010/11/24/world/middleeast/24iran.html.

———. "Iran Lets Gas Prices Soar, but Drivers Seem Unfazed." *New York Times*, December 20, 2010. www.nytimes.com/2010/12/21/world/middleeast/21iran.html?e. . . .

———. "Iran May Drop Stoning Sentence." *New York Times*, January 2, 2011. www.ny times.com/2011/01/04/world/middleeast/04iran.html.

———. "Iran Says it Arrested Computer Worm Suspects." *New York Times*, October 2, 2010. www.nytimes.com/2010/10/03/world/middleeast/03iran.html? . . .

———. "Iran's Divorce Rate Stirs Fears of Society in Crisis." *New York Times*, December 6, 2010. www.nytimes.com/2010/12/07/world/middleeast/07divorce.html.

Yong, William, and Alan Cowell. "Bomb Kills Iranian Nuclear Scientist." *New York Times*, November 29, 2010, www.nytimes.com/2010/11/30/world/middleeast/30tehran.html. . . .

Zonis, Marvin, and David Brumberg. "Shi'ism as Interpreted by Khomeini: An Ideology of Revolutionary Violence." In *Shi'ism, Resistance, and Revolution*, edited by Martin Kramer. Boulder, CO: Westview Press, 1987.

INDEX